V.T.Tinh

THE CLAY SANSKRIT LIBRARY

FOUNDED BY JOHN & JENNIFER CLAY

WWW.CLAYSANSKRITLIBRARY.COM

WWW.NYUPRESS.ORG

RĀMA'S LAST ACT
BY BHAVABHŪTI

TRANSLATED BY
SHELDON POLLOCK

NEW YORK UNIVERSITY PRESS
JJC FOUNDATION
2007

Library of Congress Cataloging-in-Publication Data
Bhavabhūti, 8th cent.
[Uttararāmacarita. English & Sanskrit]
Rama's last act / by Bhavabhuti ;
edited and translated by Sheldon Pollock.
p. cm. — (The Clay Sanskrit library)
In English and Sanskrit (romanized) on facing pages;
includes translation from Sanskrit.
Includes bibliographical references and index.
ISBN: 978-0-8147-6733-7 (cloth : alk. paper)
1. Rama (Hindu deity)—Drama.
I. Pollock, Sheldon I. II. Title.
PK3791.B58U713 2007
891'.22–dc22
2007014900

Contents

Sanskrit alphabetical order 7
CSL conventions 7

Preface 15

Foreword by Girish Karnad 17

RAMA'S LAST ACT

Introduction 27

Prologue 63
Act I: At the Painting Exhibition 73
Prelude to Act II 125
Act II: The Entrance into Pancha·vati 143
Prelude to Act III 163
Act III: The Shadow 173
Prelude to Act IV 233
Act IV: The Meeting of Kausálya and Jánaka 241
Act V: The Young Man's Valor 283
Prelude to Act VI 315
Act VI: The Recognition of the Young Men 325
Act VII: Reunion 359

Paraphrase of Prakrit *(chāyā)* 391

Notes 407
Index 443
Sandhi grid 452

CSL CONVENTIONS

SANSKRIT ALPHABETICAL ORDER

Vowels:	*a ā i ī u ū ṛ ṝ ḷ ḹ e ai o au ṃ ḥ*
Gutturals:	*k kh g gh ṅ*
Palatals:	*c ch j jh ñ*
Retroflex:	*ṭ ṭh ḍ ḍh ṇ*
Dentals:	*t th d dh n*
Labials:	*p ph b bh m*
Semivowels:	*y r l v*
Spirants:	*ś ṣ s h*

GUIDE TO SANSKRIT PRONUNCIATION

a	b*u*t
ā, â	f*a*ther
i	s*i*t
ī, î	f*ee*
u	p*u*t
ū, û	b*oo*
ṛ	vocalic *r*, American p*ur*dy or English p*re*tty
ṝ	lengthened *ṛ*
ḷ	vocalic *l*, ab*le*
e, ê, ē	m*a*de, esp. in Welsh pronunciation
ai	b*i*te
o, ô, ō	r*o*pe, esp. Welsh pronunciation; Italian s*o*lo
au	s*ou*nd
ṃ	*anusvāra* nasalizes the preceding vowel
ḥ	*visarga*, a voiceless aspiration (resembling the English *h*), or like Scottish lo*ch*, or an aspiration with a faint echoing of the last element of the preceding vowel so that *taiḥ* is pronounced *taih*^{i}
k	lu*ck*
kh	blo*ckh*ead
g	*g*o
gh	bi*gh*ead
ṅ	a*n*ger
c	*ch*ill
ch	mat*chh*ead
j	*j*og
jh	aspirated *j*, he*dgeh*og
ñ	ca*ny*on
ṭ	retroflex *t*, *t*ry (with the tip of tongue turned up to touch the hard palate)
ṭh	same as the preceding but aspirated
ḍ	retroflex *d* (with the tip of tongue turned up to touch the hard palate)
ḍh	same as the preceding but aspirated
ṇ	retroflex *n* (with the tip of tongue turned up to

	touch the hard palate)
t	French *t*out
th	ten*t h*ook
d	*d*inner
dh	guil*dh*all
n	*n*ow
p	*p*ill
ph	u*ph*eaval
b	*b*efore
bh	a*bh*orrent
m	*m*ind
y	*y*es
r	trilled, resembling the Italian pronunciation of *r*
l	*l*inger
v	*w*ord
ś	*sh*ore
ṣ	retroflex *sh* (with the tip of the tongue turned up to touch the hard palate)
s	hi*ss*
h	*h*ood

CSL PUNCTUATION OF ENGLISH

The acute accent on Sanskrit words when they occur outside of the Sanskrit text itself, marks stress, e.g. Ramáyana. It is not part of traditional Sanskrit orthography, transliteration or transcription, but we supply it here to guide readers in the pronunciation of these unfamiliar words. Since no Sanskrit word is accented on the last syllable it is not necessary to accent disyllables, e.g. Rama.

The second CSL innovation designed to assist the reader in the pronunciation of lengthy unfamiliar words is to insert an unobtrusive middle dot between semantic word breaks in compound names (provided the word break does not fall on a vowel resulting from the fusion of two vowels), e.g. Maha·bhárata, but Ramáyana (not Rama·áyana). Our dot echoes the punctuating middle dot (·) found in the oldest surviving samples of written Indic, the Ashokan inscriptions of the third century BCE.

The deep layering of Sanskrit narrative has also dictated that we use quotation marks only to announce the beginning and end of every direct speech, and not at the beginning of every paragraph.

CSL PUNCTUATION OF SANSKRIT

The Sanskrit text is also punctuated, in accordance with the punctuation of the English translation. In mid-verse, the punctuation will not alter the sandhi or the scansion. Proper names are capitalized. Most

Sanskrit metres have four "feet" *(pāda):* where possible we print the common *śloka* metre on two lines. The capitalization of verse beginnings makes it easy for the reader to recognize longer metres where it is necessary to print the four metrical feet over four or eight lines. In the Sanskrit text, we use French *Guillemets* (e.g. *«kva saṃcicīrṣuḥ?»*) instead of English quotation marks (e.g. "Where are you off to?") to avoid confusion with the apostrophes used for vowel elision in sandhi.

Sanskrit presents the learner with a challenge: *sandhi* ("euphonic combination"). Sandhi means that when two words are joined in connected speech or writing (which in Sanskrit reflects speech), the last letter (or even letters) of the first word often changes; compare the way we pronounce "the" in "the beginning" and "the end."

In Sanskrit the first letter of the second word may also change; and if both the last letter of the first word and the first letter of the second are vowels, they may fuse. This has a parallel in English: a nasal consonant is inserted between two vowels that would otherwise coalesce: "a pear" and "an apple." Sanskrit vowel fusion may produce ambiguity. The chart at the back of each book gives the full sandhi system.

Fortunately it is not necessary to know these changes in order to start reading Sanskrit. For that, what is important is to know the form of the second word without sandhi (pre-sandhi), so that it can be recognized or looked up in a dictionary. Therefore we are printing Sanskrit with a system of punctuation that will indicate, unambiguously, the original form of the second word, i.e., the form without sandhi. Such sandhi mostly concerns the fusion of two vowels.

In Sanskrit, vowels may be short or long and are written differently accordingly. We follow the general convention that a vowel with no mark above it is short. Other books mark a long vowel either with a bar called a macron (*ā*) or with a circumflex (*â*). Our system uses the macron, except that for initial vowels in sandhi we use a circumflex to indicate that originally the vowel was short, or the shorter of two possibilities (*e* rather than *ai*, *o* rather than *au*).

When we print initial *â*,	before sandhi that vowel was	*a*
	î or *ê*,	*i*
	û or *ô*,	*u*
	âi,	*e*

âu,	*o*
ā,	*ā* (i.e., the same)
ī,	*ī* (i.e., the same)
ū,	*ū* (i.e., the same)
ē,	*ī*
ō,	*ū*
ai,	*ai*
āu,	*au*

', before sandhi there was a vowel *a*

FURTHER HELP WITH VOWEL SANDHI

When a final short vowel (*a*, *i* or *u*) has merged into a following vowel, we print ' at the end of the word, and when a final long vowel (*ā*, *ī* or *ū*) has merged into a following vowel we print " at the end of the word. The vast majority of these cases will concern a final *a* or *ā*.

Examples:

What before sandhi was *atra asti* is represented as *atr' âsti*

atra āste	*atr' āste*
kanyā asti	*kany" âsti*
kanyā āste	*kany" āste*
atra iti	*atr' êti*
kanyā iti	*kany" êti*
kanyā īpsitā	*kany" ēpsitā*

Finally, three other points concerning the initial letter of the second word:

(1) A word that before sandhi begins with *ṛ* (vowel), after sandhi begins with *r* followed by a consonant: *yatha" rtu* represents pre-sandhi *yathā ṛtu*.

(2) When before sandhi the previous word ends in *t* and the following word begins with *ś*, after sandhi the last letter of the previous word is *c* and the following word begins with *ch*: *syāc chāstravit* represents pre-sandhi *syāt śāstravit*.

(3) Where a word begins with *h* and the previous word ends with a double consonant, this is our simplified spelling to show the pre-sandhi

form: *tad hasati* is commonly written as *tad dhasati*, but we write *tadd hasati* so that the original initial letter is obvious.

COMPOUNDS

We also punctuate the division of compounds (*samāsa*), simply by inserting a thin vertical line between words. There are words where the decision whether to regard them as compounds is arbitrary. Our principle has been to try to guide readers to the correct dictionary entries.

EXAMPLE

Where the Devanagari script reads:

कुम्भस्थली रक्षतु वो विकीर्णसिन्धूररेणुर्द्विरदाननस्य ।
प्रशान्तये विघ्नतमश्छटानां निष्ठ्यूतबालातपपल्लवेव ॥

Others would print:

kumbhasthalī rakṣatu vo vikīrṇasindūrareṇur dviradānanasya /
praśāntaye vighnatamaśchaṭānāṃ niṣṭhyūtabālātapapallaveva //

We print:

kumbha|sthalī rakṣatu vo vikīrṇa|sindūra|reṇur dvirad'|ānanasya
praśāntaye vighna|tamaś|chaṭānāṃ niṣṭhyūta|bāl'|ātapa|pallav" êva.

And in English:

"May Ganésha's domed forehead protect you! Streaked with vermilion dust, it seems to be emitting the spreading rays of the rising sun to pacify the teeming darkness of obstructions."

"Nava·sáhasanka and the Serpent Princess" I.3

DRAMA

Classical Sanskrit literature is in fact itself bilingual, notably in drama. There women and characters of low rank speak one of several Prakrit dialects, an "unrefined" *(prākṛta)* vernacular as opposed to the "refined" *(saṃskṛta)* language. Editors commonly provide such speeches with a Sanskrit paraphrase, their "shadow" *(chāyā)*. We mark Prakrit speeches with ⌜opening and closing⌟ corner brackets, and supply the Sanskrit *chāyā* in endnotes. Some stage directions are original to the author but we follow the custom that sometimes editors supplement these; we print them in italics (and within brackets, in mid-text).

WORDPLAY

Classical Sanskrit literature can abound in puns *(śleṣa)*. Such paronomasia, or wordplay, is raised to a high art; rarely is it a *cliché*. Multiple meanings merge *(śliṣyanti)* into a single word or phrase. Most common are pairs of meanings, but as many as ten separate meanings are attested. To mark the parallel senses in the English, as well as the punning original in the Sanskrit, we use a *slanted* font (different from *italic*) and a triple colon *(⁝)* to separate the alternatives. E.g.

yuktaṃ Kādambarīṃ śrutvā kavayo maunam āśritāḥ
Bāṇa/dhvanāv an|adhyāyo bhavat' îti smṛtir yataḥ.

It is right that poets should fall silent upon hearing the Kádambari, for the sacred law rules that recitation must be suspended when *the sound of an arrow ⁝ the poetry of Bana* is heard.

Soméshvara·deva's "Moonlight of Glory" I.15

For Allison,
tat tasya kim api dravyam…

Preface

I wish to thank Guy Leavitt for his help in preparing the Sanskrit and Prakrit text in the Clay Sanskrit Library format. Staff at the British Library and Gillian Evison and Doris Nicholson at the Oriental Institute, Oxford, provided me copies of Bhaṭṭa Nārāyaṇa's commentary, for which I am very grateful. My research assistant Shreya Vora helped gather materials for the introduction and did last-minute proofing. Allison Busch read the entire translation and her Sanskrit eyes, coupled with her literary taste, saw numerous places for improvement—some of which, alas, remain. CSL editors Isabelle Onians and Somadeva Vasudeva were ever ready with advice and guidance. I am also grateful to Dániel Balogh for his superb job of copyediting. Lastly, John Clay himself has proved to be the ideal patron, providing at once the inspiration for achieving excellence and the possibility of realizing it.

Sheldon Pollock
New York City, September, 2006

FOREWORD

In Valmíki's 'Ramáyana,' the course of Rama's life is determined by forces impinging upon him from the outside. Things happen to him, and he faces the crises according to moral precepts sanctified by tradition or advice given to him by respected elders. He hardly initiates any action of his own, except in a rare and desperate case like the killing of Vali. As a result, Rama emerges from the epic morally unsullied and psychologically unscathed, and tradition has been able to accept him as the ultimate embodiment of righteousness.

In the "Final Chapter" *(Uttarakāṇḍa)* of the 'Ramáyana,' however—a later addition to Valmíki's poem—a single act of Rama's sets the entire action rolling, and it is an act the ethical justification for which has always been ambiguous. Rama here is responsible for inflicting humiliation and pain on the queen he knows is innocent and for tearing his family apart. When in the end he receives the public rebuff of being rejected by the gentle Sita, our sympathies are all on her side. It is this anguished awareness of the responsibility he must bear for the abandonment of the woman he loves so dearly that forms the basic tenor of this section of the 'Ramáyana.'

Bhava·bhuti, in 'Rama's Last Act,' exploits the enormous emotional potential and ethical complexities of this situation. But instead of a straightforward dramatization of a fairly simple original narrative, he takes breath-taking risks with his material by refracting the narrative and projecting it from different and often conflicting angles. And, in addition, he takes immense pleasure in drawing our attention to these unusual strategies and devices.

Take for instance the lopsided organization of the narrative itself. Act One ends with Rama sending Sita off with Lákshmana to the jungle. Then the action jumps over twelve years, and in the Prelude to the next act, a female ascetic, talking to a forest deity, recounts four events from different parts of the epic, totally unrelated to each other in terms of time. Nothing is said about what actually happened to Sita, abandoned alone in the jungle—a wrenching moment for which the whole of Act One has been a build-up. Thus there is a gaping 'hole' after Act One, left unfilled till the very end, a crucial piece missing at the very centre of the jigsaw puzzle.

Before we pursue this trajectory further, it is worthwhile looking at another feature of the play which is equally striking. We are not too far into the drama before we become aware of the number of art forms that figure in it. Painting, music, sculpture, singing, poetry are all brought in. But they are not there, as often in Sanskrit plays, to emphasize the artistic and sensual vibrancy of the royal court. They play a positive role in furthering the action, almost like human characters, each form making its own specific contribution to the development of the plot.

In Act One, the central action takes place in the picture gallery, where Rama, Sita and Lákshmana are looking at paintings illustrating episodes from their past life. Moved by the memories evoked by these images, Rama calls upon the Jrímbhaka weapons to become available to Sita's children, and beseeches the goddesses, Bhagi·rathi and Príthivi

(Earth), to protect Sita should the need arise. These exclamations, purely emotional responses to the paintings, come true and decide the course of the rest of the play. Similarly, an image sculpted in gold replaces Sita by Rama's side, enabling him to remain loyal to her while launching the horse sacrifice that will ultimately bring the family together. The possession of the Jrímbhaka weapons by the twins helps confirm their parentage. Lava owes much of his recognition of the world to the books he has read. He identifies the functions of a horse from what he has read in the Vedic texts.

Thus, Bhava·bhuti designs the action to emphasize how the various art forms help toward healing the wounds inflicted by Rama's initial act. Not surprisingly, it is the epic, the 'Ramáyana,' that plays a seminal role in this recuperation.

In fact, as the action of the play unfolds in front of us, we are continually made conscious that the epic is being composed and developing in parallel in the background. Valmíki is invisible till the last few minutes of the play but we are aware of his creative presence in the wings right through. The paintings in Act One not only give a synoptic presentation of the content of the 'Ramáyana' but also consciously echo the summary provided by the sage Nárada to Valmíki at the very beginning of the epic. In Act Two we are informed that Valmíki has started composing the 'Ramáyana.' In Act Four, the composition has progressed far enough for Kusha and Lava to have started studying it. The poet has not published the entire poem yet, so while Lava knows the names of the members of his parents' generation, he is still in the dark regarding his cousins. Indeed, the process of Lava getting acquainted with his cousins takes place in the scene we are witnessing, thus intertwining the plot development in Bhava·bhuti's play with the progressive unfolding of Valmíki's epic. The encounter between Rama and his sons is continually and subtly modulated by their academic recitation of the 'Ramáyana.' Thanks to the epic, the twins, who have been brought up in the jungle, have a nuanced access to Rama's emotions which their cousin, Chandra·ketu, who has grown up with Rama in the palace, entirely lacks. And in the final act, it is the presentation of Valmíki's new play that reunites Sita with Rama and her sons.

This play-within-the-play begins, suddenly, with Sita shouting out to Rama and Lákshmana that she is alone in the wild forests, about to give birth to twins. And we immediately realize that Bhava·bhuti is here filling in the 'hole' we pointed out earlier, the piece missing at the heart of the jigsaw puzzle. That Valmíki should have chosen this scene for presentation to Rama is understandable, since Rama was not present when the event actually happened. He is now being brought up to date on what exactly transpired after he abandoned Sita. But we, the audience watching Bhava·bhuti's play, have a right to ask what point Bhava·bhuti is making by placing this scene so late in the play, dislocating it from its chronological position in the narrative.

Obviously, he is avoiding needless repetition. But there is a subtler strategy at work here. For the play-within-the play doesn't merely inform us that Sita was saved. It details how she was saved: she was saved by the two goddesses, Bhagi·rathi and Príthivi, who were responding to Rama's exclamations while viewing the paintings in Act One. This connection of the play-within-the-play with Act One is further reinforced by making the Jrímbhaka weapons appear in the scene and assure Sita that 'our destiny now lies with your sons as.... [Rama] proclaimed at the time of viewing the paintings.' As in a detective novel, the references to the viewing of the paintings are clues provided by Bhava·bhuti to make it unambiguously clear that the scene that Valmíki is presenting in 'Rama's Last Act' is in fact the 'absent Second Act' of the same play.

The play written by Valmíki then is in fact Bhava·bhuti's. Bhava·bhuti is thus asserting that he himself is Valmíki. All poets are one: through their work they give us unalloyed joy, the experience of *rasa,* the aesthetic equivalent of a mystical experience.

The question is whether this polyphonic structure of the play is merely a vehicle for the display of Bhava·bhuti's fondness for pyrotechnics—almost akin to his proclivity for prodigiously long verbal compounds—or, at the most, a means of asserting his own stature as a poet, or whether there is a more complex philosophical purpose to the exercise. Does, in short, a *prabandha dhvani*—a unified resonance—emerge from the simultaneous playing of these various themes?

As far as I know, Kirtinath Kurtkoti, the great critic of Kannada literature, was the first scholar to draw our attention to the significance of the following passage in the Prologue to the play:

DIRECTOR: *My dear fellow,*
It is our duty to act no matter what.
There is no escaping criticism.
However pure the words—or the woman—
There are always people who'll be malicious.

ACTOR: *Worse than malicious, you should have said.*
Since the people are reproaching
Vaidéhi, the queen herself.

Thus Sita personifies speech. (There is an obvious reference here to the *Nāṭyaśāstra:* 'Let Indra protect the hero and Sarásvati the heroine.') Spreading slander about such a noble person is to indulge in the abuse of speech, to distort the perception of reality and to damage the fabric of normal life. The tragedy inflicted upon Sita by her vilifiers objectifies what is being done to language itself in the same process. This is a crisis which only the Poet can resolve. 'Rama's Last Act' celebrates the Poet as one who bears the central responsibility of maintaining the purity of speech and who, when that turns turbid, can restore it to its unclouded state.

At the end of the 'Ramáyana,' Sita rejects Rama's offer of acceptance. Even in the play-within-the-play, Sita's exit line expresses similar rejection of the 'vicissitudes of this world.' But this is not a dénouement acceptable to Bhava·bhuti. When Rama faints at Sita's exit, Lákshmana turns to Valmíki and demands:

LÁKSHMANA: *Help, Valmíki, help! Is this the moral of your poem?*

Bhava·bhuti here is protesting that for him, Rama and Sita must unite. But their reunion is not merely a bow to the convention of happy endings ordained by Sanskrit dramaturgy. That is the central necessity of his philosophical position: The poet pleases our sensibilities. He heals us psychologically. But he fulfils a more universal function; he purifies the language of the tribe and brings its members together in the enjoyment of a meaningful life.

If this interpretation seems to attribute an almost godlike status to the Poet, Bhava·bhuti would be the last person to feel embarrassed. In fact, as has often been noted, in the benedictory verses at the beginning as well as at the end of the play (which should normally praise the gods), he goes out of his way to hail the Poet's prowess.

Valmíki appears on stage only a few minutes before the end of the play, almost as though to take a bow, and appropriately the final line spoken by him is,

> VALMÍKI: *Dear Rama, is there some further good turn I can do for you?*

As a playwright myself, I know that this is what every playwright would want to ask of his audience.

Finally, may I say how happy I am to be writing the Foreword to this delightfully limpid translation of a play which, for all its concern with what we do to language, is not exactly known for its pellucid style.

Girish KARNAD

INTRODUCTION

The Playwright Bhava·bhuti

As is the case with most Sanskrit poets, even the most eminent, we have scant reliable knowledge about Bhava·bhuti. The twelfth-century historian Kálhana associates him with the court of King Yasho·varman, which would place him in the celebrated cultural capital of Kanya·kubja (Kanauj) in the first third of the eighth century, and nothing in his writings speaks against this. Bhava·bhuti tells us something of himself in the prologues to his works. He was born in what is today southern Maharashtra, and was a member of a Brahman family distinguished for its Vedic learning. Indeed, his works show a degree of knowledge—especially in hermeneutics (*mīmāṃsā*) and Vedánta—that give some credence to the otherwise thin (but chronologically credible) tradition that makes him a pupil of Kumárila, the greatest hermeneutics scholar of the epoch.

If the hard documentary evidence scarcely enables us to eke out a paragraph about Bhava·bhuti's life, the personality that emerges from his work is as sharp as we can delineate for any Sanskrit poet, and his voice as individual. He was a man drawn to exploring the most vexed problems the literary tradition had bequeathed him, and to do so in a way—through a searching examination of the human heart—that sets him apart in the history of Sanskrit literature.

Bhava·bhuti wrote only three plays[1] and probably in the following order: the 'Acts of the Great Hero' (*Mahāvīra-carita*), a *nāṭaka*, or historical (epic-derived) play, on the Rama legend; 'Málati and Mádhava' (*Mālatīmādhava*), next to 'Little Clay Cart' (*Mṛcchakaṭikā*) undoubtedly the finest *prakaraṇa*, or fictional play, in the entire Sanskrit repertory, and arguably the most insightful meditation on the nature of romantic love in early India; and 'Rama's Last Act' (*Uttararāmacarita*).

'Rama's Last Act' is also a *nāṭaka*—indeed, the implicit claim that Bhava·bhuti makes at the end of the play, that it is the first formal drama based on Valmíki's poem, may well be true. At least, no unequivocally earlier examples exist.[2] Undoubtedly it is Bhava·bhuti's masterpiece, and next to Kali·dasa's 'Shakúntala' (*Abhijñānaśākuntala*), the most celebrated work of the Sanskrit theater. In the *Śṛṅgāraprakāśa* ('Light on Passion'), an encyclopedic literary treatise of the early eleventh century, the scholar-king Bhoja cites 'Rama's Last Act' more than any other work (some 235 times) except Kali·dasa's 'Birth of Kumára' (*Kumārasambhava,* 415). And the play had become famous within a few generations. Vámana, an important literary critic of Kashmir (c. 800), prized it as a touchstone of literary figuration (citing Act 1.8 as a paradigm of metaphor). Another measure of the poet's impact, besides his prominence among literary critics, is his appearance in the "praise-poems of poets," eulogies that form the closest thing Sanskrit literary culture had to a canonization process. In a twelfth-century anthology, an anonymous poet, after praising Subándhu, Kali·dasa, Pánini, Hari·chandra, Arya·shura, and Bháravi—the greatest among the earlier poets—ends by saying Bhava·bhuti transcends them all by offering the deepest, most indescribable kind of pleasure (a line no doubt imitating Bhava·bhuti). Another such poem attributes to him the mastery of the

"Way" that his contemporaries and successors such as Vak·pati·raja would follow.[3]

Bhava·bhuti's Way (*mārga*)—the term is a technical one, meaning style in the largest sense—is no easy thing to characterize. His language can be abstruse and his nominal compounding dense, though he knows precisely how and when to moderate both (the point-counterpoint in the descriptive verses of Act 2 of 'Rama's Last Act' is a good example). One less obvious dimension of his style may well be the personalized authorial voice, of the sort we find in the autobiographical section of Bana's *Harṣacarita*, or in Vak·pati's reflections on his literary art. Consider this celebrated verse from 'Málati and Mádhava':

Those quick to disparage me here
know something, I am sure,
but I don't write on their account.
Someone of like nature to me
exists or will be born
for time is endless and earth is vast.

(*Mālatīmādhava* Act 1.6)

Related in some way to this voice is Bhava·bhuti's penchant for acute psychological analysis. It is uncommon to meet anywhere in Sanskrit literature the kind of deep-felt reflection on love that we find throughout 'Rama's Last Act':

Love between a man and a woman:

Identity in joy and sorrow,
consonance in every condition,
where the heart can find respite,

whose rasa *old age cannot spoil,*
what alone abides as time
removes all veils and pure love ripens—
that singular blessing is only bestowed
on a good man, and only then with luck. (1.171 [40])

between new friends:

There is no way to counteract
a predilection that has no cause.
There is some thread of affection that knits
living things together deep within. (5.57 [17])

between parent and child:

A child marks the highest degree of love,
and the source of the parents' ultimate bonding.
Because it is the common object of a couple's love
a child is a knot of bliss that ties their hearts together.[4]
(3.105–3.106 [18])

No one in Sanskrit—except again, perhaps, Kali·dasa—demonstrates quite this level of interest in and capacity for capturing in verse the most complex states of human attachment. The hazard here, of straying into turgid and turbid psychologism, is one to which Bhava·bhuti often exposes himself as he strives to give expression to the least expressible dimensions of human feeling:

Every single time you touch me
a kind of transformation—
it can't be described as joy or sorrow,
ecstasy or sleep,
a state of intoxication

or all-suffusing poison—
confuses my senses and at once
excites and dulls my awareness. (1.154 [36])

And melodrama often threatens: the characters "fall faint" and "compose themselves" a dozen times or more, and their expressions of woe beggar the resources of contemporary English. Here the modern reader is urged to keep in mind the potentially very different standards of literary taste—and indeed, the possibility of a very different history of emotions—in the nonmodern nonWest. That said, the analyst of the human heart inevitably runs the risk of excess, in the hopes of penetrating to some important truth.

Kali·dasa's work, dating from three centuries earlier, is comparable to Bhava·bhuti's in other respects besides emotional register: it was one of Bhava·bhuti's crucial models. This fact is centrally important in understanding both the story he has told in 'Rama's Last Act' and the way he has constructed the play.

Intertext and Structure

To grasp the significance of the narrative dimension of 'Rama's Last Act' and in fact even to perceive the complexity of its formal organization, we need to take a step backward in Sanskrit literary history, and explore not just Bhava·bhuti's relationship to earlier drama but the epic literature from which that drama was derived.

In the heart of Bhava·bhuti's principal epic source, Valmíki's 'Ramáyana,' lies a formative relationship with India's other great epic, the 'Maha·bhárata' of Vyasa. The works are, in a fundamental way, complementary. For example, the 'Ramáyana' concerns the Solar lineage of kings, the 'Maha·bhárata' the Lunar (the major—though completely ideal—genealogical division among ancient Indian royalty); the 'Ramáyana' is a story of normative monogamy; the 'Maha·bhárata,' of anomalous polyandry. Both poems relate a struggle over succession to the throne, leading to the degradation of the princess and the political power she represents and (before or after that) the exile of the protagonists, war, return, and recovery of the throne. But here, too, the complementarities are telling. Most important is the agon itself: the 'Ramáyana' is a tale of "othering," the enemy is non-human, even demonic, and the war takes place in an unfamiliar, faraway world; the 'Maha·bhárata' is a tale of "brothering," the enemy are kinsmen—indeed, as the protagonists say, almost their own selves—and the war takes place at home.[5]

'Shakúntala' is a 'Maha·bhárata' play, and 'Rama's Last Act' seems designed as a 'Ramáyana' counterpart to, and competitor of, Kali·dasa's masterpiece. Like the two epics the two plays share a deep resemblance. In their core they are stories about love, rejection, recovery, and ultimately—because this is the very reason behind the rejection— political power and its perpetuation. The star-crossed love of Dushyánta and Shakúntala is mirrored in that of Rama and Sita. The women, both of whom are pregnant, are repudiated because of doubts about their fidelity and (implicitly) the paternity of the progeny they are carrying. This is followed by a soul-searing acknowledgement of guilt on the part of the husband, reunion with his wife, recognition of the legitimacy of the offspring with the aid of quasi-divine agents (Marícha in 'Shakúntala,' the magical anthropomorphic weapons in 'Rama's Last Act'), and reconciliation of husband and wife. Both works hereby aim to emend and aesthetically enhance their epic models.[6]

If some of these features may be found in other plays, nowhere else is the correspondence so intimate. But what most strikingly testifies to Bhava·bhuti's creative appropriation from 'Shakúntala' is the architectural principles behind his play. These are entirely different from the elements of traditional dramaturgical theory, which have claimed the attention of medieval commentators and modern scholars alike, but which actually do little to enhance our actual appreciation of the play as anything more than a token of a type.[7] The Kalidasan architectonics adopted in 'Rama's Last Act,' by contrast, are fundamental to our understanding the playwright's thought, despite the fact that they were never noted by traditional Indian readers or perhaps even consciously apprehended. Great poets are always smarter than their smartest readers.

No fully satisfactory account of these structural principles exists for 'Shakúntala,' one that would show how thoroughly they pervade the work from acts to scenes to verses to the most subtle verbal echoes.[8] A perfect symmetry of action balances Acts 1 and 7, 2 and 6, 3 and 5, each latter act recapitulating events, motifs, and even phrases from the former in a kind of counterpoint or antiphony. A comparable concentric construction can be found in 'Rama's Last Act.' Thus, in Act 1, the opening verse, which offers up 'Rama's Last Act' "with an expression / of homage to the poets of old"; the viewing of the picture gallery and the metaliterary framing by Rama, "It's only a painting"; the benediction that Rama pronounces regarding the magical weapons, "From now on without fail they will serve your offspring"; the reference to Sita as "dear companion in my sojourn in Dándaka wilderness"; the request that Ganga protect Sita; the artistic representation that precedes the separation; the announcement about the demon Lávana—all this has crystal-clear resonances with what occurs in Act 7: the play within the play and the metaliterary framing by Lákshmana, "This is only a play"; the mention of the magical weapons (Lákshmana directly quotes the earlier statement, "My brother did tell her, 'From now on without fail...'"); the reference to Sita as Rama's "dear companion in my sojourn in Dándaka wilderness"; Ganga's affirmation that she has protected Sita; the dramatic representation that precedes the reunion; the announcement about the demon Lávana, and the concluding verse making reference to the ancient narrative, the 'Ramáyana,' that the playwright has transfigured in his work.

The same sort of excavation could be done for the remaining acts: 2 and 6 correspond in their preludes (spoken by semidivine beings, the water spirits and the *Vidyādhara*s respectively); in individual verses—one of the poet's most often quoted insights on love is repeated verbatim:

The person need do nothing at all,
the mere joy of being together

dispels sorrow. What a gift it is,
to have someone who loves you
(Act 2.87 [19] = Act 6.14 [5]);

and in subtle resonances such as the allusion to Rama and Sita's intimate conversations (Act 2.99 = Act 6.127). Acts 3 and 5 correspond closely, too: Rama's tense dialogue with the invisible Sita is shadowed by Chandra·ketu's dialogue with the unrecognized Lava, the victory of Sita's "son," the elephant she raised from birth, by the victory of Lava (to whom Sita herself makes allusion, Act 3.98), and so on.

There is no doubt a distinct pleasure for the audience in the discovery of such concealed artistry, but that is not the only purpose of this structure. The design of the construction may be thought to recapitulate, as a sort of objective correlative, the design of the action: The lovers' separation and reunion are as carefully plotted by fate as the play is by the poet. This dimension of predestination, a dominant convention of Sanskrit theater and repeatedly emphasized in 'Rama's Last Act' no less than in 'Shakúntala,' is a major concern, or even a problem, for Bhava·bhuti given the moral calculation of responsibility that motivates his revision of Valmíki, a question I examine below. It would be unsurprising, then, to find it reflected in the dramatic structure. But in addition to offering aesthetic pleasure and providing an objective correlative for the narrative of predetermined action, the concentric, antiphonal design of the play might also be interpreted as another aspect of the playwright's concern with the reflexive appreciation of dramatic art itself and the place of art in making sense of lived experience. Not only is this concern a dominant interest of Bhava·bhuti's, but it perhaps constitutes the supreme achievement of 'Rama's Last Act.'

Bhava·bhuti's Theater of Reflexivity[9]

Bhava·bhuti is arguably the most "meta" of premodern Indian authors—and this is saying much, since the concern with reflecting *on* literature *in* literature has a distinguished genealogy in Sanskrit, beginning with the 'Maha·bhárata' (where Vyasa literally fathers the characters of his epic) and the 'Ramáyana' (where the work opens with a poetic account of Valmíki's invention of poetry). 'Rama's Last Act' is as much about the power of drama itself, about the capacity of literary narrative to make life intelligible and coherent, as it is about the problem of moral agency that the best literature aims to highlight. I see two principal dimensions to this reflexivity: one pertains, again, to the formal dimension of literature, but specifically as this resides in the purpose and paradox of representation itself; the other to its content, which in traditional Indian dramaturgical theory largely means the problem of *rasa*.

As just noted, the play is framed by two verses that celebrate the power of poets: at the start, the power of the "poets of old," Valmíki foremost among them (as any Indian audience would immediately recognize); at the end, that of Bhava·bhuti himself, "master of the sacred mystery of language," who claims primacy in turning the 'Ramáyana' into formal drama. More dramatically, the play is framed by two representations of representation: the tour of the picture gallery in Act 1 and the performance of "Valmíki's" new play in Act 7. The former is a representation of what is past and known to the viewers (Rama, Lákshmana, and Sita are seeing the painted scenes of their life in exile, effectively the main events of Valmíki's poem, of which there will be allusive reprise in Act 3). The latter—offered as a portion of the as-yet unpublished 'Ramáyana,' "the *rasa* heightened by its new form, [which] is meant for performance"—is a representation about what is past but unknown to the viewers (Rama and Lákshmana are seeing the events that occurred after Sita was abandoned in the forest). Embedded in the play-within-the-play we can find a crucial metaliterary claim of Bhava·bhuti's: He himself, of course, wrote the play he attributes to Valmíki. Thus when Valmíki declares, "Through deep insight made possible by a seer's vision we have produced a brief composition at once purifying and filled with *rasa*," and Rama concurs that "Seers have direct vision of *dharma*," and that their insights are "never found to be contradicted—and hence never to be doubted," Bhava·bhuti is asserting his own power to declare the truth—or even make it, since "In everyday life a good man's words correspond with facts / But in the case of a primal seer the facts conform with his words" (Act 1.42 [10]). It is this assertion that seems to underlie the use of the device.

In both cases the reality or truth of the representations is the paramount question. In Act 1, Sita cries out when she sees the painting of Shurpa·nakha, "Oh my husband, this is my last sight of you!" to which Rama replies, "Now, now, there's no need to be afraid of separation. It's only a painting." In Act 7, observing "Sita" on stage (played by an *apsaras*, or divine courtesan, in the troupe of the mythic director, Bharata) about to commit suicide after her brother-in-law has abandoned her in the forest,[10] Rama cries out "My queen, my queen, look, Lákshmana is here!" to which Lákshmana replies, "But brother, this is only a play." But in both instances, there are truths to be learned from something that is untrue because unreal. In the former instance, the characters relive the past and confirm the truth of their experience. In the latter, they not only learn what happened in the past but hear it correctly for the first time: They learn from Earth, Sita's mother, and the Ganga River, tutelary deity of Rama's clan, the truth of Sita's innocence (declaring her "the source of good fortune to the world" and enhancer of their own purity), and learn from the divine weapons the truth of the pedigree of the twins, Kusha and Lava. For the audience the content of this markedly reflexive form consists in coming to recognize that the representation they themselves are watching—'Rama's Last Act'—is as true as the representations, paintings or performance, that the characters themselves verify, as Rama does when he avers in Act 1, "My god, it's as if the episode at Jana·sthana were happening this very moment." It is only through narrative that we can understand our lives. Or indeed perhaps, to simplify the complex ancient theory of *śabda/brahma*, the "mystery of language" of which Bhava·bhuti is master, our lives may be nothing but verbal narrative. While it may be that art can sometimes make us, quixotically, confuse reality and representation, it also shows us that representation can sometimes be the only way the real and the true come to be known.[11]

Bhava·bhuti was obviously not the first writer in history to use this technique. Western poetry begins with Homer deriving a similar truth-claim about his representation from showing Odysseus corroborate with his tears what that bard Demodocus sang in his account—that is, of course, Homer's account—of the 'Iliad' at Phaeacia; less developed but more familiar is Vergil's adaptation of Homer in Aeneas's *lacrimae rerum* before the murals in Dido's temple depicting the sack of Troy. But Bhava·bhuti's achievement is not only as compelling as these, but even more complex, shaping as it does the whole work of art, with a skillfulness shown by no other Sanskrit dramatist, and with multiplying effects of signification that can be dizzying. And it is enhanced by the particular moral claims that, as we will see, he seeks thereby to raise.

The second dimension of Bhava·bhuti's reflexive theater pertains to content rather than form, and at first glance it stands in some tension with the subliminal persuasiveness of the former. For here the poet seems to intentionally subvert the illusion of mimetic truth that furnished the strongest proof of his power. Perhaps most dramatic is Lákshmana's exclamation over Rama when he faints at the portrayal of Sita's apparent death in the drama in Act 7: "Help, Valmíki, help! Is this the moral of your poem?"[12] Rama here ceases to be a "real" person and becomes instead a character in a story, and the whole event, the play itself no less than the play within it, is unmasked as artifice. Our suspension of disbelief is similarly defied with respect to the emotional impact of the work, its *rasa*.

Rasa literally means flavor or taste, but as a technical term refers to the emotional state created by a literary work (and that literature aims, above all else, to create such a state was never doubted). These states are canonically eight: the erotic, comic, pitiful, heroic, fearful, disgusting, furious, and wonderful. Literary works were thought, reasonably enough, to produce a single dominant emotional impact, but, again reasonably enough, to also show a range of subordinate states. Sad tales sometimes have comic interludes (Shambúka in Act 2, with his incessant, extravagant descriptions, almost certainly is meant to play a role analogous to the buffoon in the same act in the 'Shakúntala'), comedies often have an erotic dimension, horror stories a heroic one. In the case of 'Rama's Last Act,' the dominant *rasa* is identified by the poet himself as *karuṇa*, translated here as "pity."[13]

Sanskrit literary critics are in unanimous agreement that in developing a *rasa* the writer must, among other things, refrain from actually naming it in the literary text. It requires only a moment's thought to see that the erotic illusion of a scene will be destroyed by announcing, "Here is an erotic scene." Naming the *rasa*, however, and more challengingly still, openly reflecting on *rasa* is precisely what Bhava·bhuti does throughout the play:[14]

(The Múrala River speaks:)

Rama has been filled with the rasa of pity,
kept hidden by his profound demeanor,
the sharp pain of it held deep within
like a clay pot baking in embers. (3.4 [1])

* * *

(The Támasa River, in reference to Rama, effectively summarizing the emotional register of the play as a whole:)

How complex a plot this is.
There is only a single rasa—
pity—but it takes different forms
since it changes in response
to circumstances that are changing,
just the way that water forms
into whirlpool, bubble, or wave
though in the end it all remains
the same: nothing but water. (3.258 [48])

* * *

(Lava at his meeting Chandra·ketu:)

Well really, the development of the rasa *here is all muddled.*
Night-blooming lotuses rejoice when the moon begins to rise
and so do my eyes when I see him. And yet my arm—
its ghastly wounds agape, throbbing with love for the heavy bow
and its string twanging so cruelly and loud—is hankering for battle.[15] (5.78–5.79 [26])

* * *

(The director of the play within the play:)

We have produced a brief composition at once purifying and filled with rasa, *the* rasas *of pity and wonder.* (7.11)

* * *

(Rama, in perhaps the best distillation in the play of the idea of how, in the absence of narrative art, life becomes unintelligible:)

Alas for the affairs of life, their incoherent, upside-down events, that lack all rasa, *that end in frustrated love, that bring only burning pain.* (6.120)

Why does the author insist on such a disenchantment of the emotional impact of his work by constantly telling us that Rama is explicitly said to be "pity incarnate," Sita "the very image of pity," Lava "the heroic *rasa* approaching," as if he were demanding we recognize in fact, again and again, that "It's only a play"? Is it a consequence of his attempt to demonstrate the true extent of his power by drawing the viewer out of the charmed circle of *rasa* only to plunge him back in? Might this feature be understood on analogy with the thematic component just discussed and thus concern the capacity of the poet to show the characters naming, and thereby reconfirming as true, the emotional state he has so skillfully created? Whatever the adequacy of these, or other, explanations, such reflexive features are evidence of a literary practice of supreme self-awareness, something also found, though in far more conflicted form, in the key conceptual problem of the play: the place of moral responsibility in human affairs.

Rewriting and Rewriting the Ramáyana

What Bhava·bhuti attempted to achieve with his ethical rethinking in 'Rama's Last Act' becomes clearer the richer the historical context of reception we can provide. And as often, this is a context that is best reconstructed backward. So let us start from the almost-present.

In late 1947, the year of Indian partition, a young man going to work along his usual route in Bombay, Maharashtra, began to notice a number of women who had taken up living on the streets. Day after day he passed the women—he never saw any men among them—his sympathy for their misery grew. Once he stopped to ask, Who are you and why are your men not with you? and they replied, We are from Sind; as for our husbands, go ask them yourself. The young man did so, and in reply to his asking, Why are you not living with your wives? he was told, Because they have been raped, and we won't take them back. But why? he pressed, and they answered, Did Rama take back Sita? This was a moment of poetic epiphany for the young man—almost like Valmíki's in response to the sorrowful event in the epic's Prelude that marks the beginning of Indian poetry—and he decided to create a new version of the 'Ramáyana' in Marathi, and along with it, he fondly hoped, a new social dispensation.[16]

The Bombay poet was only one in a long line of Indian writers who have felt compelled to respond with creative revision to Valmíki's troubling masterpiece.[17] The literary history of rewriting began almost as soon as that work was completed. A 'Maha·bhárata' poet included a version of the 'Ramáyana' in the great epic; a Buddhist poet composed a contorted account in Pali, the *Dasaratha Jātaka*, making Rama and Sita brother and sister (this sort of subversive contortion being a common Buddhist response to Hindu texts and practices);[18] the Jain poet Vímala·suri wrote a scathing critique of Valmíki in his own reworking of the tale, the Prakrit *Paümacariyam*. Such rewriting of history—and epic is history for traditional readers—has not only a long tradition, outside of the world of the 'Ramáyana' no less than within (the 'Shakúntala' rewrites the 'Maha·bhárata'), but also clear sanction in Sanskrit literary criticism.[19] So while Bhava·bhuti thus has many revisionist predecessors as well as the authority to rewrite, he may have been the first not only to produce a reworking intended for theatrical performance, but more important, to attempt to tackle the most critical problem of the story, the abandonment of Sita, the moral valence of the act, and the precise degree of Rama's personal responsibility.

I say "attempt to tackle" because it is unclear whether this is a problem that, in the context of Indian social and political theory, admits of what can reasonably be called a solution rather than a revelation of insolubility. In the version of the episode in the *Uttarakāṇḍa*, or "Last Book," of the original 'Ramáyana' (while certainly not composed by the author of Books 2–6, it was part of the text as known to Bhava·bhuti), Sita bitterly refuses reconciliation with Rama when he meets her years later in the forest, rejecting yet another demand for a fire ordeal to test her chastity, and instead beseeching mother Earth to swallow her up (which she does). In many Sanskrit versions, such as the *Rāmābhyudaya* of Yasho·varman, Bhava·bhuti's own patron, the story ends with the triumphant return of the couple to Ayódhya; the entire episode of the abandonment has been eliminated,[20] as it was in most of the later vernacular versions, including the most celebrated (in the south, Kamban's *Irāmāvatāra*, twelfth century, Tamil; in the north, Tulsi·dasa's *Rāmcaritmānas*, sixteenth century, Avadhi). Clearly the original version posed so profound an ethical dilemma that many writers preferred to simply ignore it.

Refusing to accept the *Uttarakāṇḍa*'s tale of the wife who can recover a measure of autonomy only in the act of suicide (as in fact Kali·dasa had done before him),[21] let alone to implicitly ratify the tradition by refusing to address it, Bhava·bhuti confronted head-on the problem of reconciling not just fate with human agency but political demands with personal needs. This is a task of no small order, and it is not surprising that the contradictions—intentional tensions of the poet or not we cannot know—come fast and thick throughout. When, for example, in response to an injunction from his preceptor that as new king he is required above all to win the loyalty of his subjects, Rama declares that

Affection, compassion, pleasure… indeed, Jánaki
herself
I wouldn't scruple to renounce to propitiate the
people. (1.50 [12])

Sita herself agrees, responding, "That is why my husband is the mainstay of the Rághava dynasty." By contrast, when in the play within the play (another antiphonal moment) Earth herself, Sita's mother, reproves Rama,

But was that seemly of dear Rama?
To pay no heed to the hand he grasped
in childhood, when he was a child,
or to me or Jánaka or Fire
or her deference or his progeny. (7.42–7.43 [5])

Rama (in the audience) responds (though to no real person), "Mother Earth, I am the man you describe." (7.47) It is left to the Ganga, presiding deity of Rama's clan, to make the exonerating argument:

The dreadful infamy had spread abroad
and the purifying trial by fire
took place on Lanka—how were people here
to be expected to give it credence?
The ancestral wealth of the Ikshvákus
lies in propitiating all the world.
So in these straits, most terrible straits,
what was my child supposed to do? (7.49 [6])

Sita's abandonment was fated. Arúndhati tells Kausálya: "Your family guru… affirmed that what had happened had to be so but that it would all turn out well in the end." And Ganga herself explains Sita's abandonment by saying, "Yet what creature has the power to seal the doors / of fate when it is on the verge of bearing fruit?" In other words—if these are indeed appropriate other words—Sita's abandonment was the only way true exoneration could be secured, the necessary condition for the affirmation of her chastity in public before "the entire world of creatures, moving and unmoving."

In deciding for himself what was the right thing to do Rama remains ambivalent. His earlier confident assertion had been spoken as a king in a normative political voice, not as a husband whose very existence is unthinkable without the woman he loves. The ambivalence is sharpened by the criticism he incurs not just from Earth but from the forest deity Vasánti in Act 3; from Sita throughout, who calls her being disowned "groundless," denouncing him repeatedly; and from Rama himself, who, even while recognizing the fatedness of things ("the seed of this reproach was a consequence of fate"), calls himself evil, an untouchable, an outcaste, proclaiming his guilt ("Rama is guilty of terrible wrongdoing") to the very end—unjustly so, it nevertheless turns out.

Here an instructive parallel may be offered by the slaying of the Shudra ascetic, Shambúka (another episode deeply disturbing to later poets, Sanskrit and vernacular, who usually suppress it). The right thing for the king to do, according to the moral economy of the traditional élites, is to punish the low-caste for the capital offense of violating social norms by performing the ritual acts of a high-caste man (that it is a capital offense is shown by the fact that a Brahman's son has unaccountably predeceased him, something impossible in a perfectly moral kingdom). The righteousness of the punishment is certified by a heavenly voice demanding Shambúka's decapitation and by the divine transfiguration of Shambúka after his execution. Yet Rama again shows ambivalence (this is Bhava·bhuti's invention; Valmíki knows nothing of it in the *Uttarakāṇḍa*): Few verses in Sanskrit poetry are as caustically self-critical as the one Rama speaks as he does the deed—and which closes the circle of the analogy just drawn to his abandonment of Sita:

> *O my right hand, bring down this sword*
> *upon the Shudra monk*
> *and bring the dead son of the Brahman*
> *back to life. You are a limb*
> *of Rama's—who had it in him to drive*
> *his Sita into exile,*
> *weary and heavy with child.*
> *Why start with pity now?*
> (somehow striking a blow) *There, you have done a deed worthy of Rama...* (2.68 [10]–2.69)

In the end Rama obeys a commandment higher than and in conflict with his personal judgment, and yet is vindicated in his obedience. His personal moral sense, we feel forced to conclude, is in essence flawed, whereas doing what is truly right requires overriding that sense. The fact that the hero's moral judgment might be impaired was disturbing to later readers. An eleventh-century Kashmiri critic even argued that Bhava·bhuti "destroyed his work by his own words" in allowing Lava to criticize his (as yet unrecognized) father Rama in Act 5.[22] But surely the moral ambiguity here is the very point of the play. The same hard, even terrifying logic—renouncing the claims of personal conscience and, in a kind of Abrahamic moment, following some external authority even when this appears to be a sin—would seem to apply to Rama's abandonment of Sita as well.

Matters may not be quite so cut and dried, however. One of the things that make Bhava·bhuti a great writer is his refusal to provide any simple, and therefore necessarily simple-minded, answers to the often bitter tension between social and personal ethics. Poets are not ethicists; their business is not to offer actionable solutions but to probe the nature of the human predicament with moral dilemmas that are often irresolvable. It is only at the end of the play, which modern readers are likely to find altogether unsatisfying, that the untranscendable conventions of the Sanskrit theater get the better of Bhava·bhuti: a *deus ex machina* in the form of "the purifying miracle that Valmíki has vouchsafed" restores Sita to Rama; her innocence is proclaimed, the scandal-mongers are chastised, and everyone lives happily ever after. But the contradictions the poet so powerfully framed—between personal happiness and social obligation, between the need to act and the sense that everything has always already been enacted—remain sharp to the very end in the dispute between Earth and Ganga themselves and in Rama's almost incoherent exclamation to Sita that this fated "turn of events befell you because of Rama," and are there to gnaw at the audience as they make their way complacently from the theater.[23]

Text, Editions, Commentaries

There are more than 200 manuscripts of 'Rama's Last Act' catalogued in libraries across the Indian subcontinent and in the West, a relatively large number for a Sanskrit text, which testifies to its great popularity ('Málati and Mádhava' is extant in about half that number, 'Shakúntala' in perhaps half again as much). The work was critically edited once, by S. K. Belvalkar, but his edition suffered a curious fate.

The text and apparatus meant to constitute Parts 2 and 3 respectively of his edition for the Harvard Oriental Series were never issued (Part 1, the introduction and translation, came out in 1915). Part 2 was printed at the Nirnaya Sagar Press c. 1914 but not published as such; another edition, re-set in the identical font but somewhat less correctly, was later brought out in the Poona Oriental Series. What happened to BELVALKAR's critical apparatus remains a mystery; he was still promising it as late as 1921.[24] A copy of BELVALKAR's rare NSP version forms the basis of the text published here.

Without having access to BELVALKAR's critical apparatus it is impossible to know let alone assess the evidence behind his editorial choices. Despite his claim (in the Sanskrit preface to the Pune edition) that he exhaustively examined regional traditions and commentaries, he did not take into account the Malayalam version of the commentator Nārāyaṇa, far and away the best version of the play so far discovered. It is also clear that he relied heavily on the often less convincing northern tradition represented in the manuscripts from Nepal, though he did not have access to the best manuscript of this group, a copy in *kuṭila* script dated 1196 CE (thus among the half-dozen oldest extant manuscripts of a Sanskrit drama). He also seems to have placed too much trust in the often faulty text of the commentator Bhaṭṭa Nārāyaṇa, especially for the Prakrit portions (though this commentator provides only the Sanskrit *chāyā* and BELVALKAR's reconstructions are sometimes faulty).

Short of establishing an entirely new edition, I have adopted the following principles: I have generally followed BELVALKAR, who often presents a text that in countless places is an improvement over anything available. Where the 1196 CE Newari manuscript and Nārāyaṇa agree against BELVALKAR I have rejected him with full confidence, with somewhat less confidence where he is contradicted by the unanimous testimony of the commentators. Where a clearly superior reading was offered by one or several (though not all) of the commentators, especially Nārāyaṇa, I have tended to consider it seriously if more hesitantly, since here one's subjective view can most mislead.

Although there are commentaries on 'Málati and Mádhava' from as early as the twelfth century,[25] the oldest one available on 'Rama's Last Act,' that of the Kerala scholar Nārāyaṇa,[26] dates only from the early seventeenth. It must be counted among the more careful and perceptive ever produced for a Sanskrit play. Nārāyaṇa's text is very frequently corroborated by the eighteenth-century Andhra scholiast Vīrarāghava; the two together may be taken to represent a southern tradition. Inferior both textually and critically is the work of Ghanaśyāma of Maratha Tanjavur, arguably at once the most arrogant and ignorant of Sanskrit commentators (fl. 1725; he was earlier than and known to Vīrarāghava). I have already referred to the less reliable text of Bhaṭṭa Nārāyaṇa (also known as Nārāyaṇa Dīkṣita), son of a minor grammarian named Ranganātha Dīkṣita and resident in Varanasi in the first half of the seventeenth century; this, along with the Newari manuscript, may be taken to represent a northern tradition.[27] All this material merits far more systematic sifting than could be attempted here. Unless BELVALKAR's apparatus somehow turns up, the study of the manuscript history of 'Rama's Last Act' can scarcely be said to have begun. An analysis of its textual dynamics, especially in comparison with those of the two other plays, is a real desideratum.

Variation in the Sanskrit text is on the whole a matter of the occasional reading. There are no serious additions or omissions let alone evidence of revisions major enough to make a case for an authorial second edition, as scholars believe occurred for 'Málati and Mádhava,'[28] to say nothing of regional recensions, as are present for 'Shakúntala.' Yet these variants are often consequential and in their totality they affect our interpretation of the play in many subtle ways, as the notes to the edition and annotations show. The Prakrit text, as usual, has been rather less reliably transmitted. Again, short of reediting the entire play, I have generally followed BELVALKAR, silently correcting obvious errors (though keeping his multiple spellings of the same word) and rejecting his readings only when the commentators, in particular Nārāyaṇa, offered something that seemed patently preferable.

The text offered is not intended as a variorum let alone a critical edition. The variant readings printed as endnotes record only where I have departed from BELVALKAR's text, providing the evidence in support of my choice as well as the evidence available to me that supports BELVALKAR. The annotations have also been kept brief, in accordance with Clay Sanskrit Library style. They are intended to explain the reasons for the translation adopted and to weigh select alternatives, and do not discuss all the commentators' interpretations. I have assumed that scholars who seek more information will have access to the two most important annotated editions, those of KANE and STCHOUPAK, and, accordingly, I have refrained from repeating the information they have already provided.

NOTES

1 A number of verses ascribed to him in anthologies cannot be traced in these works, but it is doubtful they are authentic or indicate that texts were lost.

2 The so-called Bhasa plays (the *Pratimānāṭaka* and the *Abhiṣekanāṭaka* are based on the *Rāmāyaṇa*) are far later than scholars once thought. One other early Rama play, the *Kundamālā* of Dhira·naga, is almost certainly dependent on Bhava·bhuti (MIRASHI 1974: 292–305). Intriguingly, the *Rāmābhyudaya* (available only in fragments) is attributed to Yasho·varman, and may have been written as a response to Bhava·bhuti's work (see Introduction, note 19).

3 *Subhāṣitaratnakośa* 1698 (I thank Gary TUBB for the idea of parody here); 1733. On the canonizing function of the literary encomium see POLLOCK 2003: 76–80.

4 A similar interest in the poet's emotional range I now find in BELVALKAR (1915: xxxviii–xxxix).

5 POLLOCK 1993.

6 HARSHÉ seems to have been the first to compare the two plays (1938: 63–66), though his perspective is entirely different from mine. Other works of Kali·dasa are alluded to in the play, including *Vikramorvaśīya* (in Act 3) and *Meghadūta* (see endnote to 1.136 [33])

7 KANE 1986.

8 This structural element seems to have first been perceived by Walter RUBEN (1956); see also POLLOCK 2004 and VASUDEVA 2006: 22–23. A larger argument, based on the widespread independent discovery of this compositional technique, is offered in DOUGLAS 2007.

9 For quite different reflections on the theme see JASPART-PANSU 1997.

10 An innovation of Bhava·bhuti's; in the 'Ramáyana,' she explicitly rejects suicide so as not to kill the heirs to Rama's throne (STCHOUPAK 1935: 48 n.).

11 A variation on this theme is offered in Act 3: Here Sita, audience-like because made invisible by the Ganga and therefore outside the main action of the scene, learns at last the true depth of Rama's love for her.

12 Just this sort of metaliterary trope can be found even in folk literature, see RAMANUJAN 1991.

13 For many later Indian thinkers *karuṇa* is possible only if the beloved is actually dead; if he or she is merely absent, the mood is the erotic-in-separation. In addition to that problem, "pity" is an inadequate translation, since *karuṇa* does not only or even primarily concern outward-directed sadness but rather sadness for oneself. In the case of Rama this comes in part from having lost the sons that are required to help him repay the debt to his ancestors (6.28 [8]).

14 So that readers can register this fact, and also because of the inadequacy of any English term, the word *rasa* is left untranslated throughout.

15 This verse, Act 5.79 [26], and the previous, Act 3.258 [48], at the same time constitute examples of antiphony.

16 SADHALE 1988.

17 Two useful collections of essays are RICHMAN 1991 and 2000.

18 I regard as untenable the view that either the Pali or the 'Maha·bhárata' version precedes Valmíki.

19 The ninth-century theorist Anánda·várdhana authorizes poets to revise historical accounts in the interests of *rasa* (see Pollock

2003: 58). Curiously, Bhava·bhuti's patron Yasho·varman may have been one of the few who opposed the practice of radical revision, demanding *kathāmārge na cātikramaḥ*, "close adherence to the [received] storyline" (see RAGHAVAN 1961: 7).

20 RAGHAVAN 1961: 10–11.

21 *Raghuvaṃśa* 14.

22 Kṣemendra, *Aucityavicāracarcā* p. 10. Kshéméndra's statement that "the dominant *rasa* of the whole work" is the heroic, rather than the piteous, as Bhava·bhuti himself affirms, is a jaw-dropping blunder. Or did he misremember the verse as belonging to 'Acts of the Great Hero'?

23 See endnote to 7.19.

24 BELVALKAR 1921: iii–iv.

25 GRIMAL 1999.

26 A pupil of the celebrated philosopher-poet Melputtūr Nārāyaṇa Bhaṭṭari he also wrote commentaries on the works of Kali·dasa (though largely by paraphrasing the earlier commentator Aruṇagirinātha). A commentary attributed to the learned Rāmacandra Budhendra (which is unavailable to me) cannot have been written by him, since not a single manuscript of the work bearing his name is known to exist (see also KANE 1971: 43).

27 On the superiority of the southern tradition of the 'Acts of the Great Hero,' see MALL 1928: xviii.

28 COULSON 1989: xxx–xli; BELVALKAR 1915: lxxii.

Abbreviations

B = the NSP edition of Belvalkar

Bh = Bhavabhūti

BN = commentary of Bhaṭṭa Nārāyaṇa [IO 4137 = BL shelfmark IO San 1605b Oxf. ms Wilson 165c]

C = commentators

G = commentary of Ghanaśyāma

H = commentary of Harihara on MM

Index = *Index des mots de l'oeuvre de Bhavabhūti*, ed. Grimal

K = edition and notes of Kane

MM = *Mālatīmādhava*

MVC = *Mahāvīracarita*

N = commentary of Nārāyaṇa

Ne = The Newari ms of 1196 ce [National Archives, Kathmandu, 1–344, Nepal-German Manuscript Preservation Project reel-number B 15/4)]

R = *Rāmāyaṇa* of Vālmīki (crit. ed.)

S = edition and translation of Stchoupak

V = commentary of Vīrarāghava

v. = verse

v.l. = varia lectio

a, *b*, *c*, *d* = first, second, third, fourth *pāda* respectively

Bibliography and References

Editions and Commentaries of Bhavabhūti's Works

Apekṣitavyākhyāna of Bhaṭṭa Nārāyaṇa on *Uttararāmacarita*. British Library shelfmark IO San 1605b; Oxford ms. Wilson 165c.

Belvalkar, Shripad Krishna, ed. [c. 1914]. [*Bhavabhuti's Uttara-Rama-charita*]. [Bombay: Nirnaya Sagar Press].

Belvalkar, Shripad Krishna, ed. 1921. *Bhavabhuti's Uttara-Rama-charita (text only)*. Pune : Oriental Book-Supplying Agency.

COULSON, MICHAEL, ed. 1989. *A Critical Edition of the Mālatīmādhava*, rev. Roderick SINCLAIR. Delhi: Oxford University Press.

GRIMAL, FRANÇOIS, ed. 1999. *Mālatīmādhavaṭīkā: Le commentaire de Harihara sur le Mālatīmādhava de Bhavabhūti*. Pondicherry: Institut français de Pondichéry.

KANE, PANDURANGA VAMANA, ed., and C. N. JOSHI, trans. 1915. *Uttararāmacarita* [with the commentary of Ghanaśyāma]. Girgaum, Bombay, sold by the Oriental Pub. Co.; reprint Delhi, 1971.

MALL, TODAR, ed. 1928. *Mahāvīra-Caritam*. London: Humphrey Milford.

SANKARA RAMA SASTRI, C. ed. 1932. *Uttararāmacharita* [with the commentary of Nārāyaṇa]. Mylapore, Madras: Sri Balamanorama Press.

PRIMARY WORKS

Aucityavicāracarcā of Kṣemendra. 1933. Edited by DHUNDIRAJA SASTRI. Varanasi: Chaukhamba Sanskrit Series Office.

Subhāṣitaratnakośa of Vidyākara. 1957. Edited By D. D. KOSAMBI and V. V. GOKHALE. Cambridge: Harvard University Press.

Śṛṅgāraprakāśa of Bhoja. 1998–. Edited by V. RAGHAVAN. Cambridge: Harvard University Press.

SECONDARY WORKS

BELVALKAR, SHRIPAD KRISHNA, trans. 1915. *Rama's Later History or Uttara Rama Charita: An Ancient Hindu Drama*. Part 1: Introduction and Translation. Cambridge: Harvard University Press.

DOUGLAS, MARY. 2007. *Thinking in Circles: An Essay on Ring Composition*. New Haven: Yale University Press.

GRIMAL, FRANÇOIS, ed. 2005. *Index des mots de l'oeuvre de Bhavabhūti*. Pondicherry: Institut français de Pondichéry.

HARSHÉ, R. G. 1938. *Observations sur la vie et l'oeuvre de Bhavabhūti*. Paris: Editions littéraires de France.

JASPART-PANSU, CAROLE. 1997. 'La Mise en abyme dans l'Uttararāmacarita.' *Puruṣārtha* 20: 123–36.

KANE, MARGARET. 1986. *The Theory of Plot Structure in Sanskrit Drama and its Application to the Uttararāmacarita.* Dissertation, Harvard University.

MIRASHI, V. V. 1974. *Bhavabhūti.* Delhi: Motilal Banarsidass.

POLLOCK, SHELDON. 2006. *Ramáyana III: The Forest.* New York: New York University Press and the JJC Foundation.

POLLOCK, SHELDON. 2004. 'Shakuntala.' In *Longman Anthology of World Literature, Vol. A: The Ancient World*, ed. DAVID DAMROSCH *et al*. New York: Longman.

POLLOCK, SHELDON. 2003. 'Sanskrit Literature from the Inside Out.' In *Literary Cultures in History: Reconstructions from South Asia*, edited by SHELDON POLLOCK. Berkeley: University of California Press.

POLLOCK, SHELDON. 1993. '*Rāmāyaṇa* and Political Imagination in India.' *Journal of Asian Studies* 52.2: 261–97.

POLLOCK, SHELDON. 1986. *The Rāmāyaṇa of Vālmīki, Vol. II: Ayodhyā.* Princeton: Princeton University Press.

RAGHAVAN, V. 1961. *Some Old Lost Rama Plays.* Annamalainagar: Annamalai University.

RAMANUJAN, A. K. 1991. 'Three Hundred Ramayanas: Thoughts on Translation.' In RICHMAN, ed., *Many Rāmāyaṇas.*

RICHMAN, PAULA, ed. 2000. *Questioning Rāmāyaṇas: A South Asian Tradition.* Berkeley: University of California Press.

RICHMAN, PAULA, ed. 1991. *Many Rāmāyaṇas: The Diversity of a Narrative Tradition in South Asia.* Berkeley: University of California Press.

RUBEN, WALTER. 1956. *Kālidāsa. Die menschliche Bedeutung seiner Werke.* Berlin: Akademie-Verlag.

SADHALE, ANAND 1988. *Mahārāṣṭra Rāmāyaṇa: mahākāvya.* Pune: Srividya Prakasana.

STCHOUPAK, NADINE, trans. 1935. *Uttararāmacarita (La dernière aventure de Rāma).* Paris: Les belles lettres.

VASUDEVA, SOMADEVA. 2006. *The Recognition of Shakúntala.* New York: New York University Press and the JJC Foundation.

DRAMATIS PERSONÆ

Characters marked with ⌜corner brackets⌟ speak Prakrit.

Sūtradhāra:	Director
Naṭa:	Actor
Rāma:	Rama (king of Ayódhya)
⌜Sītā⌟:	Sita (wife of Rama)
Kañcukī:	Chamberlain
Aṣṭāvakara:	Ashta·vakra (a sage)
Lakṣmaṇa:	Lákshmana (Rama's younger brother)
⌜Pratīhārī⌟:	Female doorkeeper
⌜Durmukha⌟:	Dúrmukha (a harem attendant)
Ātreyī:	Atréyi (a female ascetic)
Vāsantī:	Vasánti (forest spirit)
Śambhūka:	Shambhúka (a Shudra ascetic)
Muralā:	Múrala (a river spirit)
Tamasā:	Támasa (a river spirit)
⌜Saudhātaki⌟:	Saudhátaki (a student)
Bhāṇḍāyana:	Bhandáyana (a student)
Janaka:	Jánaka (father of Sita)
Arundhatī:	Arúndhati (wife of the sage Vasíshtha)
Gṛṣṭi:	Chamberlain to Valmíki
⌜Kausalyā⌟:	Kausálya (mother of Rama)
Lava:	Lava (Rama's son)
Baṭavaḥ:	Students
Puruṣa:	An officer
Candraketu:	Chandra·ketu (Rama's nephew)
Sumantra:	Sumántra (Chandra·ketu's charioteer)
Vidyādhara:	*Vidya·dhara* man
⌜Vidyādharī⌟:	*Vidya·dhara* woman
Kuśa:	Kusha (Rama's son)
Vālmīki:	Valmíki (author of the *Ramáyana*)

In the play within the play:

Sūtradhāra:	Director
Pṛthivī:	Earth
Bhāgirathī:	Bhagi·rathi (the Ganga River)

mở đầu một vở kịch

PROLOGUE

IDAṂ KAVIBHYAḤ pūrvebhyo
namo|vākaṃ praśāsmahe.
vandemahi ca tāṃ vācam
amṛtām ātmanaḥ kalām. [1]

nāndy|ante

SŪTRA|DHĀRAḤ: alam ativistareṇa. adya khalu bhagavataḥ Kāla|priya|nāthasya yātrāyām ārya|miśrān vijnāpayāmi. evam atra|bhavanto vidāṃ kurvantu. asti tatra|bhavān Kāśyapaḥ Śrīkaṇṭha|pada|lāñchano Bhavabhūtir nāma.

yaṃ *brahmāṇam* iyaṃ devī
Vāg vaśy" êv' ânvavartata
Uttaraṃ Rāma|caritaṃ
tat|praṇītaṃ prayokṣyate. [2]

1.5 eṣo 'smi kavi|vaśād Āyodhyakas tadānīntanaś ca saṃvṛttaḥ. *(samantād avalokya)* bho bhoḥ? yadā tāvad atra|bhavataḥ Paulastya|kula|dhūma|ketor mahā|rāja|Rāmasy' âyam abhiṣeka|samayo rātrin|divam a|saṃhṛt'|ānanda|nāndīkas, tat kim adya viśrānta|cāraṇāni catvara|sthānāni?

---

[i] A town south of Kanauj; the Lord is probably the Sun god. [ii] Śiva.
[iii] Family name of the demon king Rāvaṇa.

THIS WE OFFER with an expression
of homage* to the poets of old.
Let us also pay reverence to language,
a deathless thing, a part of the soul.

At the end of the benediction

DIRECTOR: Without further ado, I must now make an announcement to this discerning audience at the festival of the Blessed Lord of Kala·priya.[i] My good sirs have no doubt heard of a man named Bhava·bhuti, who belongs to the Káshyapa family and bears the epithet* Shri·kantha.[ii]

Goddess Language has always complied with this
Brahman
as obediently *as she does Brahma,**
and it was he who composed 'Rama's Last Act,'
the play we will perform for you today.

Here I myself, in obedience to the poet,* now transform 1.5
myself into a sojourner in Ayódhya* of that day and age. *(glancing all around)* Hello, anyone there? I wonder why the musicians are no longer performing in the courtyards when for days and nights on end the joyful music never stopped for the coronation ceremony of the great king, the honorable Rama, that firestorm to the clan of Paulástya?[iii]

NAṬAḤ: *(praviśya)* bhāva, preṣitā hi te sva|gṛhān mahā|rājena Laṅkā|samara|suhṛdo mah"|ātmānaḥ plavaṅga|rākṣasāḥ sabhājan'|ôpasthāyinaś ca nānā|dig|anta|pāvanā brahma'|rṣayo deva'|rṣayaś ca, yad|ārādhanāy' âitāvato divasān utsava āsīt. samprati hi

Vasiṣṭh'|âdhiṣṭhitā devyo
gatā Rāmasya mātaraḥ
Arundhatīṃ puraskṛtya
yajñe jāmātur āśrayam. [3]

SŪTRA|DHĀRAḤ: vaideśiko 'sm' îti pṛcchāmi. kaḥ punar jāmātā?

NAṬAḤ:

kanyāṃ Daśaratho rājā
Śāntāṃ nāma vyajījanat
apatya|kṛtikāṃ rājñe
Lomapādāya yāṃ dadau. [4]

1.10 Vibhāṇḍaka|sutas tām Ṛṣyaśṛṅga upayeme. tena dvādaśa|vārṣikaṃ satram ārabdham. tad|anurodhāt kaṭhora|garbhām api vadhūṃ Jānakīṃ vimucya guru|janas tatra gataḥ.

SŪTRA|DHĀRAḤ: tat kim anena? ehi. rāja|dvāram eva sva|jāti|samayen' ôpatiṣṭhāvaḥ.

---

[i] Wife of Vasiṣṭha, family priest of Rāma's clan. [ii] The sacrifice will thus span the time frame of the play's narrative. [iii] Sītā.

Enter an ACTOR: My friend, the great allies at the battle of Lanka, the monkeys and *rákshasa*s,* have been sent home by the king. The same goes for the Brahmans and deities* who came to pay him their respects, purifying* every region through which they passed. It was to honor these guests that the festival had been going on for so many days. For now*

> The queen mothers of Rama have gone off—
> watched over by Vasíshtha
> and following Arúndhati[i]—for a ritual at their
> son-in-law's ashram.

DIRECTOR: Say—I ask because I'm not native to these parts —who is this son-in-law?

ACTOR:

> King Dasha·ratha fathered a girl named Shanta
> and bestowed her on King Loma·pada as an adoptive daughter.

She was married to Rishya·shringa, Vibhándaka's son, and 1.10
he's the one who has just initiated this twelve-year-long sacrifice.[ii] Out of deference to him the elders have gone on a visit, leaving behind their daughter-in-law Jánaki,[iii] though she is far advanced in pregnancy.

DIRECTOR: No matter, come along, we should pay court at the palace gate in accordance with our caste duty.

NAṬAḤ: tena hi nirūpayatu rājñaḥ su|pariśuddhām upasthāna|stotra|paddhatiṃ bhāvaḥ.

SŪTRA|DHĀRAḤ: māriṣa,

sarvathā vyavahartavyaṃ.
  kuto hy a|vacanīyatā?
yathā strīṇāṃ tathā vācāṃ
  sādhutve dur|jano janaḥ. [5]

I.15 NAṬAḤ: ati|dur|jana iti vaktavyam,

devyām api hi Vaidehyāṃ
  s'|âpavādo yato janaḥ:
rakṣo|gṛha|sthitir mūlam,
  agni|śuddhau tv a|niścayaḥ. [6]

SŪTRA|DHĀRAḤ: yadi punar iyaṃ kiṃ|vadantī mahā|rājaṃ prati syandet, tataḥ kaṣṭaṃ syāt.

NAṬAḤ: sarvatha" ṛṣayo devatāś ca śreyo vidhāsyanti. *(parikramya)* bho bhoḥ? kv' êdānīṃ mahā|rājaḥ? *(ākarṇya)* evaṃ janāḥ kathayanti:

---

[i] Sītā.

ACTOR: Well then, my friend had better come up with a courtly panegyric whose style* is utterly flawless.

DIRECTOR: My dear fellow,

It is our duty to act no matter what.*
There is no escaping criticism.
However pure the words—or the woman—
there are always people who'll be malicious.

ACTOR: Worse than malicious, you should have said, 1.15

Since the people are reproaching
Vaidéhi,[i] the queen herself. The reason?
The fact that she lived in the *rákshasa*'s house
and their doubts about the fire ordeal.*

DIRECTOR: It would be awful if this gossip were ever to reach the king.

ACTOR: At all events the seers and deities will see to their welfare. *(walks around)* Hello, anyone there? Where is the king at present? *(listening)* The people are saying

snehāt sabhājayitum etya dināny amūni
nītv" ôtsavena Janako 'dya gato Videhān.
devyās tato vimanasaḥ parisāntvanāya
dharm'|āsanād viśati vāsa|gṛhaṃ nar'|êndraḥ. [7]

1.20 *niṣkrāntau.*

Prastāvanā

---

[i] Father of Sītā.

Jánaka[i] came to pay his respects out of deep
affection,
passed some days in celebration, and now has
returned to Vidéha.
The queen is therefore distraught, and to
console her the king
has left the throne of *dharma* and gone back to his
dwelling.

Exeunt both. 1.20

End of the Prologue

ACT I
AT THE PAINTING EXHIBITION

tataḥ praviśaty upaviṣṭo RĀMAḤ, SĪTĀ *ca.*

RĀMAḤ: devi Vaidehi, samāśvasihi samāśvasihi. te hi guravo na śaknuvanty asmān vimoktum.

kin tv anuṣṭhāna|nityatvaṃ
svātantryam apakarṣati.
saṅkaṭā hy āhit'|âgnīnāṃ
pratyavāyair gṛhasthatā. [8]

1.25 SĪTĀ: ⌜jāṇāmi, ajja|utta, jāṇāmi. kin du sandāva|āriṇo bandhu|aṇa|vippaoā honti.⌟

RĀMAḤ: evam etat. ete hi hṛdaya|marma|cchidaḥ saṃsāra| bhāgā yebhyo bībhatsamānāḥ santyajya sarvān kāmān araṇye viśrāmyanti manīṣiṇaḥ.

KAÑCUKĪ: *(praviśya)* Rāma|bhadra... *(ardh'|ôkte s'|āśaṅkam)* mahā|rāja...

RĀMAḤ: *(sa|smitam)* ārya, nanu «Rāma|bhadra ity» eva māṃ praty upacāraḥ śobhate tāta|parijanasya. tad yath"|âbhyāsam ucyatām.

KAÑCUKĪ: Ṛṣyaśṛṅg'|āśramād Aṣṭāvakraḥ samprāptaḥ.

1.30 SĪTĀ: ⌜ajja, tado kiṃ vilambīadi?⌟

RĀMAḤ: tvaritaṃ praveśaya.

KAÑCUKĪ *niṣkrāntaḥ.*

The scene opens on RAMA, *seated, and* SITA.

RAMA: Queen Vaidéhi, please don't be upset. It wasn't easy for our elders to leave us.

> But the constant press of observances restricts one's freedom.
> For the religious, domestic life is fraught with obstacles.*

SITA: I know, my husband, I know. It's just that parting 1.25
from loved ones is a source of such sadness.

RAMA: It's true. These are the things of life that tear at the heart's soft core and make sensitive people feel such revulsion* they're ready to give up all objects of desire and seek peace in the wilderness.

Enter the CHAMBERLAIN: Dear Rama... *(breaks off, then anxiously)* Your Majesty...

RAMA: Good man, come now, the salutation "dear Rama" for me is entirely appropriate from someone of my father's retinue. So speak to me as was your habit of old.

CHAMBERLAIN: Ashta·vakra has arrived from Rishya·shringa's ashram.

SITA: Good man, why then the delay? 1.30

RAMA: Show him in at once.

Exit CHAMBERLAIN.

AṢṬĀVAKRAḤ: *(praviśya)* svasti vām.

RĀMAḤ: bhagavann, abhivādaye. ita āsyatām.

1.35 SĪTĀ: ⌜ṇamo de. avi kusalaṃ me samaggassa guru|aṇassa, ajjāe a Santāe?⌟

RĀMAḤ: nirvighnaḥ soma|pītī āvutto me bhagavān Ṛṣyaśṛṅgaḥ, āryā ca Śāntā?

SĪTĀ: ⌜amhe vā sumaradi?⌟

AṢṬĀVAKRAḤ: *(upaviśya)* atha kim? devi, bhagavān Vasiṣṭhas tvām āha:

«Viśvambharā bhagavatī bhavatīm asūta.
rājā Prajāpati|samo Janakaḥ pitā te.
teṣāṃ vadhūs tvam asi, nandini, pārthivānāṃ
yeṣāṃ gṛheṣu Savitā ca gurur vayaṃ ca. [9]

1.40 tat kim anyad āśāsmahe? kevalaṃ vīra|prasavā bhūyāḥ.»

RĀMAḤ: anugṛhītāḥ smaḥ.

laukikānāṃ hi sādhūnām
arthaṃ vāg anuvartate.
ṛṣīṇāṃ punar ādyānāṃ
vācam artho 'nudhāvati. [10]

---

i A beverage consumed in a solemn Vedic rite. ii The sun was considered the primal ancestor of Rāma's lineage.

Enter ASHTA·VAKRA: My blessings on you both.

RAMA: Greetings, blessed one. Please be seated.

SITA: Homage to you. Is all well with my elders and my sister-in-law Shanta? 1.35

RAMA: Is my brother-in-law Rishya·shringa, a man who has drunk *soma*,[i] prospering as well as my sister Shanta?

SITA: Has she remembered herself to us?

ASHTA·VAKRA: *(taking his seat)* To be sure. Queen, Vasíshtha has this to say to you:

> "It was the blessed Earth herself,
> the All-supporting, who gave you birth,
> your father is King Jánaka,
> peer of the cosmic demiurge,
> and you are the daughter-in-law,
> my child, of a family of kings
> who have two gurus in their home:
> ourselves and the very Sun.[ii]

What else, then, could we wish for you aside from giving birth to heroes?" 1.40

RAMA: We are deeply gratified.

> In everyday life a good man's words correspond with facts.
> But in the case of a primal seer the facts conform with his words.

AṢṬĀVAKRAḤ: idaṃ bhagavaty" Ârundhatyā, devībhiḥ, Śāntayā ca bhūyo bhūyaḥ sandiṣṭam: «yaḥ kaś cid garbha|dohado 'syā bhavati so 'vaśyam a|cirān mānayitavyaḥ.»

RĀMAḤ: kriyate yad eṣā kathayati.

1.45 AṢṬĀVAKRAḤ: nanānduḥ patyā ca devyāḥ sandiṣṭam Ṛṣyaśṛṅgeṇa: «vatse, kaṭhora|garbh" êti n' ânīt" âsi. vatso 'pi Rāma|bhadras tvad|vinod'|ârtham eva sthāpitaḥ. tat putra|pūrṇ'|ôtsaṅgām āyuṣmatīṃ drakṣyāmaḥ.»

RĀMAḤ: *(sa|harṣa|lajjā|smitam)* tath" âstu. bhagavatā punar Vasiṣṭhena na kiṃ cid ādiṣṭo 'smi?

AṢṬĀVAKRAḤ: śrūyatām:

«jāmātṛ|yajñena vayaṃ niruddhās.
   tvaṃ bāla ev' âsi, navaṃ ca rājyam.
yuktaḥ prajānām anurañjane syās.
   svasmād yaśo yat paramaṃ dhanaṃ vaḥ.» [11]

ASHTA·VAKRA: Arúndhati, the queens, and Shanta were insistent on directing you as follows: "Whatever cravings Sita may have in her pregnancy are to be satisfied without hesitation."

RAMA: We will do whatever she asks.

ASHTA·VAKRA: Rishya·shringa, the husband of her sister-in- 1.45
law, directed the queen as follows: "Child, you were not asked to come because your pregnancy is so far advanced.* Dear Rama, our son, was charged with the sole task of providing you some diversion. We hope to see you soon, flourishing, with a son filling your embrace."

RAMA: *(smiling with joy and embarrassment)* So be it. Has Vasíshtha sent me no message?

ASHTA·VAKRA: Listen:

"We have been detained at the sacrifice of your
brother-in-law.
You are but a child and your kingship has just
begun.
Dedicate yourself to the conciliation of your
subjects
since reputation is a treasure more precious than
life itself."*

RĀMAḤ: yath" āha bhagavān Maitrāvaruṇiḥ:

1.50 sneham dayāṃ ca saukhyaṃ ca
yadi vā Jānakīm api
ārādhanāya lokasya
muñcato n' âsti me vyathā. [12]

SĪTĀ: ⌜ado jjevva Rāhava|dhurandharo ajja|utto.⌟

RĀMAḤ: kaḥ ko 'tra bhoḥ? viśrāmyatām Aṣṭāvakraḥ.

AṢṬĀVAKRAḤ: *(utthāya, parikramya)* aye, kumāra | Lakṣmaṇaḥ prāptaḥ. *(niṣkrāntaḥ)*

LAKṢMAṆAḤ: *(praviśya)* jayatv āryaḥ. ārya, tena citra|kareṇ' âsmad | upadiṣṭam asyāṃ vīthikāyām āryasya caritam abhilikhitam. tat paśyatv āryā.

1.55 RĀMAḤ: jānāsi, vatsa, durmanāyamānāṃ devīṃ vinodayitum. tat kiyantam avadhiṃ yāvat?

LAKṢMAṆAḤ: yāvad āryāyā hut'|āśane viśuddhiḥ.

RĀMAḤ: śāntam.

utpatti|paripūtāyāḥ
kim asyāḥ pāvan'|ântaraiḥ?
tīrth'|ôdakaṃ ca vahniś ca
n' ânyataḥ śuddhim arhataḥ. [13]

---

[i] Vasiṣṭha.

RAMA: It will be as Maitra·váruni[i] says.

> Affection, compassion, pleasure… indeed, Jánaki herself 1.50
> I wouldn't scruple to renounce to propitiate the people.*

SITA: That is why my husband is the mainstay of the Rághava dynasty.

RAMA: Hello, anyone there? Have Ashta·vakra take his rest.

ASHTA·VAKRA: *(stands and walks around)* Ah, Prince Lákshmana has arrived. *(exit)**

Enter LÁKSHMANA: Long live my brother. The painter has completed his depiction of your life story in the picture gallery, just as we recounted it to him.* Sister-in-law is invited to view it.

RAMA: Dear brother, you're good at finding ways to divert 1.55
our dejected queen. How far does the story go?

LÁKSHMANA: Up to sister-in-law's purification by fire.

RAMA: Silence!

> What need had she of absolution who was wholly absolved at birth?
> Neither holy water nor fire requires cleansing from some secondary source.

devi deva|yajana|sambhave, prasīda. eṣa te jīvit'|âvadhiḥ praṇāmaḥ.

1.60 kaṣṭo janaḥ kula|dhanair anurañjanīyas.
tan me yad uktam a|śivaṃ na hi tat kṣamaṃ te.
naisargikī surabhiṇaḥ kusumasya siddhā
mūrdhni sthitir na caraṇair avatāḍitāni. [14]

SĪTĀ: ⌜bhodu, ajja|utta, bhodu. ehi pekkhamha dāva de caridaṃ.⌟

utthāya parikrāmati.

LAKṢMAṆAḤ: idaṃ tad ālekhyam.

SĪTĀ: *(nirvarṇya)* ⌜ke dāṇiṃ ede uvari ṇirantara|ṭṭhidā uvatthuṇanti via ajja|uttaṃ?⌟

1.65 LAKṢMAṆAḤ: etāni tāni sa|rahasya|Jṛmbhak'|âstrāṇi yāni bhagavataḥ Kṛśāśvāt Kauśikam ṛṣiṃ viśvasya mitraṃ Viśvāmitram upasaṅkrāntāni. tena ca Tāṭakā|vadhe prasādī|kṛtāny āryasya.

RĀMAḤ: vandasva, devi, divy'|âstrāṇi.

---

[i] "Soporific" literally, "Yawn-maker." [ii] An ancient sage. [iii] A female demon who had been disrupting Viśvāmitra's ritual practices.

Dear queen, you who were born at a sacred rite, I beg your forgiveness. This deference I pay to you I will pay for the rest of my life.*

> Those for whom true wealth is family honor 1.60
> must conciliate their critics.
> The ungodly thing I thus was forced to ask
> should never have been asked of you.
> As everyone knows the most natural place
> to display a rare and fragrant flower
> is on the very crown of the head,
> not lying trampled underfoot.*

SITA: Let it be, my husband, let it be. Come, let's just have a look at your life story.

He stands up and walks around. *

LÁKSHMANA: The murals are over here.

SITA: *(gazing)* Who are the beings in this episode crowding together overhead and appearing to sing my husband's praises?

LÁKSHMANA: Those are the magic Jrímbhaka[i] weapons with their secret invocations. Krisháshva[ii] bestowed them upon the seer, Káushika Vishva·mitra, "friend to all the world,"* and he gifted them to brother upon his killing Tátaka.[iii] 1.65

RAMA: Queen, do obeisance to the divine weapons.

Brahm'|ādayo brahma|hitāya taptvā
  paraḥ|sahasrāḥ śaradas tapāṃsi
etāny apaśyan guravaḥ purāṇāḥ
  svāny eva tejāṃsi tapomayāni. [15]

SĪTĀ: ⌜ṇamo edāṇaṃ.⌟

RĀMAḤ: sarvath" êdānīṃ tvat|prasūtim upasthāsyanti.

1.70 SĪTĀ: ⌜aṇugahida mhi.⌟

LAKṢMAṆAḤ: eṣa Mithilā|vṛttāntaḥ.

SĪTĀ: ⌜amhahe. dalanta|ṇava|ṇīl'|uppala|sāmala|siṇiddha|masiṇa|maṃsaleṇa deha|sohaggeṇa vimhaa|tthimida|tāda|dīsanta|somma|sundara|sirī aṇ|ādara|kkhuḍida|Saṅkara|sar'|âsaṇo sihaṇḍa|muddha|maṇḍaṇo ajja|utto ālihido.⌟

LAKṢMAṆAḤ: ārye, paśya paśya:

sambandhino Vasiṣṭh'|ādīn
  eṣa tātas tav' ârcati,
Gautamaś ca Śatānando
  Janakānāṃ puro|hitaḥ. [16]

---

[i] Śiva. [ii] The reference is to the tonsure worn by boys.

Brahma and the other gods, for the good of the Vedic way of life,
undertook ascetic acts for a thousand years and more,
and what those ancient gurus then were able to behold
were these very weapons, their own ascetic energies.

SITA: Homage to them.

RAMA: From now on without fail they will serve your offspring.

SITA: I am honored. 1.70

LÁKSHMANA: Here is the Míthila episode.

SITA: Ah, there my husband is depicted. He has just broken the bow of Shánkara[i] with utter nonchalance,* and my father is staring at the gentle splendor of his appearance, almost speechless with astonishment at his physical beauty, smooth and soft and strapping and dark as a blossoming blue lotus, with the simple ornamentation of his single forelock.[ii]

LÁKSHMANA: Have a look at this:

Here your father pays his respects to his new relations, Vasíshtha and the others,*
and so does Shatánanda Gáutama, the family priest of all the Jánaka kings.

1.75 RĀMAḤ: draṣṭavyam etat.

> Janakānāṃ Raghūṇāṃ ca
> sambandhaḥ kasya na priyaḥ,
> yatra dātā grahītā ca
> svayaṃ Kuśika|nandanaḥ? [17]

SĪTĀ: ⌜ede kkhu tak|kāla|kida|go|dāṇa|maṅgalā cattāro vi bhādaro vivāha|dikkhidā tumhe. ammo, jāṇāmi tassiṃ jevva padese tassiṃ jevva kāle vattāmi.⌟

RĀMAḤ:

> samayaḥ sa vartata iv' āiṣa yatra māṃ
> samanandayat, su|mukhi, Gautam'|ârpitaḥ
> ayam āgṛhīta|kamanīya|kaṅkaṇas
> tava mūrtimān iva mah"|ôtsavaḥ karaḥ. [18]

LAKṢMAṆAḤ: iyam āryā, iyam apy āryā Māṇḍavī, iyam api vadhūḥ Śrutakīrtiḥ.

1.80 SĪTĀ: ⌜vaccha, iaṃ vi avarā kā?⌟

LAKṢMAṆAḤ: *(sa|lajjā|smitam, apavārya)* aye, Ūrmilāṃ pṛcchaty āryā. bhavatu. anyataḥ sañcārayāmi. *(prakāśam)* ārye, dṛśyatāṃ, draṣṭavyam etat. ayaṃ ca bhagavān Bhārgavaḥ.

SĪTĀ: ⌜kampida mhi.⌟

---

[i] Viśvāmitra. In most genealogies he is the son of Gādhi and great-grandson of one Kuśa. [ii] The wives of Bharata and Śatrughna, respectively. [iii] Lakṣmaṇa's wife. [iv] The Brahman ascetic Paraśurāma.

RAMA: This is something worth seeing. 1.75

> Who would not welcome the bond between the
> Raghus and the Jánakas,
> where the son of Kúshika[i] was both giver and
> receiver?*

SITA: Here are the four brothers, after presenting the ceremonial gift of a cow required on the occasion. And here you all are consecrated for the wedding. Why, I almost feel as if I were now there and this was then.

RAMA:

> It is almost as if it were now the very moment,
> my lovely wife, when Gáutama delighted me
> in extending—like the rite itself in physical form—
> this hand of yours aglitter with the marriage
> bracelet.*

LÁKSHMANA: Here you are, and here is our other sister-in-law Mándavi, as well as our daughter-in-law* Shruta·kirti.[ii]

SITA: And who, dear boy, is this other girl? 1.80

LÁKSHMANA: *(smiling with embarrassment; aside*)* Oh, my sister-in-law must be asking about Úrmila.[iii] Well, I'll turn their attention elsewhere. *(aloud)* Oh look, this is worth seeing. It's Bhárgava.[iv]

SITA: I shudder to look.

RĀMAḤ: ṛṣe, namas te.

LAKṢMAṆAḤ: ārye, paśya paśya. ayam asāv āryeṇa…

1.85 RĀMAḤ: *(s'|ākṣepam)* ayi, bahutaraṃ draṣṭavyam. anyato darśaya.

SĪTĀ: *(sa|sneha|bahumānaṃ nirvarṇya)* ⌜suṭṭhu sohasi, ajja|utta, ediṇā viṇaa|māhappeṇa.⌟

LAKṢMAṆAḤ: ete vayam Ayodhyāṃ prāptāḥ.

RĀMAḤ: *(s'|âsram)* smarāmi, hanta, smarāmi.

> jīvatsu tāta|pādeṣu
>   nūtane dāra|saṅgrahe
> mātṛbhiś cintyamānānāṃ…
>   te hi no divasā gatāḥ. [19]

1.90 iyam api tadā Jānakī

> patana|viralaiḥ prānt'|ônmīlan|
>   manohara|kuḍmalair
>   daśana|kusumair mugdh'|ālokaṃ
>   śiśur dadhatī mukham
> lalita|lalitair jyotsnā|prāyair
>   a|kṛtrima|vibhramair
>   a|kṛta madhurair aṅgānāṃ me
>   kutūhalam aṅgakaiḥ. [20]

LAKṢMAṆAḤ: eṣā Mantharā…

RĀMAḤ: *(an|uttaram anyato gatvā)* devi Vaidehi,

RAMA: Seer, homage to you.

LÁKSHMANA: Look, here my brother's about to...

RAMA: *(testily*)* Come now, there's so much more worth seeing. Show us something else. 1.85

SITA: *(gazing with affection and admiration)* How well this noble modesty becomes you, my husband.

LÁKSHMANA: This is us returning to Ayódhya.

RAMA: *(tearfully)* I remember, alas, how well I remember.

> The days when father was alive,
> and married life was new,
> and our mothers worried over us...
> days now gone forever.

And here is Jánaki at the time, 1.90

> A child with a face lit up with innocence,
> a few flowerlike teeth—
> her baby ones had fallen out—emerging
> in front, budding beautifully,
> and with her tender little limbs ever so graceful,
> sheer moonlight, with charms
> taught by nature, exciting the curiosity
> of these limbs* of mine.

LÁKSHMANA: Here is Mánthara...

RAMA: *(without answering moving elsewhere)* Queen Vaidéhi,

iṅgudī|pādapaḥ so 'yaṃ
  Śṛṅgavera|pure purā
Niṣāda|patinā yatra
  snigdhen' āsīt samāgamaḥ. [21]

1.95 LAKṢMAṆAḤ: *(vihasya, sva|gatam)* aye, madhyam'|âmbā|vṛttam antaritam āryeṇa.

SĪTĀ: ⌜ammo, eso jaḍā|sañjamaṇa|vuttanto.⌟

LAKṢMAṆAḤ:

putra|saṅkrānta|lakṣmīkair
  yad vṛddh'|Âikṣvākubhir dhṛtam
dhṛtaṃ bālye tad āryeṇa
  puṇyam āraṇyakaṃ vratam. [22]

SĪTĀ: ⌜esā pasaṇṇa|puṇṇa|salilā bhaavadī Bhāīradhī.⌟

RĀMAḤ: devi, Raghu|kula|devate, namas te.

1.100 turaga|vicaya|vyagrān urvī|bhidaḥ Sagar'|âdhvare
  Kapila|mahas" â|marṣāt pluṣṭān pituś ca pitāmahān
a|gaṇita|tanū|tāpaṃ taptvā tapāṃsi Bhagīratho
  bhagavati tava spṛṣṭān adbhiś cirād udatītarat.
[23]

sā tvam, amba, snuṣāyām Arundhat" îva Sītāyāṃ śiv'|ânudhyānā bhava.

[i] The Gaṅgā, literally "descendent of Bhagīratha."

Here is the *íngudi* tree in Shringavéra·pura, where long ago
we met with our dear friend, the overlord of the Nishádas.

LÁKSHMANA: *(laughing; aside)* Ah, so brother is trying to skip over the episode with our middle mother!* 1.95

SITA: Why, here is the episode of tying up the ascetic's hair you were forced to wear.

LÁKSHMANA:

The vow Ikshvákus of old observed
once power was passed on to their sons
brother observed in childhood—
the holy vow of wilderness life.

SITA: Here is Bhagi·rathi[i] with her clear holy water.

RAMA: Goddess, deity of the Raghu clan, homage to you.

Singlemindedly they sought the horse 1.100
at Ságara's rite, boring through the earth
until burnt to ash by mighty Kápila
in a rage, long ago, those great grandfathers
of Bhagi·ratha. It was his fierce acts
of asceticism, without the least regard
for his body, that saved his ancestors at last—
when your waters touched them, blessed one.*

Mother, I beg you to be as kindly disposed to your daughter-in-law Sita as Arúndhati is.

LAKṢMAṆAḤ: ayam asau Bharadvāj'|āvedita|Citrakūṭa|yāyini vartmani vanas|patiḥ Kālindī|taṭa|vaṭaḥ Śyāmo nāma.

SĪTĀ: ⌜sumaradi edaṃ padesaṃ ajja|utto?⌟

RĀMAḤ: ayi, kathaṃ vismaryate?

1.105 alasa|lulita|mugdhāny adhva|saṃpāta|khedād
a|śithila|parirambhair datta|saṃvāhanāni
parimṛdita|mṛṇālī|durbalāny aṅgakāni
tvam urasi mama kṛtvā yatra nidrām avāptā. [24]

LAKṢMAṆAḤ: eṣa Vindhy'|âṭavī|mukhe Virādha|saṃrodhaḥ.

SĪTĀ: ⌜alaṃ dāṇiṃ dāva ediṇā. pekkhāmi dāva ajja|utta|sa|hatta|dharida|tāla|vatt'|ādava|vāraṇaṃ attaṇo akkhīhiṃ dakkhiṇ'|âraṇṇa|ppavesaṃ.⌟

RĀMAḤ:

etāni tāni giri|nirjhariṇī|taṭeṣu
vaikhānas'|āśrita|tarūṇi tapo|vanāni
yeṣv ātitheya|paramāḥ śamino bhajante
nīvāra|muṣṭi|pacanā gṛhiṇo gṛhāṇi. [25]

---

[i] A *rākṣasa* who tried to abduct Sita and was slain by Rama.

LÁKSHMANA: Here is Shyama, that "Black" banyan tree on the bank of the Kálindi along the road leading to Chitra·kuta, where Bharad·vaja directed us.

SITA: My husband remembers this place, doesn't he?

RAMA: Why, how could I forget?

It was there your soft limbs grew tired and sore* 1.105
from the hardships of traveling* the road, and then
  you placed them,
limp as trampled lotuses, in my lap and I massaged
  them
with firm strokes, until you fell fast asleep.

LÁKSHMANA: Here is Virádha[i] blocking the way at the entrance to the Vindhya wilderness.

SITA: Please, no more of that! Here I see myself entering the southern wilderness, as if it were before my very eyes, with my husband holding over me a palm leaf for a parasol.*

RAMA:

These are the groves on the banks by the mountain
  waterfalls
where hermits would perform ascetic acts beneath
  the trees,
where householders in search of peace would make
  their homes,
men kind to guests, while living on a handful of
  grain a day.

LAKṢMAṆAḤ: ayam a|viral'|ânokaha|nivaha|nirantara|snigdha|nīla|parisar'|âraṇya|parirabdha|Godāvarī|mukhara|kandaraḥ satatam abhiṣyandamāna|megha|medurita|nīlimā Janasthāna|madhya|go giriḥ Prasravaṇaḥ.

RĀMAḤ:

1.110 smarasi, su|tanu, tasmin parvate Lakṣmaṇena
prativihita|saparyā|svasthayos tāny ahāni?
smarasi sa|rasa|nīrāṃtatra Godāvarīṃ vā?
smarasi ca tad|upānteṣv āvayor vartanāni? [26]

api ca,

kim api kim api mandaṃ mandam āsakti|yogād
a|vicalita|kapolaṃ jalpator a|krameṇa
a|śithila|parirambha|vyāpṛt'|âik'|âika|doṣṇor
a|vidita|gata|yāmā rātrir eva vyaraṃsīt. [27]

LAKṢMAṆAḤ: eṣā Pañcavaṭyāṃ Śūrpaṇakhā.

SĪTĀ: ⌜hā ajja|utta. ettikaṃ de daṃsaṇaṃ.⌟

LÁKSHMANA: This is Mount Prásravana in the middle of Jana·sthana. Its caves echoed with the sound of the Godávari River where it lay in the embrace of the surrounding forest, a lush black forest dense with thickets of trees, and the mountain's own darkness thickened still more by the ever-gathering clouds.

RAMA:

Do you remember, my lovely wife, those days upon the mountain 1.110
when Lákshmana saw to our needs and we felt so much at home?
Do you remember the nearby Godávari with its fresh water,*
and do you remember our many walks upon its banks?

And more,

How we would lie cheek by cheek in our deep passion
talking of this and that at random ever so softly,
holding each other tight in our embrace, while the hours
passed unnoticed till night—and night alone—had ended.*

LÁKSHMANA: Here is Shurpa·nakha at Pancha·vati.

SITA: Oh my husband, this is the last sight I'll have of you!

1.115 RĀMAḤ: ayi viprayoga|traste. citram etat.

SĪTĀ: ⌜jadhā tadhā bhodu. duj|jaṇo a|suhaṃ uppādedi.⌟

RĀMAḤ: hanta, vartamāna iva Janasthāna|vṛttāntaḥ pratibhāti.

LAKṢMAṆAḤ:

ath' êdaṃ rakṣobhiḥ
  kanaka|hariṇa|cchadma|vidhinā
tathā vṛttaṃ pāpair
  vyathayati yathā kṣālitam api.
Janasthāne śūnye
  vikala|karaṇair ārya|caritair
api grāvā rodity
  api dalati vajrasya hṛdayam. [28]

SĪTĀ: *(s'|âsram, ātma|gatam)* ⌜aï deva Rahu|ul'|āṇanda. evaṃ mama kāraṇādo kilanto āsi.⌟

1.120 LAKṢMAṆAḤ: *(*RĀMAṂ *nirvarṇya, s'|ākūtam)* ārya, kim etat?

ayaṃ te bāṣp'|âughas truṭita iva muktā|maṇi|saro
  visarpan dhārābhir lagati dharaṇīṃ jarjara|kaṇaḥ
niruddho 'py āvegaḥ sphurad|adhara|nāsā|puṭatayā
  pareṣām unneyo bhavati ca bhar'|ādhmāta|hṛdayaḥ.
[29]

RAMA: Now, now, so afraid of separation. It's only a painting. 1.115

SITA: That may be, but bad people can cause trouble.*

RAMA: My, it's as if the episode at Jana·sthana were actually taking place.

LÁKSHMANA:

> Now, here those evil *rákshasa*s, with their trick
> of the golden deer,
> committed the deed that still brings heartache
> though avenged in full.
> My brother's half-mad acts when Jana·sthana was
> left deserted
> can still make a stone shed tears and break a heart
> of iron.*

SITA: *(tearfully, aside)* Ah my lord, delight of the Raghu clan, how troubled you were on my account!

LÁKSHMANA: *(gazing at* RAMA*; with curiosity)* Brother, what is this now? 1.120

> This flood of tears welling up in streams
> is splashing on the ground
> in drops that shatter like a broken
> necklace of fine pearls
> and your distress, though you repress it,
> is perfectly clear to others
> from your quivering lips and nostrils,
> and your chest heaving under the burden.

RĀMAḤ: vatsa,

tat|kālaṃ priya|jana|viprayoga|janmā
tīvro 'pi pratikṛti|vāñchayā visoḍhaḥ.
duḥkh'|âgnir manasi punar vipacyamāno
hṛn|marma|vraṇa iva vedanāṃ karoti. [30]

SĪTĀ: ⌜haddhī, haddhī! ahaṃ vi adibhūmiṃ gadeṇa raṇaraṇaeṇa ajja|utta|suṇṇaṃ via attāṇaaṃ pekkhāmi.⌟

1.125 LAKṢMAṆAḤ: *(sva/gatam)* bhavatv, anyataḥ kṣipāmi. *(citraṃ vilokya, prakāśam)* tad etan manvantara|purāṇa|gṛdhra|rājasya tatra|bhavatas tāta|Jaṭāyuṣaś caritra|vikram'|ôdāharaṇam.

SĪTĀ: ⌜hā tāda ṇivvūḍho de avacca|siṇeho.⌟

RĀMAḤ: hā tāta Kāśyapa śakunta|rāja, kva punas tvādṛśasya mahatas tīrthasya sādhoḥ sambhavaḥ?

LAKṢMAṆAḤ: ayam asau Janasthāna|paścimaś Citrakuñjavān nāma danu|Kabandh'|âdhiṣṭhito Daṇḍak"|âraṇya|bhāgaḥ. tad idam Ṛṣyamūka|parvate Mataṅgasy' âśrama|padam. iyaṃ ca Śramaṇā nāma siddha|Śabarī. tad etat Pamp"|âbhidhānaṃ padma|saraḥ.

RAMA: Dear brother,

> At the time, the fire of sorrow ignited by losing the one I love,
> though sharp, was something the thirst for vengeance made bearable.
> But it continued to ripen in my mind and now produces
> the pain of a wound that reaches to the softest core of my heart.

SITA: Oh dear god, in boundless terror I am seeing myself left alone without my husband!

LÁKSHMANA: *(aside)* Well, I had better distract them. *(glanc- 1.125
ing at the painting; aloud)* Here is an illustration of the heroism of father Jatáyus, the vulture-king, older than the ages.

SITA: Alas, father, you met the obligations of affection to your child.

RAMA: Alas, father, king of birds, son of Káshyapa. Where shall we ever again find the likes of so great a benefactor?

LÁKSHMANA: Over there lying to the west of Jana·sthana is the part of Dándaka wilderness called Chitra·kúnjavat. It was haunted by the headless monster Kabándha.* This is the ashram of the sage Matánga, atop Mount Rishya·muka, and here is the wonder-working Shábara woman named Shrámani.* That over there is the lotus pond called Pampa.*

SĪTĀ: ⌜ettha kila ajja|utteṇa vicchaḍḍid'|âmarisa|dhīrattaṇaṃ pamukka|kaṇṭhaṃ ruṇṇaṃ āsi.⌟

1.130 RĀMAḤ: devi, ramaṇīyam etat saraḥ.

etasmin mada|kala|mallikākṣa|pakṣa|
  vyādhūta|sphurad|uru|daṇḍa|puṇḍarīkāḥ
bāṣp'|âmbhaḥ|paripatan'|ôdgam'|ântarāle
  sandṛṣṭāḥ kuvalayino mayā vibhāgāḥ. [31]

LAKṢMAṆAḤ: ayam āryo Hanūmān.

SĪTĀ: ⌜eso so cira|ṇivviṇṇa|jīa|loa|samuddharaṇa|garu'|ôvaārī mahā|bhāo Mārudī.⌟

RĀMAḤ:

diṣṭyā so 'yaṃ mahā|bāhur
  Añjan"|ānanda|vardhanaḥ
yasya vīryeṇa kṛtino
  vayaṃ ca bhuvanāni ca. [32]

1.135 SĪTĀ: ⌜vaccha, eso kusumida|kaamba|taṇḍavida|barahiṇo kiṃ|ṇāma|dheo girī jattha aṇubhāva|sohagga|metta|parisesa|dhūsara|sirī mucchanto tue paruṇṇeṇa avalambido taru|ale ajja|utto ālihido?⌟

SITA: It was here, I'm told, my husband could no longer master anger* and cried at the top of his lungs.

RAMA: My queen, it was a beautiful pond. 1.130

There were patches of white lotuses, their broad stems swaying
when stirred by the wings of geese honking lustily,
but they seemed dark blue as I* looked in the interval
between one tear falling and the next welling up.

LÁKSHMANA: This is the noble Hánuman.

SITA: Yes, here he is, the Wind god's great son, who did such signal service in rescuing this long-suffering world.

RAMA:

Thank god for the mighty son of Ánjana
whose power secured us—and the worlds—our welfare.

SITA: Dear boy, what's the name of this mountain, where 1.135
the peacocks were roused to do their wild *tándava* dance on the blooming *kadámba* trees?* My husband is depicted here at the foot of a tree, with you in tears lending support and him on the point of fainting, his natural glow dulled, a mere vestige of his once-captivating majesty.

LAKṢMAṆAḤ:

so 'yaṃ śailaḥ kakubha|surabhir
Mālyavān nāma yasmin
nīla|snigdhaḥ śrayati śikharaṃ
nūtanas toya|vāhaḥ... [33]

RĀMAḤ:

vats' âitasmād virama viram' âtaḥ
paraṃ na kṣamo 'smi.
pratyāvṛttaḥ punar iva sa me
Jānakī|viprayogaḥ. [34]

LAKṢMAṆAḤ: ataḥ param āryasya tatra|bhavatāṃ ca kapi|rākṣasānām a|saṃkhyātāny uttar'|ôttarāṇi karm'|âścaryāṇi. pariśrāntā c' êyam āryā. tad vijñāpayāmi, viśrāmyatām.

SĪTĀ: ⌜ajja|utta, ediṇā citta|daṃsaṇeṇa paccuppaṇṇa|dohalāe atthi me viṇṇappaṃ.⌟

1.140 RĀMAḤ: nanv ājñāpaya.

SĪTĀ: ⌜jāṇe puṇo vi pasaṇṇa | gambhīrāsu vaṇa | rāisu viharissaṃ, pavitta|somma|sisir'|âvagāhaṃ ca bhaavadiṃ Bhāīradhiṃ avagāhissaṃ.⌟

RĀMAḤ: vatsa Lakṣmaṇa?

LAKṢMAṆAḤ: eṣo 'smi.

RĀMAḤ: acira|sampādanīyo dohada, iti sampraty eva gurubhiḥ sandiṣṭam. tad a|skhalita|sukha|sampātaṃ ratham upasthāpaya.

LÁKSHMANA:

> That is Mount Mályavan, fragrant with *kákubha*
> flowers,
> its peak dark and moist with ever-fresh clouds...*

RAMA:

> Dear brother, stop, please stop, I cannot take any
> more.
> Separation from Jánaki seems all but to befall me
> once again.

LÁKSHMANA: From here on there are countless miraculous feats for viewing, each one greater than the next, of brother and the monkeys and *rákshasas*. But sister-in-law must be tired; I would ask her to rest now.

SITA: Husband, looking at the paintings has awakened a craving in me, and I have a favor to ask.

RAMA: You've only to command. 1.140

SITA: I feel like visiting the unspoiled deep forest and bathing in the pure, placid, cool waters of the Bhagi·rathi.

RAMA: Dear Lákshmana?

LÁKSHMANA: At your service.

RAMA: Our elders just directed us to satisfy her cravings instantly. So bring the smooth-riding, comfortable chariot.

1.145 SĪTĀ: ⌜ajja|utta tumhehiṃ pi tahiṃ gantavvam.⌟

RĀMAḤ: ayi kaṭhiṇa|hṛdaye, etad api vaktavyam eva?

SĪTĀ: ⌜teṇa hi piaṃ me.⌟

LAKṢMAṆAḤ: yad ājñāpayaty āryaḥ. *(niṣkrāntaḥ)*

RĀMAḤ: priye, ito vāt'|âyan'|âpavartake muhūrtaṃ saṃviṣṭau bhavāvaḥ.

1.150 SĪTĀ: ⌜evvaṃ bhodu. ohīrāmi kkhu parissama|jaṇidāe ṇiddāe.⌟

RĀMAḤ: tena hi nirantaram avalambasva mām anugamanāya.

jīvayann iva sa|sādhvasa|śrama|
  sveda|bindur adhikaṇṭham arpyatām
bāhur aindava|mayūkha|cumbita|
  syandi|candra|maṇi|hāra|vibhramaḥ. [35]

(tathā kārayan, s'|ānandam) priye, kim etat?

viniścetuṃ śakyo
    na sukham iti vā duḥkham iti vā
  pramoho nidrā vā
    kim u viṣa|visarpaḥ kim u madaḥ?
tava sparśe sparśe
    mama hi parimūḍh'|êndriya|gaṇo
  vikāraś caitanyaṃ
    bhramayati ca sammīlayati ca. [36]

---

[i] Moonstones were represented as liquifying when brought into moonlight.

SITA: Husband, won't you come along too?

RAMA: Why, hard-hearted lady, do you even need to ask?

SITA: I'm so pleased at that.

LÁKSHMANA: As my brother wishes. *(exit)*

RAMA: Let's sit a minute in the recess of this window.

SITA: Yes, alright. I am actually tired from all the exertions.

RAMA: So come, lean your full weight on me and let me lead you.

> Place your arm round my neck—it seems to revive
> me.
> Beaded with sweat from your exertions and your
> fright
> your arm is like a necklace of moonstones running
> with liquid when kissed by the rays of the moon.[i]

(doing so; blissfully) My beloved, what can this be?

> Every single time you touch me
> a kind of transformation—
> it can't be described as joy or sorrow,
> ecstasy or sleep,
> a state of intoxication
> or all-suffusing poison—
> confuses my senses and at once
> excites and dulls my awareness.*

I.155 SĪTĀ: *(vihasya)* ⌜thira|ppasādā tumhe. ido dāṇiṃ kiṃ avaraṃ?⌟

RĀMAḤ:

mlānasya jīva|kusumasya vikāsanāni
  santarpaṇāni sakal'|êndriya|mohanāni
etāni te su|vacanāni saroruh'|âkṣyāḥ
  karṇ'|âmṛtāni manasaś ca rasāyanāni. [37]

SĪTĀ: ⌜piaṃ | vada, ehi saṃvisamha.⌟ *(śayanāya samantato nirūpayati)*

RĀMAḤ: ayi kim anveṣṭavyam?

ā vivāha|samayād gṛhe vane
  śaiśave tad|anu yauvane punaḥ
svāpa|hetur an|upāśrito 'nyayā
  Rāma|bāhur upadhānam eṣa te. [38]

I.160 SĪTĀ: *(nidrāṃ nāṭayantī)* ⌜atthi edaṃ ajja | utta, atthi edaṃ...⌟ *(svapiti)*

RĀMAḤ: kathaṃ, priya|vacanā vakṣasi supt" āiva? *(nirvarṇya, sa|sneham)*

SITA: *(laughing)* You have always been constant in your affection for me. What could it be but that? 1.155

RAMA:

> They make the faded flower of life
> bloom for me again,
> they reinvigorate me
> and infatuate my every sense,
> those sweet words of my lotus-eyed wife,
> ambrosia to the ears, elixir to the mind.

SITA: My sweet-talker, come let's relax. *(looking this way and that for a place to lie down)*

RAMA: But there's no need to search:

> From the moment we were wed,
> at home or in the forest,
> in childhood and then in youth,
> this sole cause of repose,
> where not a single other woman
> has ever laid her head,
> this very arm of Rama here
> will serve you as a pillow.

SITA: *(miming falling asleep)** That's true, my husband, that's true... *(sleeps)* 1.160

RAMA: What's this, has my sweet-talking wife fallen fast asleep on my chest? *(gazing; affectionately)*

iyaṃ gehe Lakṣmīr, iyam amṛta|vartir nayanayor,
asāv asyāḥ sparśo vapuṣi bahalaś candana|rasaḥ.
ayaṃ kaṇṭhe bāhuḥ śiśira|masṛṇo mauktika|saraḥ.
kim asyā na preyo yadi param a|sahyas tu virahaḥ? [39]

PRATĪHĀRĪ: *(praviśya)* ⌜deva, uvatthido.⌟

RĀMAḤ: ayi kaḥ?

PRATĪHĀRĪ: ⌜āsaṇṇa|paricārao Dummuho devassa.⌟

RĀMAḤ: *(sva|gatam)* śuddh'|ântacārī Durmukhaḥ? sa mayā paura|jānapadān apasarpituṃ prayuktaḥ. *(prakāśam)* āgacchatu.

PRATĪHĀRĪ *niṣkrāntā.*

DURMUKHAḤ: *(praviśya, sva|gatam)* ⌜hā kadhaṃ dāṇiṃ Sīdā|deviṃ antareṇa īdisaṃ a|cintaṇijjaṃ jaṇ'|âvavādaṃ devassa kadhaïssaṃ? ahavā ṇioo kkhu me eriso manda|bhāassa.⌟

SĪTĀ: *(utsvapnāyate)* ⌜hā ajja|utta somma, kahiṃ si?⌟

RĀMAḤ: aye s" âiva raṇaraṇaka|dāyinī citra|darśanād viraha|bhāvanā devyāḥ svapn'|ôdvegaṃ karoti. *(sa|snehaṃ parāmṛśan)*

---

[i] Goddess of wealth and royalty. [ii] Literally "Gloomy-looking" (perhaps also/or "Defamer").

She is Lakshmi[i] herself living
in my house, ambrosial balm
for my eyes, the touch of rich sandalwood
cream upon my body;
this arm of hers around my neck
is a cool and smooth pearl necklace.
What don't I love about her—except
the torture of being apart?

Enter female DOORKEEPER: Present, my lord.

RAMA: Present? What is present?*

DOORKEEPER: My lord's personal attendant, Dúrmukha.[ii] 1.165

RAMA: *(aside)* Dúrmukha, the harem attendant? I employed him to gather intelligence among the people of the city and countryside. *(aloud)* Show him in.

Exit DOORKEEPER.

Enter DÚRMUKHA: *(aside)* How in the world am I going to report to the king these unspeakable rumors about Queen Sita? But such is my charge, cursed as I am.

SITA: *(crying out in her sleep)* Oh my gentle husband, where are you?

RAMA: Those terrifying anxieties of separation roused by viewing the paintings are disturbing the queen's dreams. *(stroking her affectionately)* 1.170

a|dvaitaṃ sukha|duḥkhayor anuguṇaṃ
sarvāsv avasthāsu yad
viśrāmo hṛdayasya yatra jarasā
yasminn a|hāryo rasaḥ
kālen' āvaraṇ'|âtyayāt pariṇate
yat sneha|sāre sthitaṃ
bhadraṃ tasya su|mānuṣasya katham apy
ekaṃ hi tat prāpyate. [40]

DURMUKHAḤ: *(upasṛtya)* ⌜jaadu devo.⌟

RĀMAḤ: brūhi yad upalabdham.

DURMUKHAḤ: ⌜uvatthuṇanti devaṃ pora | jāṇavadā visumarāvidā amhe mahā|rāa|Dasaradhassa Rāma|deveṇatti.⌟

1.175 RĀMAḤ: artha|vāda eṣaḥ. doṣaṃ tu kaṃ cit kathaya yena pratividhīyate.

DURMUKHAḤ: *(s'|âsram)* ⌜suṇādu devo.⌟ *(karṇe, evam eva)*

RĀMAḤ: ahaha tīvra|saṃveśo vāg|vajraḥ. *(mūrchati)*

DURMUKHAḤ: ⌜assasadu devo.⌟

RĀMAḤ: *(āśvasya)*

Identity in joy and sorrow,
consonance in every condition,
where the heart can find respite,
whose *rasa* old age cannot spoil,
what alone abides as time
removes all veils and pure love ripens—
that singular blessing is only bestowed
on a good man, and only then with luck.*

DÚRMUKHA: *(approaching)* Long live the king!

RAMA: Tell me what you have learned.

DÚRMUKHA: The people of the city and countryside sing my lord's praises, saying "Lord Rama has made us forget the great king Dasha·ratha."

RAMA: That is mere flattery. Inform me of any lapses so that 1.175
countermeasures can be taken.

DÚRMUKHA: *(tearfully)* Listen, my lord. *(in his ear, explaining*)*

RAMA: Oh god, your words are thunderbolts piercing me to the quick! *(falls faint)*

DÚRMUKHA: My lord, compose yourself!

RAMA: *(regaining his composure)*

1.180 hā hā dhik! para|gṛha|vāsa|dūṣaṇaṃ yad
Vaidehyāḥ praśamitam adbhutair upāyaiḥ
etat tat punar api daiva|dur|vipākād
ālarkaṃ viṣam iva sarvataḥ prasṛptam. [41]

tat kim atra manda|bhāgyaḥ karomi? *(vimṛśya, sa|karuṇam)* atha vā kim anyat?

satāṃ ken' âpi kāryeṇa
lokasy' ārādhanaṃ vratam
yat pūritaṃ hi tātena
māṃ ca prāṇāṃś ca muñcatā. [42]

sampraty eva bhagavatā Vasiṣṭhena sandiṣṭam. api ca:

yat Sāvitrair dīpitaṃ bhūmi|pālair
loka|śreṣṭhaiḥ sādhu śuddhaṃ caritram
mat|sambandhā kaśmalā kiṃ|vadantī
syāc ced asmin hanta dhiṅ mām a|dhanyam. [43]

1.185 hā devi deva|yajana|sambhave. hā sva|janm'|ânugraha|pavitrita|vasundhare. hā Nimi|Janaka|vaṃśa|nandini. hā Pāvaka|Vasiṣṭh'|Ârundhatī|praśasta|śīla|śālini. hā Rāmamaya|jīvite. hā mah"|âraṇya|vāsa|priya|sakhi. hā tāta|priye. hā priya|stoka|vādini. katham evaṃ|vidhāyās tav' âyam īdṛśaḥ pariṇāmaḥ?

---

[i] Indian kings traditionally have traced their origins either to the sun or the moon. [ii] An ancestor of Janaka.

No, oh no! The scandal of living in another man's house 1.180
had been wiped away by Vaidéhi—and by wondrous means—
but here it has reappeared through a fated turn of events,
to spread far and wide like the poison of a rabid dog.

What am I to do about it, cursed as I am? *(reflecting; with pity)* But then, what else can I do?

A good man's vow is to propitiate
the people by any necessary means.
This is the vow my own father fulfilled
at the cost of losing me—and his own life.*

And that is what Vasíshtha just directed me to do. Then,

If the pure good conduct made lustrous
by the eminent Solar[i] kings of old
should be stained by slander connected with me
then truly am I doomed, and damned as well.

Oh my queen, you who were born at a sacred rite, you purified Earth herself by honoring her with your birth, you brought joy to the lineage of Jánaka and Nimi.[ii] Your good character has been praised by Fire, Vasíshtha, and Arúndhati. Rama is your whole life, you were the dear companion in my sojourn in the deep wilderness, the darling of my father, with your sweet and measured words… How could such a woman as you suffer a reversal such as this? 1.185

tvayā jaganti puṇyāni,
tvayy a|puṇyā jan'|ôktayaḥ.
nāthavantas tvayā lokās,
tvam a|nāthā vipatsyase. [44]

Durmukha, brūhi Lakṣmaṇam eṣa te nūtano rājā Rāmaḥ samājñāpayati. *(karṇe, evam eva)*

DURMUKHAḤ: ⌈kahaṃ dāṇiṃ aggi | parisuddhāe gabbha | ṭṭhida|pavitta|Rahu|ula|santāṇāe devīe dujjaṇa|vaaṇādo evvaṃ vavasidaṃ deveṇa?⌋

RĀMAḤ: śāntam! kathaṃ durjanāḥ paura|jānapadāḥ?

1.190 Ikṣvāku|vaṃśo 'bhimataḥ prajānāṃ
jātaṃ ca daivād vacanīya|bījam
yac c' âdbhutaṃ karma viśuddhi|kāle
pratyetu kas tad yadi dūra|vṛttam? [45]

tad gaccha.

DURMUKHAḤ: ⌈hā devi!⌋ *(niṣkrāntaḥ)*

RĀMAḤ: hā kaṣṭam! atibībhatsa|karmā nṛ|śaṃso 'smi saṃvṛttaḥ.

Because of you all beings in the world are blessed
and yet on you these cursed rumors have fallen;
in you the people have a true protector
yet you face ruin yourself all unprotected.

Dúrmukha, tell Lákshmana that the novice* king Rama has an order for him. *(in his ear, explaining)*

DÚRMUKHA: The queen, already purified by fire, is purified the more by the continuation of the Raghu line she carries in her womb. How can my lord have reached such a decision* on the basis of malicious gossip about her?

RAMA: Silence!* How dare you call the people of the city and countryside malicious?

The Ikshváku dynasty has earned the people's esteem; 1.190
the seed of this reproach was a consequence of fate;
as for the wondrous act at the time of purification,
who could give it credence since it occurred far away?

Go then!

DÚRMUKHA: Alas, my queen! *(exit)*

RAMA: How awful! What a repulsive deed I am about to do, what a cruel man I have become!

śaiśavāt prabhṛti poṣitāṃ priyaiḥ
  sauhṛdād a|pṛthag|āśayāṃ priyām
chadmanā paridadāmi mṛtyave
  sauniko gṛha|śakuntikām iva. [46]

1.195 tat kim a|sparśanīyaḥ pātakī devīṃ dūṣayāmi? *(SĪTĀYĀḤ śiraḥ svairam unnamayya bāhum ākarṣan)*

a|pūrva|karma|cāṇḍālam,
  ayi mugdhe, vimuñca mām.
śrit" âsi candana|bhrāntyā
  durvipākaṃ viṣa|drumam. [47]

(utthāya) hanta, samprati viparyasto jīva|lokaḥ. paryavasitaṃ jīvita|prayojanaṃ Rāmasya. śūnyam adhunā jīrṇ'|âraṇyaṃ jagat. a|sāraḥ saṃsāraḥ. kāṣṭha|prāyaṃ śarīram. a|śaraṇas tu kiṃ karomi? kā gatiḥ? atha vā:

duḥkha|saṃvedanāy' âiva
  Rāme caitanyam āhitam.
marm'|ôpaghātibhiḥ prāṇair
  vajra|kīlāyitaṃ sthiraiḥ. [48]

From childhood my delicate love fed on delicacies
and was never parted* from me because of our deep affection.
And now I am ready to use deceit and deliver her over
to death, like a man who butchers a small pet bird.

How dare I then—an untouchable and outcaste myself— 1.195
pollute the queen with my touch? *(carefully lifting* SITA'*s head and withdrawing his arm)*

Innocent woman, let go of me,
a pariah capable of anything.
You thought you were reposing on sandalwood,
and not a noxious poison tree.

(standing) My god, this world has now been turned upside down. There is no longer any point to Rama's living. Suddenly the earth is empty, a desolate wilderness. Life is lifeless, this body mere matter. I have no recourse, what am I to do? Where am I to turn? I suppose

It was only to let him register pain
that Rama was endowed with consciousness.
Life itself is wounding me to the quick*
and seems bolted in place by an iron bolt.

amba Arundhati, bhagavantau Vasiṣṭha|Viśvāmitrau, bhagavan Pāvaka, devi Bhūtadhātri, hā tāta, hā Janaka, hā mātaraḥ, hā priya|sakha mahā|rāja Sugrīva, hā saumya Hanuman, hā param'|ôpakārin Laṅk"|âdhipate Vibhīṣaṇa, hā sakhi Trijaṭe, muṣitāḥ stha, paribhūtāḥ stha Rāma|hatakena. atha vā, kaś ca teṣām aham idānīm āhvāne?

1.200 te hi manye mah"|ātmānaḥ
kṛta|ghnena dur|ātmanā
mayā gṛhīta|nāmānaḥ
spṛśyanta iva pāpmanā. [49]

yo 'ham

visrambhād urasi nipatya labdha|nidrām
unmucya priya|gṛhiṇīṃ gṛhasya śobhām
ātaṅka|sphurita|kaṭhora|garbha|gurvīṃ
kravyādbhyo balim iva nirghṛṇaḥ kṣipāmi. [50]

(SĪTĀYĀḤ pādau śirasi kṛtvā) devi devi, ayam a|paścimas te Rāmasya śirasā pāda|paṅkaja|sparśaḥ. *(roditi)*

NEPATHYE: a|brahmaṇyam! a|brahmaṇyam!

1.205 RĀMAḤ: jñāyatām, bhoḥ kim etat?

---

[i] King of the monkeys and ally of Rāma. [ii] Monkey scout and ally of Rāma. [iii] Rāvaṇa's brother and ally of Rāma. [iv] A female *rākṣasa* who took pity on Sītā.

Mother Arúndhati, blessed Vasíshtha and Vishva·mitra, and Fire, and goddess Earth that bears all creatures! Oh father, Jánaka, mothers, dear friend King Sugríva,[i] gentle Hánuman,[ii] best benefactor and lord of Lanka, Vibhíshana,[iii] dear friend Tri·jata[iv]—you have all been deceived and disgraced by this contemptible Rama. But then, who am I to invoke these people now?

> For me even to use their names, 1.200
> base ingrate that I am,
> is tantamount to defiling
> these high persons with my own sin.

I who

> Push her from my chest where she had fallen peacefully asleep,
> this beloved wife of mine, this ornament to my house,
> heavy with unborn child—how anxiously it kicked!—
> and throw her unpitied to the dogs, like an offering of meat.

(bowing his head to SITA*'s feet)* My queen, my queen, this is the very last time that Rama will touch his head to your lotus feet. *(weeps)*

OFFSTAGE: Sacrilege! What sacrilege!

RAMA: Find out, someone, what is going on. 1.205

PUNAR NEPATHYE:

> ṛṣīṇām ugra|tapasāṃ
> Yamunā|tīra|vāsinām
> Lavaṇa|trāsitaḥ stomaḥ
> śaraṇyaṃ tvām upasthitaḥ. [51]

RĀMAḤ: āḥ katham ady' âpi rākṣasa|trāsaḥ? tad yāvad asya dur|ātmanaḥ Kumbhīnasī|putrasy' ônmūlanāya Śatrughnaṃ preṣayāmi. *(kati cit padāni gatvā, punaḥ pratinivṛtya)* hā devi, katham evaṃ|gatā bhaviṣyasi? bhagavati Vasundhare, śūnyāṃ duhitaram avekṣasva Jānakīm,

> Janakānāṃ Raghūṇāṃ ca
> yat kṛtsnaṃ gotra|maṅgalam
> yāṃ deva|yajane puṇye
> puṇya|śīlām ajījanaḥ. [52]

(niṣkrāntaḥ)

1.210 SĪTĀ: *(svapnāyate)* ⌜hā somma ajja|utta...⌟ *(sahas" ôtthāya)* ⌜haddhī, haddhī! dus|siviṇaena vippaladdhā ahaṃ ajja|uttaṃ akkandāmi.⌟ *(vilokya)* ⌜haddhī, haddhī! eāiṇiṃ maṃ pasuttaṃ ujjhia gado ajja|utto. kiṃ dāṇiṃ edaṃ? bhodu. se kuppissaṃ—jaï taṃ pekkhantī attaṇo pahavissaṃ. ko ettha pariaṇo?⌟

DURMUKHAḤ: *(praviśya)* ⌜devi, kumāra|Lakkhaṇo viṇṇavedi: «sajjo radho. āruhadu devī.»⌟

---

i A female *rākṣasa*, sister of Rāvaṇa.

STILL OFFSTAGE:

> A host of seers, mighty ascetics who live on the banks of the Yámuna,
> have been terrified by Lávana and have taken refuge with you.

RAMA: What, are *rákshasas* still causing trouble? I had better send Shatrúghna to root out Kumbhi·nasi's[i] son. *(taking a few steps forward, then returning)* Oh my queen, what will become of you in these desperate straits? Blessed Earth, watch over your helpless* daughter Jánaki,

> The good fortune entire of the Raghu and Jánaka clans,
> the blessed child you gave birth to at the blessed sacrifice of the gods.

(exit)

SITA: *(dreaming)* Dear husband... *(suddenly rising)* Oh dear 1.210
god, I had a nightmare that I became separated from my husband and was crying out for him. *(looking around)* But where has he gone leaving me asleep and alone? I'll show him some anger—if I can remain mistress of my heart when I set eyes on him. Who is in attendance?

Enter DÚRMUKHA: Your Highness, Prince Lákshmana wishes to inform you that the chariot is all set for Your Highness to board.

SĪTĀ: ⌜iaṃ āruhāmi.⌟ *(utthāya)* ⌜paripphuradi via me gabbha|bhāro. saṇiaṃ gacchamha.⌟

DURMUKHAḤ: ⌜ido ido devī.⌟

SĪTĀ: ⌜ṇamo Rahu|ula|devadāṇaṃ.⌟

1.215 *niṣkrāntau.*

iti mahā|kavi|śrī|Bhavabhūti|praṇīta Uttara|Rāma|carita|nāṭake Citra|darśano nāma prathamo 'ṅkaḥ.

SITA: I'm ready to board. *(standing)* My baby keeps kicking, we must go slowly.

DÚRMUKHA: This way, Your Highness.

SITA: Homage to the deities of the Raghu clan!

Exeunt both. 1.215

End of Act I

I think, this is a test for Rama that when someone critize his wife the one who he love,
This is how Rama deal with.

PRELUDE TO ACT II

NEPATHYE: sv|āgataṃ tapo|dhanāyāḥ.

tataḥ praviśaty adhvaga|veṣā TĀPASĪ.

TĀPASĪ: aye, vana|devat" êyaṃ phala|kusuma|pallav'|ârghyeṇa mām upatiṣṭhate.

VANA|DEVATĀ: *(praviśya, arghyaṃ vikīrya)*

2.5 yath"|êcchā|bhogyaṃ vo
vanam idam. ayaṃ me su|divasaḥ.
satāṃ sadbhiḥ saṅgaḥ
katham api hi puṇyena bhavati.
taru|cchāyā toyaṃ
yad api tapaso yogyam aśanaṃ
phalaṃ vā mūlaṃ vā
tad api na par'|âdhīnam iha vaḥ. [1]

TĀPASĪ: kim atr' ôcyate?

priya|prāyā vṛttir,
vinaya|madhuro vāci niyamaḥ,
prakṛtyā kalyāṇī
matir, an|avagītaḥ paricayaḥ,
puro vā paścād vā
tad idam a|viparyāsita|rasaṃ
rahasyaṃ sādhūnām
an|upadhi viśuddhaṃ vijayate. [2]

upaviśataḥ.

VANA|DEVATĀ: kāṃ punar atra bhavatīm avagacchāmi?

OFFSTAGE: Welcome, holy one!

Enter a female ASCETIC *dressed as a traveler.*

ASCETIC: Ah, the forest deity herself is here to wait on me with an offering of fruits and flowers and fronds.

Enter the FOREST DEITY: *(spreading out the offering)*

Enjoy this forest to your heart's content. 2.5
This is a happy day for me:
It is rare for good people to meet
and happens only thanks to merit.
Shade of a tree, water, whatever
food is fit for ascetic acts—
fruits and roots and the rest—
is all at your disposal.

ASCETIC: What can I say?

Loving ways, measured speech
sweetened with courtesy,
a heart well-disposed by nature,
and ungrudging service,
a *rasa* that never goes bad,
before or after—long live
this secret of the holy ones,
which knows no pretence or stain.

The two sit.

FOREST DEITY: Who am I to understand my honored guest to be?

2.10 TĀPASĪ: Ātreyy asmi.

VANA|DEVATĀ: ārye Ātreyi, kutaḥ punar ih' āgamyate? kim|prayojano vā Daṇḍak"|âraṇya|pracāraḥ?

ĀTREYĪ:

asminn Agastya|pramukhāḥ pradeśe
  bhūyāṃsa udgītha|vido vasanti.
tebhyo 'dhigantuṃ nigam'|ânta|vidyāṃ
  Vālmīki|pārśvād iha paryaṭāmi. [3]

VANA|DEVATĀ: yadā tāvad anye 'pi munayas tam eva hi purāṇa|brahma|vādinaṃ Prācetasam ṛṣiṃ brahma|pārāyaṇāy' ôpāsate, tat ko 'yam āryāyāḥ pravāsaḥ?

ĀTREYĪ: tatra mahān adhyayana|pratyūha ity eṣa dīrgha|pravāso 'ṅgī|kṛtaḥ.

2.15 VANA|DEVATĀ: kīdṛśaḥ?

ĀTREYĪ: tasya bhagavataḥ ken' âpi devatā|viśeṣeṇa sarva|prakār'|âdbhutaṃ stanya|tyāga|mātrake vayasi vartamānaṃ dāraka|dvayam upanītam. tat khalu na kevalaṃ tasya, api tu sa|car'|âcarāṇāṃ bhūtānām āntarāṇi tattvāny upasnehayati.

VANA|DEVATĀ: api tayor nāma|saṃvijñānam asti?

ĀTREYĪ: tay" âiva kila devatayā tayoḥ «Kuśa|Lavāv» iti nāmanī prabhāvaś c' ākhyātaḥ.

---

[i] Vālmīki.

ASCETIC: I am Atréyi. 2.10

FOREST DEITY: Atréyi, where do you come from, and for what purpose are you wandering the Dándaka wilderness?

ATRÉYI:

In this region there live many masters
of the Veda's essence,* Agástya and others.
It is to learn Vedánta knowledge from them
that I am roaming here, far from Valmíki.

FOREST DEITY: But since other sages worship that ancient spiritual master, the seer who is son of Prachétas,[i] in order to attain spiritual mastery, why is the noble woman absenting herself from him?

ATRÉYI: I have resigned myself to this long absence because there is now a major obstacle to studying with him.

FOREST DEITY: Of what sort? 2.15

ATRÉYI: Some deity—it was a wonder—once brought the blessed one a set of twin boys who had barely been weaned. And as you can imagine they won his heart, and not just his but that of all moving and unmoving beings.

FOREST DEITY: Is anything known about their names?

ATRÉYI: They say the deity itself revealed to him their names —Kusha and Lava—and their power.

VANA|DEVATĀ: kīdṛśaḥ prabhāvaḥ?

2.20 ĀTREYĪ: tayoḥ kila sa|rahasya|Jṛmbhak'|âstrāṇy ā|janma|siddhāni.

VANA|DEVATĀ: iti hi bhoś citram!

ĀTREYĪ: tau ca bhagavatā Vālmīkinā dhātrī|karma vastutaḥ parigṛhya poṣitau parirakṣitau ca. vṛtta|cūḍau ca trayī|varjam itarās tisro vidyāḥ s'|âvadhānena paripāṭhitau. samanantaraṃ ca garbh'|âikādaśe varṣe kṣātreṇa kalpen' ôpanīya trayī|vidyām adhyāpitau. na hy etābhyām atipradīpta|prajñā|medhābhyām asmad|ādeḥ sah' âdhyayana|yogo 'sti. yataḥ:

vitarati guruḥ prājñe vidyāṃ
yath" âiva tathā jaḍe,
na tu khalu tayor jñāne śaktiṃ
karoty apahanti vā.
bhavati ca punar bhūyān bhedaḥ
phalaṃ prati. tad yathā:
prabhavati śucir bimb'|ôdgrāhe
maṇir na mṛdāṃ cayaḥ. [4]

VANA|DEVATĀ: ayam asāv adhyayana|pratyūhaḥ?

2.25 ĀTREYĪ: aparaś ca.

FOREST DEITY: What sort of power?

ATRÉYI: They say that magic weapons along with their secret invocations were at their disposal from the moment of their delivery. 2.20

FOREST DEITY: Remarkable indeed.

ATRÉYI: And Valmíki accepted what was effectively the task of a nurse and raised the two of them and cared for them. After their tonsure ceremony had taken place he attentively schooled them in the three forms of knowledge,* the triple Veda excepted; eventually, on their eleventh birthday, he initiated them according to Kshatriya custom and taught them the triple sacred knowledge. It is hardly proper to have people like us studying alongside two boys of such luminous understanding and insight. For

A guru transmits knowledge to the dull
no less than to the bright
but he can neither make nor break
their aptitude for learning,
and a great difference in outcome
arises between them.
A polished gem can reflect an image;
a clump of dirt cannot.

FOREST DEITY: This is the obstacle to study, then?

ATRÉYI: There is another. 2.25

VANA|DEVATĀ: ath' âparaḥ kaḥ?

ĀTREYĪ: atha sa brahma'|ṛṣir ekadā madhyan|dina|savane nadīṃ Tamasām anuprapannaḥ. tatra yugma|cāriṇoḥ krauñcayor ekaṃ vyādhena vidhyamānam apaśyat. ākasmika|pratyavabhāsāṃ devīṃ vācam a|vyatikīrṇa|varṇām ānuṣṭubhena cchandasā paricchinnām abhyudairayat.

> «mā niṣāda pratiṣṭhāṃ tvam
> agamaḥ śāśvatīḥ samāḥ,
> yat krāuñca|mithunād ekam
> avadhīḥ kāma|mohitam.» [5]

VANA|DEVATĀ: citram, an|āmnāyo nūtanaś chandasām avatāraḥ.

2.30 ĀTREYĪ: tena khalu punaḥ samayena taṃ bhagavantam āvirbhūta|śabda|brahma|prakāśam ṛṣim upasaṅkramya bhagavān bhūta|bhāvanaḥ padma|yonir avocat, «ṛṣe, prabuddho 'si vāg|ātmani brahmaṇi. tad brūhi Rāma|caritam. a|vyāhata|jyotir ārṣaṃ te prātibhaṃ cakṣuḥ. ādyaḥ kavir asi,» ity uktv" ântarhitaḥ. atha bhagavān Prācetasaḥ prathamaṃ manuṣyeṣu śabda|brahmaṇas tādṛśaṃ vivartam itihāsaṃ Rāmāyaṇam ṛṣiḥ praṇināya.

---

[i] Brahmā.

FOREST DEITY: And what is that?

ATRÉYI: Well, once upon a time the Brahman seer went down to the Támasa River for his noontime bath, and there he saw a hunter killing one of a pair of cranes. Suddenly the goddess Language flashed before his mind's eye, each sound distinct and measured by the eight-syllable meter, and he gave voice to her thus:

"Nisháda man, may you never
for all of time find fulfillment*
since you've slain one of this pair
of cranes in the very act of love."

FOREST DEITY: How remarkable, a new* incarnation of verse forms unconnected with the Vedas.

ATRÉYI: On the same occasion when the light of the sacred 2.30
mystery of language had manifested itself to the seer, he was approached by the god born in the lotus,[i] the enlivener of living things, who spoke as follows: "O seer, you have gained knowledge of the mystery known as language. Tell then the story of Rama. You will possess the eye of inspiration, the seer's eye whose light is never dimmed. You are the primal poet," and with this, he vanished into thin air. Then the seer, the son of Prachétas, composed the 'Ramáyana,' a history that represents the first such manifestation among men of the mystery of language.

VANA|DEVATĀ: hanta, maṇḍitaḥ saṃsāraḥ.

ĀTREYĪ: tasmād avocaṃ, «tatra mahān adhyayana|pratyūha,» iti.

VANA|DEVATĀ: yujyate.

ĀTREYĪ: viśrānt" âsmi, bhadre. sampraty Agasty'|āśramasya panthānaṃ brūhi.

2.35 VANA|DEVATĀ: itaḥ Pañcavaṭīm anupraviśya gamyatām anena Godāvarī|tīreṇa.

ĀTREYĪ: *(sa|bāṣpam)* apy etat tapo|vanaṃ Pañcavaṭī? api sarid iyaṃ Godāvarī? apy ayaṃ giriḥ Prasravaṇaḥ? api Janasthāna|devatā Vāsantī tvam?

VĀSANTĪ: tad etat sarvam.

ĀTREYĪ: vatse Jānaki,

sa eṣa te vallabha|vastu|vargaḥ,
  prāsaṅginīnāṃ viṣayaḥ kathānām,
tvāṃ nāma|śeṣām api dṛśyamānaḥ
  pratyakṣa|dṛśyām iva naḥ karoti. [6]

2.40 VĀSANTĪ: *(sa|bhayam, sva|gatam)* kathaṃ, «nāma|śeṣām,» ity āha? *(prakāśam)* ārye, kim atyāhitaṃ Sītā|devyāḥ?

ĀTREYĪ: na kevalam atyāhitaṃ, s'|âpavādam api. *(karṇe, evam eva)*

FOREST DEITY: Ah, life itself has been enriched.

ATRÉYI: That's why I spoke of a great obstacle to study.

FOREST DEITY: That's understandable.

ATRÉYI: My good lady, I am rested. Tell me now the way to the ashram of Agástya.

FOREST DEITY: From here you enter Pancha·vati and go along the bank of the Godávari. 2.35

ATRÉYI: *(tearfully)* Is that Pancha·vati, the celebrated penance grove? Is that river the Godávari, and that mountain Prásravana—and are you Vasánti, the deity of Jana·sthana?

VASÁNTI: It is all just as you say.

ATRÉYI: O child Jánaki,

> This is the host of things you cherished,
> object of so many passing conversations,
> and as I behold them they seem to make you
> visible—
> though nothing is left of you now but your name!

VASÁNTI: *(fearfully, aside)* What does she mean, "nothing... but your name?" *(aloud)* Noble lady, has some calamity befallen Queen Sita? 2.40

ATRÉYI: Not just a calamity, but a calumny as well. *(in her ear, explaining)*

VĀSANTĪ: ahaha, dāruṇo daiva|nirghātaḥ. *(mūrchati)*

ĀTREYĪ: bhadre, samāśvasihi, samāśvasihi!

VĀSANTĪ: hā priya|sakhi, hā mahā|bhāge, īdṛśas te nirmāṇa|bhāgaḥ. Rāma|bhadra, Rāma|bhadra... atha v" âlaṃ tvayā! ārye Ātreyi, atha tasmād araṇyāt parityajya nivṛtte Lakṣmaṇe Sītāyāḥ kiṃ vṛttam, iti kā cid asti pravṛttiḥ?

2.45 ĀTREYĪ: na hi, na hi.

VĀSANTĪ: hā kaṣṭam. Arundhatī|Vasiṣṭh'|âdhiṣṭhiteṣu Raghu|kadambakeṣu, jīvantīṣu ca vṛddhāsu rājñīṣu, katham idaṃ jātam?

ĀTREYĪ: Ṛṣyaśṛṅg'|āśrame guru|janas tad" āsīt. samprati parisamāptaṃ tad dvādaśa|vārṣikaṃ satram. Ṛṣyaśṛṅgeṇa ca visarjitāḥ sampūjya guravaḥ. tato bhagavaty Arundhatī, «n' âhaṃ vadhū|virahitām Ayodhyāṃ gamiṣyāmi,» ity āha. tad eva Rāma|mātṛbhir anumoditam. tad|anurodhād bhagavato Vasiṣṭhasya pariśuddhā matir yathā: «Vālmīki|tapo|vanaṃ gatvā tatra vatsyāma,» iti.

VĀSANTĪ: atha sa rājā kim|ācāraḥ samprati?

ĀTREYĪ: tena rājñā kratur aśva|medhaḥ prakrāntaḥ.

2.50 VĀSANTĪ: hā dhik. pariṇītam api?

ĀTREYĪ: śāntam, śāntam.

VASÁNTI: Oh no! What a cruel blow of fate. *(falls faint)*

ATRÉYI: Compose yourself, dear woman, I beg you!

VASÁNTI: Oh my beloved friend and most honorable woman, that such should be your lot in life. Dear Rama, dear Rama... No, enough of you! Atréyi, is there any news of what happened to Sita when Lákshmana left her and returned from the wilderness?

ATRÉYI: Alas, none at all. 2.45

VASÁNTI: How awful. How could such a thing have happened with Arúndhati and Vasíshtha presiding over the Raghu clan, and the aged queens still alive?

ATRÉYI: At the time, the elders were away at the ashram of Rishya·shringa. Now the twelve-year-long sacrifice has been concluded, and Rishya·shringa, after honoring the elders, was about to send them home when Arúndhati declared, "I will not return to an Ayódhya bereft of my daughter-in-law," and Rama's mothers concurred. And in compliance with her Vasíshtha, too, expressed the sensible view that they should all go to Valmíki's penance grove and stay there.

VASÁNTI: As for the king, what is he doing?

ATRÉYI: The king has commenced the Horse Sacrifice.*

VASÁNTI: Dear god, has he already remarried then? 2.50

ATRÉYI: Heaven forbid, no.

VĀSANTĪ: kā tarhi yajñe saha|dharma|cāriṇī?

ĀTREYĪ: hiraṇmayī Sītā|pratikṛtiḥ.

VĀSANTĪ: hanta bhoḥ.

2.55 vajrād api kaṭhorāṇi,
mṛdūni kusumād api,
lok'|ôttarāṇāṃ cetāṃsi
ko hi vijñātum arhati? [7]

ĀTREYĪ: visṛṣṭaś ca Vāmadev'|âbhimantrito medhyo 'śvaḥ. upakalpitāś ca yathā|śāstraṃ tasya rakṣitāraḥ. teṣām adhiṣṭhātā Lakṣmaṇ'|ātmajaś, Candraketur, avāpta|divy'|âstra|saṃpradāyaś catur|aṅga|sādhan'|ânvito 'nuprahitaḥ.

VĀSANTĪ: *(sa|sneha|kautuk'|âsram)* kumāra|Lakṣmaṇasy' âpi putraḥ? hanta, mātar, jīvāmi.

ĀTREYĪ: atr'|ântare brāhmaṇena mṛtaṃ putram āropya rāja|dvāri s'|ôras|tāḍam «a|brahmaṇyam» udghoṣitam. tato «na rāj'|âpacāram antareṇa prajāyām a|kāla|mṛtyuś carat',» îty ātma|doṣaṃ nirūpayati karuṇāmaye Rāma|bhadre sahas" âiv' â|śarīriṇī vāg udacarat:

«Śambūko nāma vṛṣalaḥ
pṛthivyāṃ tapyate tapaḥ.
śīrṣa|cchedyaḥ sa te Rāma.
taṃ hatvā jīvaya dvijam.» [8]

---

[i] A family priest substituting for Vasiṣṭha.

VASÁNTI: Then who is the wife in *dharma* at the ritual?*

ATRÉYI: A golden image of Sita.

VASÁNTI: My word,

Who can possibly fathom the minds 2.55
of such supernatural men?
They can at once be harder than steel
and softer by far than flowers.

ATRÉYI: The sacrificial horse has been released, duly blessed by Vama·deva,[i] and guardians have been assigned for it, in accordance with the ritual texts. They are led by Lákshmana's son Chandra·ketu, who has acquired the tradition of the divine weapons. He has been sent on ahead with an army of four divisions.

VASÁNTI: *(tearfully, with affection and surprise)* Prince Lákshmana has a son, too? Ah mother, this gives me strength.

ATRÉYI: In the midst of all these goings-on, a Brahman came and laid his dead son before the palace gate and exclaimed "Sacrilege!" with a breast-beating cry. At that point, while dear Rama—pity incarnate he seemed—was reflecting on the fact that an untimely death could never befall one of his subjects in the absence of some wrong-doing on the part of the king himself, a disembodied voice suddenly proclaimed,

A lowcaste man named Shambúka
is practicing austerities somewhere on earth.
You must behead him, Rama, for only
by slaying him can you revive the Brahman child.

2.60 ity upaśrutya kṛpāṇa|pāṇiḥ Puṣpakaṃ vimānam āruhya sarvā diśo vidiśaś ca śūdra|tāpas'|ânveṣaṇāya jagat|patiś caritum ārabdhavān.

VĀSANTĪ: Śambūko nāma dhūmapaḥ śūdro 'sminn eva Janasthāne tapaś carati. tad api nāma Rāma|bhadraḥ punar idaṃ vanam alaṅkuryāt?

ĀTREYĪ: bhadre, gamyate 'dhunā.

VĀSANTĪ: ārye Ātreyi, evam astu. kaṭhorī|bhūtas tu divasaḥ. tathā hi:

kaṇḍūla|dvipa|gaṇḍa|piṇḍa|kaṣaṇ'|ā-
kampena sampātibhir
gharma|sraṃsita|bandhanaiḥ sva|kusumair
arcanti Godāvarīm
chāy"|âpaskiramāṇa|viṣkira|mukha|
vyākṛṣṭa|kīṭa|tvacaḥ
kūjat|klānta|kapota|kukkuṭa|kulāḥ
kūle kulāya|drumāḥ. [9]

2.65 *parikramya niṣkrānte.*

viṣkambhakaḥ

[i] Rāvaṇa's flying chariot.

When he heard this the lord of the world, sword in hand, ascended the Púshpaka chariot,[i] and set out to search far and wide for the ascetic Shudra. 2.60

VASÁNTI: There is a Shudra named Shambúka who is engaged in austerities in Jana·sthana itself, breathing in smoke as a penance. If only dear Rama might once again adorn this forest.

ATRÉYI: Dear woman, I must be going now.

VASÁNTI: So be it, Atréyi, though the day has turned brutally hot:

> On the riverbanks the nesting trees pay worship
> to the Godávari with offerings of their own flowers
> dropping in heaps from heat-softened stems
> when shaken by elephants come to rub
> their swollen itchy cheeks; and in the trees
> the birds scratch about in the shade
> and draw insects from the bark with their beaks,
> while heat-stricken doves and cocks are moaning.*

Walking about, exeunt both. 2.65

End of the Prelude

ACT II
THE ENTRANCE INTO PANCHA·VATI

tataḥ praviśati Puṣpaka|sthaḥ sa|day"|ôdyata|khaḍgo RĀMAḤ.

RĀMAḤ:

> he hasta dakṣiṇa, mṛtasya śiśor dvijasya
> jīvātave visṛja śūdra|munau kṛpāṇam.
> Rāmasya gātram asi. durvaha|garbha|khinna|
> Sītā|pravāsana|paṭoḥ karuṇā kutas te? [10]

(katham cit prahṛtya) kṛtaṃ Rāma|sadṛśaṃ karma. api jīvet sa brāhmaṇa|putraḥ!

2.70 DIVYA|PURUṢAḤ: *(praviśya)* jayati, jayati devaḥ.

> datt'|âbhaye tvayi Yamād api daṇḍa|dhāre
> sañjīvitaḥ śiśur asau, mama c' êyam ṛddhiḥ.
> Śambūka eṣa śirasā caraṇau natas te.
> sat|saṅga|jāni nidhanāny api tārayanti. [11]

RĀMAḤ: dvayam api priyaṃ naḥ. tad anubhūyatām ugrasya tapasaḥ paripākaḥ.

---

[i] The god of death.

The scene opens on RAMA *aboard the Púshpaka, filled with compassion, his sword upraised.*

RAMA:

O my right hand, bring down this sword
upon the Shudra monk
and bring the dead son of the Brahman
back to life. You are a limb
of Rama's—who had it in him to drive
his Sita into exile,
weary and heavy with child.
Why start with pity now?

(somehow striking a blow) There, you have done a deed worthy of Rama. Let the Brahman's son live again!*

Enter a HEAVENLY BEING: Long live the king. 2.70

Thanks to you, who grant safety from Yama[i]
himself,
by meting out just punishment
that child has been revived—and I too have been
exalted:
Here Shambúka bows his head to your feet.
Whatever comes from contact with the good,
be it death itself, will bring salvation.

RAMA: Both outcomes are welcome to me. Enjoy then the fruition of your fierce austerities.

yatr' ānandāś ca modāś ca
yatra puṇy'|âbhisambhavaḥ,
Vairājā nāma te lokās
taijasāḥ santu te dhruvāḥ. [12]

ŚAMBŪKAḤ: yuṣmat|pāda|prasādan'|ôpāya eṣa mahimā. kim atra tapasaḥ? atha vā mahad upakṛtaṃ tapasā.

2.75 anveṣṭavyo yad asi bhuvane
bhūta|nāthaḥ śaraṇyo
mām anviṣyann iha vṛṣalakaṃ
yojanānāṃ śatāni
krāntvā prāptaḥ sa iha tapasaḥ
saṃprasādo. 'nyathā cet,
kv' Âyodhyāyāḥ punar upagamo
Daṇḍakāyāṃ vane vaḥ? [13]

RĀMAḤ: kiṃ nāma Daṇḍak" êyam? *(sarvato 'valokya)* ām.

snigdha|śyāmāḥ kva cid aparato
bhīṣaṇ'|ābhoga|rūkṣāḥ,
sthāne sthāne mukhara|kakubho
jhāṅkṛtair nirjharāṇām,
ete tīrth'|ā śrama|giri|sarid|
garta|kāntāra|miśrāḥ
sandṛśyante paricita|bhuvo
Daṇḍakā|Vindhya|bhāgāḥ. [14]

---

[i] A divine feminine power of the Vedic pantheon. [ii] A mountain range in central India.

May the refulgent heavenly worlds of Viraj[i] be
yours forever,
worlds of bliss and pleasure accumulated through
merit.*

SHAMBÚKA: This high status was made possible by the reverence paid to your feet— austerities have no role. Then again, austerities may have been of great service to me:

I would have had to search the earth 2.75
for you, lord of beings and my refuge,
but you instead sought me, a lowcaste,
traversing hundreds of leagues to reach me.
That can only be a blessing
conferred by my austerities—
why else should you have left Ayódhya
to come once more to Dándaka Forest?

RAMA: What, do you mean to say this is Dándaka? *(looking all around)* Yes,

Here soft and dark green meadows, and there rough
menacing tracts,
in every quarter echoing to the horizons with the
roar of rushing rivers,
with fords, ashrams, mountains, streams, caves, and
forests interspersed...
yes, the grounds I see here are familiar: the Dándaka
side of the Vindhyas.[ii]

ŚAMBŪKAḤ: Daṇḍak" âiv' êyam. atra kila pūrvaṃ nivasatā devena

caturdaśa sahasrāṇi
rakṣasāṃ bhīma|karmaṇām
trayaś ca Dūṣaṇa|Khara|
Trimūrdhāno raṇe hatāḥ, [15]

2.80 yena siddha|kṣetre Janasthāne mādṛśām api bhīru|janānām a|kuto|bhayaḥ saṃcāro jātaḥ.

RĀMAḤ: na kevalaṃ Daṇḍakā, Janasthānam api?

ŚAMBŪKAḤ: bāḍham. etāni khalu sarva|bhūta|loma|harṣaṇāny unmatta|caṇḍa|śvāpada|kul'|ākrānta|vikaṭa|giri|gahvarāṇi Janasthāna|paryanta|dīrgh'|âraṇyāni dakṣiṇāṃ diśam abhivartante. tathā hi:

niṣkūja|stimitāḥ kva cit, kva cid api
proccaṇḍa|sattva|svanāḥ
sv'|êcchā|supta|gabhīra|ghora|bhujaga|
śvāsa|pradīpt'|âgnayaḥ
sīmānaḥ pradar'|ôdareṣu vilasat|
svalp'|âmbhaso yāsv ayaṃ
tṛṣyadbhiḥ pratisūryakair ajagara|
sveda|dravaḥ pīyate. [16]

SHAMBÚKA: This is indeed Dándaka. They say that when my lord was living here

He killed fourteen thousand fearsome *rákshasas* in battle—
and three more: Dúshana, Khara, and Tri·shiras.

This made Jana·sthana a holy land where even fearful folk like me could move about in safety. 2.80

RAMA: What, not only Dándaka, but Jana·sthana too?

SHAMBÚKA: Yes of course. Those vast stretches of wilderness—they will make your hair stand on end no matter who you are, with their gruesome mountain caves swarming with packs of vicious wild dogs—border on Jana·sthana and lead to the south.*

Its tracts are deathly silent in one place,
in another, wild animals howl;
fires are ignited by the hissing
of huge, dreadful snakes sleeping peacefully,*
and water is scarce there, to be found
only deep within crevasses,
and thirsty lizards drink the sweat
from the very backs of serpents.

RĀMAḤ:

paśyāmi ca Janasthānaṃ
bhūta|pūrvaṃ Khar'|ālayam,
pratyakṣān iva vṛttāntān
pūrvān anubhavāmi ca. [17]

2.85 *(sarvato vilokya)* priya|Rāmā hi sarvathā Vaidehy āsīt. etāni tāni nāma kāntārāṇi. kim ataḥ paraṃ bhayānakasya? *(s'/ âsram)*

«tvayā saha nivatsyāmi
vaneṣu madhu|gandhiṣu»
it' îh' âramat' âiv' âsau.
snehas tasyāḥ sa tādṛśaḥ. [18]

a|kiñ|cid api kurvāṇaḥ
saukhyair duḥkhāny apohati.
tat tasya kim api dravyaṃ
yo hi yasya priyo janaḥ. [19]

ŚAMBŪKAḤ: tad alam ebhir dur|āsadaiḥ. ath' âitāni mada|kala|mayūra|kaṇṭha|komala|cchavibhir avakīrṇāni parvatair a|virala|niviṣṭa|nīla|bahala|cchāya|taruṇa|taru|ṣaṇḍa|maṇḍitāny a|sambhrānta|vividha|mṛga|yūthāni paśyatu mah"|ânubhāvaḥ praśānta|gambhīrāṇi madhyam'|âraṇyāni.

RAMA:

As I gaze at Jana·sthana, the place where Khara used
to live,
I relive the events that once occurred as if they were
right before my eyes.

(looking all around) How deep was Vaidéhi's love for Rama:* 2.85
Here are those very forests, for heaven's sake, what could be more terrifying? *(tearfully)*

Yet she said, "I will live with you
in the honey-scented woods," and indeed
she actually enjoyed it here—
such was the measure of her affection.

The person need do nothing at all,
the mere joy of being together
dispels sorrow. What a gift it is,
to have someone who loves you.

SHAMBÚKA: Have done with memories that bring only pain. Let my lord turn his eye toward the wilderness in the middle distance, calm and deep woods surrounded by mountains the color of the soft neck of a lusty-throated peacock, adorned with clumps of thickly packed, dark and dense shade-trees, with herds of animals of every sort calmly reposing.

iha sa|mada|śakunt'|ākrānta|vānīra|vīrut|
prasava|surabhi|śīta|svaccha|toyā vahanti
phala|bhara|pariṇāma|śyāma|jambū|nikuñja|
skhalana|mukhara|bhūri|srotaso nirjhariṇyaḥ.

[20]

2.90 api ca:

dadhati kuhara|bhājām atra bhallūka|yūnām
anurasita|gurūṇi styānam ambū|kṛtāni.
śiśira|kaṭu|kaṣāyaḥ styāyate śallakīnām
ibha|dalita|vikīrṇa|granthi|niṣyanda|gandhaḥ.

[21]

RĀMAḤ: *(sa|bāṣpa|stambham)* bhadra, śivās te panthānaḥ. deva|yānaṃ pratipadyasva puṇyebhyo lokebhyaḥ.

ŚAMBŪKAḤ: yāvat purāṇa|brahma'|rṣim Agastyam abhivādya śāśvataṃ padam anupraviśāmi.

niṣkrāntaḥ.

Here mountain streams run with water cold and clear and fragrant
with the flowers of vines and rushes shaken by the lusty birds,
and their strong currents noisily tumble amidst the arbors
of rose-apple trees dark with their ripened loads of fruit.

What's more, 2.90

On the mountains there are caves
where bear cubs have their lairs,
and their growls are amplified
by their resounding echo;
amplified as well is the scent
of succulent *shállaki* leaves,
cool and sharp and tangy, torn
from stems and scattered by elephants.

RAMA: *(choking with sobs)* Good fellow, may your path be an auspicious one, may you follow the heavenly route* to the worlds of merit.

SHAMBÚKA: After I pay my respects to the ancient Brahman seer Agástya I shall enter the eternal abode.

Exit.

RĀMAḤ:

2.95 etat tad eva hi punar vanam adya dṛṣṭaṃ
yasminn abhūma ciram eva purā vasantaḥ,
āraṇyakāś ca gṛhiṇaś ca ratāḥ sva|dharme,
sāṃsārikeṣu ca sukheṣu vayaṃ rasajñāḥ. [22]

ete ta eva girayo viruvan|mayūrās,
tāny eva matta|hariṇāni vana|sthalāni,
āmañju|vañjula|latāni ca tāny amūni
nīrandhra|nīla|niculāni sarit|taṭāni. [23]

megha|māl" êva yaś c' âyam
ārād api vibhāvyate,
giriḥ Prasravaṇaḥ so' yaṃ
yatra Godāvarī nadī. [24]

asy' âiv' āsīn mahati śikhare
gṛdhra|rājasya vāsas.
tasy' âdhastād vayam api ratās
teṣu parṇ'|ôṭajeṣu
Godāvaryāḥ payasi vitat|ā-
nokaha|śyāmala|śrīr
antaḥ|kūjan|mukhara|śakuno
yatra ramyo van'|ântaḥ. [25]

RAMA:

This is the very same forest I am seeing again today 2.95
where once—it was many years ago—I long
sojourned,
both hermit and householder devoted to my own
dharma,
who came to know the sweet taste of worldly
pleasures.

Those are the same mountains, where peacocks
used to cry,
those, the same forest-reaches with their deer in
heat,
those, the riverbanks with their lovely reeds and
vines
and rushes blue-black and thickly clumped
together.

And what looms in the distance there like a wreath
of clouds
is Mount Prásravana, where the Godávari River
runs.

On that mountain's high peak the king of vultures
once lived
and on the lower slopes we enjoyed our leaf-
thatched huts
by the Godávari, where the forest lay spread out
alive with cooing birds, splendid with dark trees.

atr' âiva sā Pañcavaṭī yatra cira|nivāsena vividha|visrambh'|âtiprasaṅga|sākṣiṇaḥ pradeśāḥ priyāyāḥ priya|sakhī Vāsantī ca. tat kim idam āpatitam adya Rāmasya? samprati hi:

2.100 cirād veg'|ârambhī
prasṛta iva tīvro viṣa|rasaḥ,
kutaś cit saṃvegāc
calita iva śalyasya śakalaḥ,
vraṇo rūḍha|granthiḥ
sphuṭita iva hṛn|marmaṇi punar,
purā|bhūtaḥ śoko
vikalayati māṃ nūtana iva. [26]

tath" âpi tān pūrva|suhṛdo bhūmi|bhāgān paśyāmi. *(nirūpya)* aho, an|avasthito bhū|sanniveśaḥ.

purā yatra srotaḥ
pulinam adhunā tatra saritāṃ.
viparyāsaṃ yāto
ghana|virala|bhāvaḥ kṣiti|ruhām.
bahor dṛṣṭaṃ kālād
aparam iva manye vanam idaṃ.
niveśaḥ śailānāṃ
tad idam iti buddhiṃ draḍhayati. [27]

hanta, pariharantam api mām itaḥ Pañcavaṭī|sneho balād ākarṣat' îva. *(sa|karuṇam)*

Right here is Pancha·vati, whose different locales witnessed, in the course of our long residence, our many intimate conversations, and where my beloved's friend Vasánti lives. But what's happening to Rama?* For now

Like a slow-working poison that spreads 2.100
with sharp and sudden potency
or an arrowhead lodged deep within
that moves from some external shock
or a wound within the heart's soft core
scarred over but bursting apart again,
my ancient* grief has suddenly
begun anew to tear me apart.

Still, I want to visit those expanses of land that were once our friends. *(looking)* My, how the lay of the land has changed.

Where once there was a flowing stream
is now dry riverbed,
where once the trees were dense they're sparse,
and sparse where once they were dense.
Seen after so long a time I find
this forest completely changed—
the placement of the hills alone
persuades me it's the same.

Ah, despite my unwillingness my affection for Pancha·vati seems to draw me on by force. *(with pity)*

yasyāṃ te divasās tayā saha tathā
nītāḥ punaḥ sve gṛhe
yat|sambandhi|kathābhir eva satataṃ
dīrghābhir asthīyata,
ekaḥ samprati nāśita|priyatamas
tām eva Rāmaḥ kathaṃ
pāpaḥ Pañcavaṭīṃ vilokayatu vā
gacchatv a|sambhāvya vā? [28]

2.105 ŚAMBŪKAḤ: *(praviśya)* jayatu devaḥ. bhagavān Agastyo mattaḥ śruta|bhavat|sannidhānas tvām āha: «parikalpit'|âvataraṇa|maṅgalā pratīkṣate vatsalā Lopāmudrā sarve ca maha"|rṣayaḥ. tad ehi sambhāvay" âsmān. atha prajavinā Puṣpakeṇa sva|deśam upagamy' âśva|medhāya sajjo bhav'» êti.

RĀMAḤ: yath" ājñāpayati bhagavān.

ŚAMBŪKAḤ: itas tarhi devaḥ pravartayatu Puṣpakam.

RĀMAḤ: bhagavati Pañcavaṭi, guru|jan'|ôparodhāt kṣaṇaṃ kṣamyatām atikramo Rāmasya.

ŚAMBŪKAḤ: deva, paśya paśya:

The place where all those days were passed with her,
and which later, when at home,
was a topic constantly brought up, a subject
of endless conversation—
how can evil Rama—all alone now
that he killed* his most beloved—
either behold Pancha·vati or pass by
without paying his respects?

Enter SHAMBÚKA: Long live the king. Agástya learned of 2.105
your presence from me and addresses you as follows: "Lopa·mudra has made all the necessary welcome preparations and awaits you affectionately in the company of the great seers. Do come and honor us with a visit. You can then return to your own country on the swift Púshpaka chariot and prepare yourself for the Horse Sacrifice."

RAMA: As the blessed one wishes.

SHAMBÚKA: Then let my lord turn the Púshpaka in this direction.

RAMA: Pancha·vati, please forgive for a moment the disrespect Rama must show in order to comply with his elders.

SHAMBÚKA: Look, my lord, look:

2.110 guñjat|kuñja|kuṭīra|kauśika|ghaṭā|
ghūtkāravat|kīcaka|
stamb'|āḍambara|mūka|maukuli|kulaḥ
Krauñcāvato 'yaṃ giriḥ.
etasmin pracalākināṃ pracalatām
udvejitāḥ kūjitair
udvellanti purāṇa|rohiṇa|taru|
skandheṣu kumbhīnasāḥ. [29]

api ca,

ete te kuhareṣu gadgada|nadad|
Godāvarī|vārayo
megh'|ālambita|mauli|nīla|śikharāḥ
kṣoṇī|bhṛto dakṣiṇāḥ.
anyonya|pratighāta|saṅkula|calat|
kallola|kolāhalair
uttālās ta ime gabhīra|payasaḥ
puṇyāḥ sarit|saṅgamāḥ. [30]

niṣkrāntau.

*iti mahā|kavi|śrī|Bhavabhūti|praṇīta
Uttara|Rāma|carita|nāṭake
Pañcavaṭī|praveśo nāma
dvitīyo 'ṅkaḥ.*

There's Mount Kraunchávata,* where flocks of crows 2.110
are silenced by the raucous din
of wind in the bamboo groves redoubled
by owls hooting in the rustling bowers;
where the snakes hanging in the branches
of the ancient sandalwood trees
writhe about frightened by the cries
of peacocks strutting down below.

What's more,

Over there are the southern mountains,
the waters of the Godávari
gurgling in their caves, their summits
darkened by clouds hovering on the peaks;
and there are the holy spots where the rivers meet,
their deep waters roaring with the crash
of waves that rise helter skelter
as the currents meet head on.

Exeunt both.

End of Act II

PRELUDE TO ACT III

tataḥ praviśati NADĪ*|dvayam.*

EKĀ: sakhi Murale kim asi sambhrānt" êva?

MURALĀ: bhagavati Tamase, preṣit" âsmi bhagavato 'gastyasya patnyā Lopāmudrayā sarid|varāṃ Godāvarīm abhidhātum: «jānāsy eva yathā vadhū|tyāgāt prabhṛti

a|nirbhinno gabhīratvād
antar|gūḍha|ghana|vyathaḥ
puṭa|pāka|pratīkāśo
Rāmasya karuṇo rasaḥ. [1]

3.5 tena ca tathā|vidh'|êṣṭa|jana|kaṣṭa|vinipāta|janmanā prakarṣaṃ gatena dīrgha|śoka|santānena samprati nitarāṃ parikṣīṇo Rāma|bhadraḥ. tam avalokya kampitam iva sa|bandhanaṃ me hṛdayam. adhunā ca pratinivartamānena Rāma|bhadreṇa niyatam eva Pañcavaṭī|vane vadhū|saha|vāsa|visrambha|sākṣiṇaḥ pradeśā draṣṭavyāḥ. teṣu ca nisarga|dhīrasy' âpy evaṃ|vidhāyām avasthāyām atigambhīr'|ābhoga|śoka|kṣobha|saṃvegāt pade pade mahānti pramāda|sthānāni śaṅkanīyāni. tad, bhagavati Godāvari, tvayā tatra s'|âvadhānayā bhavitavyam.

vīcī|vātaiḥ śīkara|kṣoda|śītair
ākarṣadbhiḥ padma|kiñjalka|gandhān
mohe mohe Rāma|bhadrasya jīvaṃ
svairaṃ svairaṃ preritais tarpay',» êti. [2]

*Enter two rivers.**

FIRST: Múrala my friend, you seem somehow distraught.

MÚRALA: Támasa, I have been sent by Lopa·mudra, wife of Agástya, with a message for Godávari, the best of rivers: "You are well aware how, from the moment he disowned my daughter-in-law,

> Rama has been filled with the *rasa* of pity,
> kept hidden* by his profound demeanor,
> the sharp pain of it held deep within
> like a clay pot baking in embers.

And as a result, an unending stream of grief, springing from 3.5
the calamity that befell that cherished woman and growing with such intensity, has now completely shattered dear Rama. My heartstrings almost break to look at him. Today he is set to return to Pancha·vati forest to have a last look at the places that witnessed the intimacies of his sojourn with my daughter-in-law. He is self-possessed by nature but still, one fears that the shock of overwhelming grief in such a place will produce great turmoil for him every step of the way. Be on the watch for this, Godávari.

> The breeze off your waves cooled with water
> droplets
> and wafting the scent of lotus filaments—
> ever so gently direct it toward dear Rama
> and soothe his soul if ever he grows faint."

TAMASĀ: ucitam eva dākṣiṇyaṃ snehasya. sañjīvan'|ôpāyas tu maulika eva Rāma|bhadrasy' âdya sannihitaḥ.

MURALĀ: katham iva?

TAMASĀ: śrūyatām: purā kila Vālmīki|tapo|van'|ôpakaṇṭhāt parityajya nivṛtte Lakṣmaṇe Sītā|devī prāpta|prasava|vedanam ātmānam atiduḥkha|saṃvegād Gaṅgā|pravāhe nikṣiptavatī. tad" âiva tatra dāraka|dvayaṃ prasūtā. bhagavatībhyāṃ Pṛthivī|Jāhnavībhyām abhyupapannā rasā|talaṃ ca nītā. stanya|tyāgāt pareṇa ca dāraka|dvayaṃ tasyāḥ Prācetasasya maha"|rṣer Gaṅgā|devyā svayaṃ samarpitam.

3.10 MURALĀ: *(sa|vismayam)*

idṛśāṃ vinipāto 'pi
jāyate param'|âdbhutaḥ
yatr' ôpakaraṇībhāvam
āyāty evaṃ|vidho janaḥ. [3]

TAMASĀ: idānīṃ tu Śambūka|vṛttānten' ânena sambhāvita| Janasthāna|gamanaṃ Rāma|bhadraṃ Sarayū|mukhād upaśrutya bhagavatī Bhāgīrathī yad eva bhagavatyā Lopāmudrayā snehād āśaṅkitaṃ tad ev' āśaṅkya Sītā|sametā kena cid iva grah'|âpacāra|vyapadeśena Godāvarīṃ vilokayitum āgatā.

---

[i] The Gaṅgā. [ii] The river that flows on the outskirts of Ayodhyā, Rāma's capital city. [iii] By the ritual of the birthday bracelets mentioned below.

TÁMASA: Such thoughtfulness is entirely in keeping with Lopa·mudra's affection. But a more basic means of revitalizing dear Rama is at hand right now.

MÚRALA: How so?

TÁMASA: Listen. Years ago, they say, no sooner had Lákshmana returned from Valmíki's penance grove after disowning her than Queen Sita went into labor, and such was the force of her pain that she hurled herself in the Ganga River.* But right then and there she gave birth to two little boys. Earth and Ganga came to her aid and spirited her away to the underworld. After the boys were weaned, Goddess Ganga herself committed them to the care of the great seer, the descendent of Prachétas.

MÚRALA: *(in astonishment)* 3.10

For such persons even ruin* is a source of sheer
wonder,
with beings of that sort coming to their aid.

TÁMASA: Now Bhagi·rathi[i] learned from the Sárayu[ii] that dear Rama was likely to have come to Jana·sthana because of the Shambúka affair, and she was seized with the very same tender-hearted worries as Lopa·mudra. Along with Sita and under the pretext of warding off the evil eye[iii] she has therefore come to pay a visit to the Godávari.

MURALĀ: su|vicintitaṃ bhagavatyā. rāja|dhānī|sthitasya khalu tais tair jagatām ābhyudayikaiḥ kāryair vyāpṛtasya Rāma|bhadrasya niyatāś citta|vikṣepāḥ. a|vyagrasya punar asya śoka|mātra|dvitīyasya Pañcavaṭī|praveśo mahān anartha iti. tat katham idānīṃ Sītā|devyā Rāma|bhadra āśvāsanīyaḥ syāt?

TAMASĀ: uktam atra bhagavatyā Bhāgīrathī|devyā: «vatse, deva|yajana|sambhave Sīte, adya khalv āyuṣmatoḥ Kuśa|Lavayor dvādaśasya janma|saṃvatsarasya saṅkhyā|maṅgala|granthir abhivardhate. tad ātmanaḥ purāṇa|śvaśuram etāvato mānavasya rāja'|rṣi|vaṃśasya prasavitāraṃ Savitāram apahata|pāpmānaṃ devaṃ sva|hast'|âvacitaiḥ puṣpair upatiṣṭhasva. na ca tvām avani|pṛṣṭha|vartinīm asmat|prabhāveṇa devatā api drakṣyanti, kiṃ punar martyāḥ?» iti. ahaṃ c' ājñāpitā: «Tamase, tvayi prakṛṣṭa|prem" âiva vadhūr vatsā Jānakī. atas tvam ev' âsyāḥ praty antarī|bhava» iti. s" âham adhunā yath"|ādiṣṭam anutiṣṭhāmi.

3.15 MURALĀ: aham apy amuṃ vṛttāntaṃ bhagavatyai Lopāmudrāyai nivedayāmi. Rāma|bhadro 'py āgata ev', êti tarkayāmi.

TAMASĀ: tad iyaṃ Godāvarī|hradān niṣkramya,

---

[i] The amulet bracelet would be tied around the boys' wrists. [ii] The Gaṅgā is often represented as the mother of the Raghu clan.

MÚRALA: That was very prescient of Ganga: Of course, so long as King Rama remained in the royal capital and was preoccupied with the many pressing affairs of his subjects, he would certainly have been distracted. But now that he has nothing to divert him and no companion other than his grief, his return to Pancha·vati is fraught with danger. Is there then some way Queen Sita might be able to comfort dear Rama?

TÁMASA: The goddess Bhagi·rathi has already anticipated this. "My child Sita," she said to her, "you who were born at a sacred rite: Today, as you know, the amulet for counting the birthdays of Kusha and Lava (long may they live!) has reached twelve.[i] You must accordingly collect some flowers with your own hands and worship the stainless Sun, who is both progenitor of the Mánavas, your sons' royal lineage, and your own primeval father-in-law. Thanks to my power no god, let alone mortal, will be able to perceive that you are present here on earth." And she gave me the following order: "Támasa, the child Jánaki, my daughter-in-law,[ii] is especially fond of you, so it's up to you to attend upon her." And now I am doing as I was directed.

MÚRALA: I will inform the Lopa·mudra of this plan. I sus- 3.15
pect that dear Rama himself has already arrived.

TÁMASA: And there, emerging from a pond by the Godávari,

paripāṇḍu|durbala|kapola|sundaraṃ
dadhatī vilola|kabarīkam ānanam
karuṇasya mūrtir atha vā śarīriṇī
viraha|vyath" êva vanam eti Jānakī. [4]

MURALĀ: iyaṃ hi sā,

kisalayam iva mugdhaṃ bandhanād vipralūnaṃ
hṛdaya|kusuma|śoṣī dāruṇo dīrgha|śokaḥ
glapayati paripāṇḍu kṣāmam asyāḥ śarīraṃ
śaradi|ja iva dharmaḥ ketakī|garbha|patram. [5]

3.20 *parikramya niṣkrānte.*

viṣkambhakaḥ

Her face covered by her disheveled hair,
all the more beautiful for her wan and sunken
cheeks,
the very image of pity, the embodiment of the pain
of love's parting, is Jánaki entering the woods.

MÚRALA: Yes, that must be her,

Like a tender bud sheared off from its stem
her pallid and haggard body has been withered
by long hard grief parching her heart's flower
like autumn heat a leaf in a *kétaki* bud.*

Walking about, exeunt both. 3.20

End of the Prelude

ACT III
THE SHADOW

NEPATHYE: pramādaḥ! pramādaḥ!

tataḥ praviśati puṣp'|âvacaya|vyagrā, sa|karuṇ'|autsukyam ākarṇayantī SĪTĀ.

SĪTĀ: ⌜ammahe, jāṇāmi pia|sahī me Vāsantī vāharadi?⌟

NEPATHYE:

3.25 Sītā|devyā sva|kara|kalitaiḥ
śallakī|pallav'|âgrair
agre lolaḥ kari|kalabhako
yaḥ purā poṣito 'bhūt, [6ab]

SĪTĀ: ⌜kiṃ tassa?⌟

PUNAR NEPATHYE:

vadhvā sārdhaṃ payasi viharan
so 'yam anyena darpād
uddāmena dvirada|patinā
sannipaty' âbhiyuktaḥ. [6cd]

SĪTĀ: *(sa|sambhramaṃ kati cit padāni dadhatī)* ⌜ajja|utta, parittāāhi, parittāāhi mama taṃ puttaaṃ!⌟ *(smṛtim abhinīya, sa|vaiklavyam)* ⌜haddhī, haddhī! tāiṃ jevva cira|paricidāiṃ akkharāiṃ Pañcavaḍī|daṃsaṇeṇa maṃ manda|bhāiṇiṃ aṇubandhanti. hā ajja|utta!⌟ *(mūrchati)*

TAMASĀ: *(praviśya)* vatse, samāśvasihi samāśvasihi.

OFFSTAGE: Danger! Danger!

Enter SITA *engrossed in picking flowers and listening with growing pity and anxiety.*

SITA: What, is it the voice of my beloved friend Vasánti that I'm hearing?

STILL OFFSTAGE:

The elephant that long ago 3.25
Queen Sita raised as a calf
on *shállaki* leaf tips picked by hand—
and how impatient it stood before her—

SITA: What about him?

STILL OFFSTAGE:

was busy playing with his mate
in the river when an elephant,
a wild bull, fell upon him
in the most brazen attack.

SITA: *(in alarm taking a few steps forward)* Husband, save my little son, save him! *(miming the return of her memory; crestfallen)* Oh dear god, the sight of Pancha·vati has brought back to me, cursed as I am, those words familiar from long ago. Oh my husband! *(falls faint)*

Enter TÁMASA: My child, compose yourself, I beg you.

3.30 NEPATHYE: vimāna|rāja, atr' âiva sthīyatām.

SĪTĀ: *(āśvasya, sa|sādhvas'|ôllāsam)* ⌜ammahe, jala|bharida|meha|manthara|tthaṇida|gambhīra|maṃsalo kudo ṇu eso bhāradī|ṇigghoso bharanto kaṇṇa|vivaraṃ maṃ pi manda|bhāiṇiṃ jhatti uddhūsarei?⌟

TAMASĀ: *(sa|smit'|âsram)* ayi, vatse,

a|parisphuṭa|nikvāṇe
 kutastye 'pi tvam īdṛśī
stanayitnor mayūr" îva
 cakit'|ôtkaṇṭhitaṃ sthitā? [7]

SĪTĀ: ⌜bhaavadi, kiṃ bhaṇāsi, «a|paripphuḍaṃ» ti? mae uṇa sara|sañjoeṇa paccabhiāṇidaṃ ajja|utto jjevva vāharadi.⌟

3.35 TAMASĀ: śrūyate: «tapasyataḥ śūdrasya daṇḍa|dhāraṇ'|ârtham Aikṣvāko rājā Janasthānam āgataḥ» iti.

SĪTĀ: ⌜diṭṭhiā a|parihīṇa|rāa|dhammo kkhu so rāā.⌟

NEPATHYE:

yatra drumā api mṛgā api bandhavo me
 yāni priyā|saha|caraś ciram adhyavātsam,
etāni tāni bahu|nirjhara|kandarāṇi
 Godāvarī|parisarasya gires taṭāni. [8]

---

[i] An ancestor of Rāma; the name is also used for Rāma's dynasty.

OFFSTAGE: King of chariots, station yourself right here. 3.30

SITA: *(regaining her composure; with a flash of panic)* Why, how is it that this sound of human speech, rich and deep as the low rumble of a water-laden cloud, should fill my ears and all of a sudden unsettle* me, cursed as I am?

TÁMASA: *(smiling and crying at once)* Ah my child,

How can someone like you become so uneasy and
wistful
at a sound so indistinct and uncertain, like a peahen
at distant thunder?

SITA: Blessed one, why do you say "indistinct"? It can only be my husband speaking, I recognize the sound of his voice.

TÁMASA: I've heard that an Ikshváku[i] king has come to Jana·sthana to punish a Shudra for practicing austerities. 3.35

SITA: How fortunate the king has not renounced the practice of kingly *dharma*.*

OFFSTAGE:

A place where the trees and beasts themselves were
kinsmen,
where I sojourned so long with my beloved...
there are the mountain slopes by Godávari
studded with caves, crisscrossed by rushing streams.

SĪTĀ: *(dṛṣṭvā)* ⌜hā kadhaṃ, pabhāda|canda|maṇḍal'|āvaṇḍura|parikkhāma|dubbaleṇa āāreṇa aaṃ ṇia|somma|gambhīr'|âṇubhāva|metta|paccabhiāṇaṇīo ajja|utto jjevva. tā maṃ dhārehi.⌟ (TAMASĀM *āśliṣya mūrchati)*

TAMASĀ: *(dhārayantī)* vatse, samāśvasihi, samāśvasihi.

3.40 NEPATHYE: anena Pañcavaṭī|darśanena

antar|līnasya duḥkh'|âgner
  ady' ôddāmaṃ jvaliṣyataḥ
utpīḍa iva dhūmasya
  mohaḥ prāg āvṛṇoti mām. [9]

hā, priye Jānaki!

TAMASĀ: *(sva|gatam)* idaṃ tad āśaṅkitaṃ guru|janen' âpi.

SĪTĀ: *(samāśvasya)* ⌜hā, kadhaṃ edaṃ?⌟

3.45 NEPATHYE: hā devi Daṇḍak"|âraṇya|vāsa|priya|sakhi. hā Videha|rāja|putri.

SĪTĀ: ⌜haddhī, haddhī. maṃ manda|bhāiṇiṃ vāharia āmīlanta|ṇetta|ṇīl|uppalo mucchido jjevva. hā kadhaṃ dharaṇi*|vaṭṭhe ṇirussāha|ṇīsahaṃ vipalhattho? bhaavadi Tamase, parittāāhi, parittāāhi. jīvāvehi ajja|uttaṃ.⌟ *(pādayoḥ patati)*

---

[i] The Gaṅgā.

SITA: *(observing)* Oh, what in the world... a form pale, wasted, and weak as the disk of the moon at dawn but with a gentle yet profound bearing all its own—the only thing that enables me to recognize... yes, it must be my husband. Take hold of me. *(falls faint in* TÁMASA*'s embrace)*

TÁMASA: *(holding her)* My child, compose yourself, I beg you.

OFFSTAGE: The sight of Pancha·vati 3.40

Rekindles now the fire of sorrow
that had long been dormant in my heart
but first, like a dense pall of smoke,
a delirium envelops me.

Oh my beloved Jánaki!

TÁMASA: *(aside)* This is exactly what my guru[i] feared.

SITA: *(regaining her composure)* Oh, how is this possible?

OFFSTAGE: Oh my queen, beloved companion in my sojourn in Dándaka wilderness. Oh princess of Vidéha. 3.45

SITA: Dear god, with my name on his lips—the name of cursed me—his dark blue lotus eyes rolled back and he fainted dead away. How can we leave him lying sprawled upon the naked ground, friendless and helpless? Save him, Támasa, save him. Bring my husband back to life. *(falls at her feet)*

TAMASĀ:

tvam eva nanu kalyāṇi
sañjīvaya jagat|patim.
priya|sparśo hi pāṇis te
tatr' âiva niyato bharaḥ. [10]

SĪTĀ: ⌜jaṃ bhodu taṃ bhodu. jadhā bhaavadī āṇavedi.⌟ *(sa|sambhramaṃ niṣkrāntā)*

tataḥ praviśati bhūmau nipatitaḥ s'|âsrayā SĪTAYĀ *spṛśyamānaḥ s'|āhlād'|ôcchvāso* RĀMAḤ.

3.50 SĪTĀ: *(kiṃ cit sa|harṣam)* ⌜jāṇe puṇo vi paccāgadaṃ via jīvidaṃ telloassa.⌟

RĀMAḤ: hanta, bhoḥ, kim etat?

praścyotanaṃ nu hari|candana|pallavānāṃ?
niṣpīḍit'|êndu|kara|kandala|jo nu sekaḥ?
ātapta|jīvita|punaḥ|paritarpaṇo me
sañjīvan'|auṣadhi|raso nu hṛdi prasiktaḥ? [11]

TÁMASA:

But surely only you, my lovely child,
can bring the lord of the world back to life.
Beloved is the touch of your hand
and on it alone the entire burden rests.*

SITA: Whatever will be will be. As the blessed one wishes. *(exit in alarm)*

The scene opens on RAMA, *collapsed on the ground, being stroked by the weeping* SITA, *and recovering with an expression of bliss.*

SITA: *(with muted joy)* I feel as if the life of the entire uni- 3.50
verse has returned.

RAMA: But, what is happening here?

Is this some kind of distillation
of heavenly sandalwood leaves,
or are these droplets come from stalks
of moonbeams squeezed in a press?
Or is someone dripping on my heart,
to soothe again a life once burned,
the extract of the magic herb
that brings the dead back to life?

sparśaḥ purā paricito niyataṃ sa eṣa
  sañjīvanaś ca manasaḥ parimohanaś ca,
santāpa|jāṃ sapadi yaḥ pratihatya mūrchām
  ānandanena jaḍatāṃ punar ātanoti. [12]

SĪTĀ: *(sa|sādhvasa|karuṇam apasṛtya)* ⌜ettikaṃ jevva dāṇiṃ me bahudaraṃ.⌟

3.55 RĀMAḤ: *(upaviśya)* na khalu vatsalayā devy" âbhyupapanno 'smi?

SĪTĀ: ⌜haddhī, haddhī. kiṃ ti ajja|utto maṃ bhaṇisadi?⌟

RĀMAḤ: bhavatu, paśyāmi.

SĪTĀ: ⌜bhaavadi Tamase, osaramha! jadi dāva maṃ pekkhissadi tado aṇ|abbhaṇuṇṇāda|saṇṇidhāṇeṇa adhiaṃ mama rāā kuppissadi.⌟

TAMASĀ: ayi vatse, Bhāgīrathī|vara|prasādād devatānām apy a|dṛśyā saṃvṛtt" âsi.

3.60 SĪTĀ: ⌜āṃ. atthi edaṃ⌟

RĀMAḤ: priye Jānaki! nanu priye Jānaki....

SĪTĀ: *(sa|manyu|gadgadam)* ⌜ajja|utta, a|sarisaṃ khu edaṃ imassa vuttantassa.⌟ *(s'|âsram)* ⌜aha vā kiṃ ti vajjamaïā jammantare vi puṇo a|sambhāvida|laddha|daṃsaṇassa

Surely I am familiar with this
from long ago, this touch
that both restores my consciousness
and induces a deep delirium:
no sooner does it dispel the faintness
arising from my anguish
than it produces the stupefaction
of an absolute bliss.

SITA: *(withdrawing in apprehension and pity)* This is as far as I should go for now.

RAMA: *(taking his seat)* Surely it cannot be that the queen in her affection for me has come to my aid?

SITA: Oh dear, why should my husband be talking* about me now?

RAMA: Well, let me just look around.

SITA: Támasa, we must leave! If the king sees me he'll be furious I am here without his permission.

TÁMASA: But dear child, the grace of Bhagi·rathi has made you invisible, even to gods.

SITA: Ah yes, you are right.

RAMA: Beloved Jánaki! Surely, beloved Jánaki…

SITA: *(her voice breaking with anger)* My husband, really, this is hardly in keeping with all that has happened. *(tearfully)* But then why should I be so hard-hearted and pitiless toward my husband when it is me, cursed me, he's affectionately addressing and when I never thought maṃ jevva manda|bhāiṇiṃ uddisia vacchalassa evvaṃ| vādiṇo ajja|uttassa uvari ṇiraṇukkosā bhavissaṃ? ahaṃ edassa hiaaṃ jāṇāmi, mama eso tti.⌟

RĀMAḤ: *(sarvato 'valokya, sa|nirvedam)* hā, na kaś cid atra.

SĪTĀ: ⌜bhaavadi Tamase, tadhā ṇikkāraṇa|pariccāiṇo vi edassa evvaṃ|vidheṇa daṃsaṇeṇa kīlisīo via me hia'|âvatthā tti ṇa āṇāmi.⌟

3.65 TAMASĀ: jānāmi vatse, jānāmi.

taṭa|sthaṃ nairāśyād,
 api ca kaluṣaṃ vipriya|vaśād,
viyoge dīrghe 'smiñ
 jhaṭiti ghaṭanāt stambhitam iva,
prasannaṃ saujanyād,
 dayita|karuṇair gāḍha|karuṇaṃ,
dravī|bhūtaṃ premṇā
 tava hṛdayam asmin kṣana iva. [13]

RĀMAḤ: devi,

prasāda iva mūrtas te
 sparśaḥ sneh'|ārdra|śītalaḥ
ady' âpy ānandayati māṃ.
 tvaṃ punaḥ kv' âsi, nandini? [14]

for a moment that I would see him again,* not even in a future life? I know his heart—as he knows mine.

RAMA: *(looking all around; despondently)* No, no one is there.

SITA: O Támasa, though he disowned me like that so groundlessly, when I see him in this state my heart reacts in ways I cannot understand.

TÁMASA: I know, my child, I know. 3.65

Cold because of your despair,
bitter because of his unkindness,
in a state of near paralysis
at meeting after long separation;
forgiving because of your goodness,
with deep sympathy for all your husband's pathos,
melted by love—such is your heart
and all, it seems, in a single moment.

RAMA: O my queen,

Your touch is like forgiveness incarnate,
cool as it is and moist with love.
It is there to delight me in spite of all—
but where are you, my heart's delight?

SĪTĀ: ⌜ede kkhu de a|gādha|daṃsida|siṇeha|sahāā āṇanda|ṇīsandiṇo Sītāmaā ajja|uttassa ullāvā jāṇaṃ paccaeṇa ṇikkāraṇa|pariccāa|sallido vi bahu|mado me jamma|lāho.⌟

3.70 RĀMAḤ: atha vā kutaḥ priyatamā? nūnaṃ saṅkalp'|âbhyāsa|pāṭav'|ôpādāna eṣa Rāmasya bhramaḥ.

NEPATHYE: pramādaḥ! pramādaḥ!

> Sītā|devyā sva|kara|kalitaiḥ
> śallakī|pallav'|âgrair
> agre lolaḥ kari|kalabhako
> yaḥ purā poṣito 'bhūt, [15ab]

RĀMAḤ: *(sa|karuṇ'|autsukyam)* kiṃ tasya?

PUNAR NEPATHYE:

> vadhvā sārdhaṃ payasi viharan
> so 'yam anyena darpād
> uddāmena dvirada|patinā
> sannipaty' âbhiyuktaḥ. [15cd]

3.75 SĪTĀ: ⌜ko dāṇiṃ abhiujjissadi?⌟

RĀMAḤ: kv' âsau, kv' âsau durātmā yaḥ priyāyāḥ putrakaṃ vadhū|dvitīyam abhibhavati? *(utthiṣṭhati)*

VĀSANTĪ: *(praviśya, sambhrāntā)* kathaṃ, devo Raghu|nandanaḥ?

SITA: My husband's protestations over Sita are filled with a deep affection and overflow with love's bliss. To believe them is to make me think that being born was worth it—however sharp the arrow of having been groundlessly disowned.*

RAMA: But then, what would my beloved be doing here? 3.70
This is a pure delusion on Rama's part, brought on by his long-honed skill in wishful thinking.

OFFSTAGE: Danger! Danger!

> The elephant that long ago
> Queen Sita raised as a calf
> on *shállaki* leaf tips picked by hand—
> and how impatient it stood before her—

RAMA: *(with growing pity and anxiety)* What about him?

STILL OFFSTAGE:

> was busy playing with his mate
> in the river when an elephant,
> a wild bull, fell upon him
> in the most brazen attack.

SITA: Who can come to the rescue now? 3.75

RAMA: Where's the wretch that dares assault my beloved's little son and his mate? *(stands up)*

Enter VASÁNTI *in alarm* Can it be king Raghu·nándana?

SĪTĀ: ⌜kahaṃ, pia|sahī me Vāsantī.⌟

VĀSANTĪ: jayatu devaḥ.

3.80 RĀMAḤ: *(nirūpya)* kathaṃ, devyāḥ priya|sakhī Vāsantī.

VĀSANTĪ: deva, tvaryatāṃ, tvaryatām. ito Jaṭāyu|śikharasya dakṣiṇena Sītā|tīrthena Godāvarīm avatīrya sambhāvayatu devyāḥ putrakaṃ devaḥ.

SĪTĀ: ⌜hā tāda Jaḍāo. suṇṇaṃ tue viṇā Jaṇaṭṭhāṇam.⌟

RĀMAḤ: ahaha, hṛdaya|marma|cchidaḥ khalv amī kath"|ôdghātāḥ.

VĀSANTĪ: ita ito devaḥ.

3.85 SĪTĀ: ⌜bhaavadi, saccakaṃ jevva vaṇa|devadā vi maṃ ṇa pekkhandi.⌟

TAMASĀ: ayi vatse, sarva|devatābhyaḥ prakṛṣṭam aiśvaryaṃ Mandākinī|devyāḥ. tat kim ity āśaṅkase?

SĪTĀ: ⌜tado aṇusaramha.⌟

parikrāmataḥ.

RĀMAḤ: bhagavati Godāvari, namas te.

---

[i] The Gaṅgā.

SITA: Why, it's my beloved friend Vasánti.

VASÁNTI: Long live the king.

RAMA: *(looking)* Why, it's the queen's beloved friend Vasánti. 3.80

VASÁNTI: Hurry, my lord, hurry. If you head out from here and go down to the Godávari by Sita's Ford to the south of Jatáyus' Peak you will see the queen's little son.

SITA: Oh father Jatáyus. Without you Jana·sthana is empty.

RAMA: Ah, allusions that tear at my heart's soft core.

VASÁNTI: This way, my lord, this way.

SITA: Blessed one, it's really true, even the forest deities can't see me. 3.85

TÁMASA: Dear child, Mandákini's[i] power far surpasses that of all other deities. There's no need to worry.

SITA: So let's follow behind.

The two walk about.

RAMA: Blessed Godávari, homage to you.

3.90 VĀSANTĪ: *(nirūpya)* deva, modasva vijayinā vadhū|dvitīyena devyāḥ putrakeṇa.

RĀMAḤ: vijayatām āyuṣmān.

SĪTĀ: ⌜ammahe, īdiso so saṃvutto.⌟

RĀMAḤ: devi, diṣṭyā vardhase.

yen' ôdgacchad|bisa|kisalaya|
snigdha|dant'|âṅkureṇa
vyākṛṣṭas te, su|tanu, lavalī|
pallavaḥ karṇa|mūlāt
so 'yaṃ putras tava mada|mucāṃ
vāraṇānāṃ vijetā
yat kalyāṇaṃ vayasi taruṇe
bhājanaṃ tasya jātaḥ. [16]

3.95 SĪTĀ: ⌜a|viutto dāṇiṃ dīh'|āū imāe somma|daṃsaṇāe bhodu.⌟

RĀMAḤ: sakhi Vāsanti, paśya paśya. kānt"|ânuvṛtti|cāturyam apy ardhaṃ śikṣitaṃ vatsena:

līl"|ôtkhāta|mṛṇāla|kāṇḍa|kavala|
cchedeṣu sampāditāḥ
puṣyat|puṣkara|vāsitasya payaso
gaṇḍūṣa|saṅkrāntayaḥ
sekaḥ śīkariṇā kareṇa vihitaḥ
kāmaṃ virāme punar
na snehād an|arāla|nāla|nalinī|
patr'|ātapatraṃ dhṛtam. [17]

VASÁNTI: *(looking)* My lord, rejoice that the queen's little son along with his mate has won the day. 3.90

RAMA: Victory and long life to him.

SITA: My, how big he's grown.

RAMA: My queen, how fortunate you are.

That son of yours, my lovely wife,
who once would pluck the *lávali* leaf
from behind your ear with his budding sprout
of a tusk glossy as a lotus petal
has now won a victory
over rutting bull elephants—
clearly he continues to enjoy
the good fortune* of his childhood.

SITA: Long may he live and from this day on may he never be separated from his kindly mate. 3.95

RAMA: Look, friend Vasánti, look: The child has almost learned the art of deferring to his beloved.

In the intervals between her chewing morsels
of lily stalks dug up in play,
he offers her mouthfuls of water scented
with just-blooming lotuses,
spraying water from his drop-filled trunk.
And yet at rest he fails to show
the proper concern by shading her
with the leaf of a straight-stemmed lotus.*

SĪTĀ: ⌜bhaavadi Tamase, aaṃ dāva īdiso jādo. te uṇa ṇa āṇāmi Kusa|Lavā ettikeṇa kāleṇa kīdisā via honti.⌟

TAMASĀ: yādṛśo 'yaṃ tādṛśau tāv api.

3.100 SĪTĀ: ⌜īdisī ahaṃ manda|bhāiṇī jāe ṇa kevalaṃ ṇirantaro ajja|utta|viraho putta|viraho vi.⌟

TAMASĀ: bhavitavyat" êyam īdṛśī.

SĪTĀ: ⌜kiṃ vā mae pasūdāe jeṇa tādisaṃ pi mama puttakāṇaṃ īsi|kalida |virala|komala|dhavala|dasaṇ|ujjala|kavolaṃ aṇubaddha|muddha|kāalī|vihasidaṃ ṇibaddha|kāa|sihaṇḍaaṃ amala|muha|puṇḍarīa|jualaaṃ ṇa paricumbidaṃ ajja|utteṇa?⌟

TAMASĀ: astu devatā|prasādāt.

SĪTĀ: ⌜bhaavadi Tamase, ediṇā avacca|sambharaṇeṇa ussasida|paṇhuda|tthaṇī tāṇaṃ ca piduṇo saṇṇidhāṇeṇa khaṇa|mettaṃ saṃsāriṇi mhi saṃvuttā.⌟

3.105 TAMASĀ: kim atr' ôcyate? prasavaḥ khalu prakarṣa|paryantaḥ snehasya. paraṃ c' âitad anyonya|saṃśleṣaṇaṃ pitroḥ.

antaḥ|karaṇa|tattvasya
  dampatyoḥ sneha|saṃśrayāt
ānanda|granthir eko 'yam
  apatyam iti badhyate. [18]

SITA: Támasa, when I see how much he has grown I think about Kusha and Lava and what they might look like after all this time.

TÁMASA: They are just like him.*

SITA: How cursed can I be to have been so cruelly separated 3.100
not only from my husband but from my sons as well.

TÁMASA: So was it meant to be.

SITA: What good was having children if my husband will never be able to kiss the faces of his sons—faces like two fresh lotuses, shining with the glow of a few delicate bright white teeth just appearing,* the innocent laughs and lisps and tufted hair of childhood?

TÁMASA: May the deities show their grace.

SITA: Támasa, at the mere memory of my children my breasts swell with milk, and the presence of their father makes me feel, for a moment, as if I were back among the living.*

TÁMASA: What is there to say? A child marks the highest 3.105
degree of love, and the source of the parents' ultimate bonding.

> Because it is the common object of a couple's love*
> a child is a knot of bliss that ties their hearts
> together.

VĀSANTĪ: ito 'pi devaḥ paśyatu.

a|tulita|pada|tāṇḍav'|ôtsav'|ânte
svayam acir'|ôdgata|mugdha|lola|barhaḥ
maṇi|mukuṭa iv' ôcchikhaḥ kadambe
nadati sa eṣa vadhū|sakhaḥ śikhaṇḍī. [19]

SĪTĀ: *(sa|kautuk'|âsram)* ⌜eso so!⌟

3.110 RĀMAḤ: modasva vatsa, modasva.

SĪTĀ: ⌜evvaṃ bhodu.⌟

RĀMAḤ:

bhramiṣu kṛta|puṭ'|ântar|maṇḍal'|āvṛtti cakṣuḥ
pracalita|catura|bhrū|tāṇḍavair maṇḍayantyā
kara|kisalaya|tālair mugdhayā nartyamānaṃ
sutam iva manasā tvāṃ vatsalena smarāmi. [20]

hanta, tiryañco 'pi paricayam anurudhyante.

katipaya|kusum'|ôdgamaḥ kadambaḥ
priyatamayā parivardhito ya āsit— [21ab]

3.115 SĪTĀ: *(nirūpya, s'|âsram)* ⌜suṭṭhu paccabhiāṇidaṃ ajja|utteṇa.⌟

VASÁNTI: Look over there as well, my lord:

> The very same peacock is calling to his mate
> from high in the *kadámba* tree, like a jeweled crest,
> with his soft tail feathers just now fanning out
> at the end of his festive, incomparable *tándava* dance.*

SITA: *(tearfully, with surprise)* It is him!

RAMA: All happiness to you, dear child.

SITA: Yes, so be it.

RAMA:

> I remember you with a fatherly affection:
> my simple-hearted wife would make you dance
> like her child by marking the beat with her hands
> and rolling her eyes to make you swirl:
> whirling like mandalas in their sockets,
> and with all the movements of a *tándava*
> in the skilful flutter of her brows.*

Why, even animals acknowledge old acquaintances:

> This *kadámba* tree just now coming into flower
> was grown from seed by my beloved queen—

SITA: *(looking; tearfully)* How sharp my husband's powers of recognition.

RĀMAḤ:

smarati giri|mayūra eṣa devyāḥ
sva|jana iv' âtra yataḥ pramodam eti. [21cd]

VĀSANTĪ: atra tāvad āsana|parigraham karotu devaḥ.

etat tad eva kadalī|vana|madhya|varti
kāntā|sakhasya śayanīya|śilā|talaṃ te
atra sthitā tṛṇam adād bahuśo yad ebhyaḥ
Sītā tato hariṇakair na vimucyate sma. [22]

RĀMAḤ: idam a|śakyaṃ draṣṭum. *(anyato rudann upaviśati)*

3.120 SĪTĀ: ⌜sahi Vāsanti, kiṃ tue kidaṃ ajja|uttassa mama a edaṃ daṃsaantīe? haddhī, haddhī. so jjevva ajja|utto, taṃ jevva Pañcavaḍī|vaṇaṃ, sā jevva pia|sahī Vāsantī, te jjevva viviha|vissambha|sakkhiṇo Godāvarī|kāṇaṇ|uddesā, te jjevva jāda|ṇivvisesā mia|pakkhi|pādavā. mama uṇa manda|bhāiṇīe dīsantaṃ pi savvaṃ jevva edaṃ ṇatthi. īdiso jīa|loassa parivatto.⌟

VĀSANTĪ: sakhi Sīte, kathaṃ na paśyasi Rāmasy' âvasthām?

RAMA:

> and the peacock is surely remembering her
> in treating the tree as if it were a brother.

VASÁNTI: Let my lord sit here a moment.

> Here is the stone bench in the *kádali* grove
> where you and your beloved would rest,
> where Sita would feed the fawns so much grass
> that they would never let her go.

RAMA: I can't bear to look at this. *(sits elsewhere, weeping)*

SITA: Vasánti, my friend, what are you doing to my husband, and to me, by showing this? Dear god, here is my husband, the very same husband, the same Pancha·vati forest, the same friend Vasánti, the same stretches of forest by the Godávari that witnessed our many intimacies, the same trees and birds and animals that were like my own offspring—all right before my eyes, and, cursed as I am, it has all ceased to exist for me. How utterly my world has been turned upside down. 3.120

VASÁNTI: Oh my friend Sita, don't you see the state Rama is in?*

kuvalaya|dala|snigdhair aṅgair
dadau nayan'|ôtsavaṃ
satatam api te sv'|êcchā|dṛśyo
navo nava eva yaḥ
vikala|karaṇaḥ pāṇḍu|śyāmaḥ
śucā paridurbalaḥ
katham api sa ity unnetavyas
tath" âpi dṛśāṃ priyaḥ. [23]

SĪTĀ: ⌜pekkhāmi, sahi, pekkhāmi.⌟

TAMASĀ: putri, paśyantī priyaṃ bhūyāḥ.

3.125 SĪTĀ: ⌜hā devva, eso mae viṇā, ahaṃ pi edeṇa viṇ" êtti keṇa sambhāvidaṃ āsi? tā muhuttakaṃ pi jamm|antarādo via laddha|daṃsaṇaṃ bāha|salil|antaresu pekkhāmi dāva vacchalaṃ ajja|uttaṃ.⌟ *(paśyantī sthitā)*

TAMASĀ: *(sa|sneh'|âsraṃ pariṣvajya)*

vilulitam atipūrair
bāṣpam ānanda|śoka|
prabhavam avasṛjantī
tṛṣṇay" ôttāna|dīrghā
snapayati hṛday'|ēśaṃ
sneha|niṣyandinī te
dhavala|bahala|mugdhā
dugdha|kuly" êva dṛṣṭiḥ. [24]

When his body was fresh as a blue lotus petal
he gave the eyes something to celebrate,
and even when you could gaze at him
to your heart's content, he seemed ever new.
And now, when almost senseless, pale and dark at once,
and so weak with grief it is almost impossible
to tell it is him, he still delights the eyes.*

SITA: But I do see, my friend, I do.

TÁMASA: My daughter, may you long continue to behold your beloved.*

SITA: Oh lord, who would ever have believed that he could 3.125
be without me and I without him? Let me just look at my dear husband a moment longer—being able to see him* is like being reborn—in the gaps between my falling tears. *(continues to look)*

TÁMASA: *(embracing her, weeping affectionately)*

A flood of tears surging in spate
arising from your bliss and grief
is released by your eyes wide with longing,
and your glances flowing with love,
white and sweet and innocent,
are drenching the lord of your heart
as if they were a stream of milk.*

VĀSANTĪ:

dadatu taravaḥ puṣpair arghyaṃ
phalaiś ca madhu|ścyutaḥ.
sphuṭita|kamal'|āmoda|prāyāḥ
pravāntu van'|ânilāḥ.
kalam a|viralaṃ rajyat|kaṇṭhāḥ
kvaṇantu śakuntayaḥ.
punar idam ayaṃ devo Rāmaḥ
svayaṃ vanam āgataḥ. [25]

RĀMAḤ: ehi, sakhi Vāsanti. nanv itaḥ sthīyatām.

3.130 VĀSANTĪ: *(upaviśya, s'|âsram)* Mahā|rāja, api kuśalaṃ kumāra|Lakṣmaṇasya?

RĀMAḤ: *(a|śrutim abhinīya)*

kara|kamala|vitīrṇair ambu|nīvāra|śaṣpais
taru|śakuni|kuraṅgān Maithilī yān apuṣyat,
bhavati mama vikāras teṣu dṛṣṭeṣu ko 'pi
drava iva hṛdayasya prasrav'|ôdbheda|yogyaḥ.
[26]

VĀSANTĪ: mahā|rāja, nanu pṛcchāmi: kuśalaṃ kumāra|Lakṣmaṇasya?

RĀMAḤ: *(sva|gatam)* aye, «mahā|rāj",» êti niṣpraṇayam āmantraṇa|padam. Saumitri|mātre ca bāṣpa|skhalit'|âkṣaraḥ kuśal'|ânupraśnaḥ. tathā manye: vidita|Sītā|vṛttānt" êyam iti. *(prakāśam)* āṃ, kuśalaṃ kumārasya. *(roditi)*

[i] Lakṣmaṇa's.

VASÁNTI:

> Let the trees offer a welcoming gift of flowers
> and fruits, drizzling them with honey.
> Let the forest breezes blow, bearing the full scent
> of freshly blooming lotuses.
> And let the birds begin a sweet unbroken song
> in full-throated warbling.
> For once again King Rama himself has come
> on a visit to this forest.

RAMA: Come, Vasánti my friend. Why don't we sit over here?

VASÁNTI: *(taking her seat; tearfully)* Your Majesty, I trust 3.130
Prince Lákshmana is well?

RAMA: *(miming not having heard)*

> Máithili would give these trees and birds and deer
> water, seeds, and grass from her lotus hand,
> and to see them again transforms me, as if my heart
> were liquefied, ready to burst open and gush forth.*

VASÁNTI: But Your Highness, I was asking whether Prince Lákshmana is well.

RAMA: *(aside)* Ah, "Your Highness," how cold the salutation. She asks only after Saumítri's[i] welfare, and her words are sob-choked. I assume she must know what happened to Sita. *(aloud)* Yes, the prince is well. *(begins to weep)*

3.135 VĀSANTĪ: ayi deva, kimiti dāruṇaḥ khalv asi?

SĪTĀ: ⌜sahi Vāsanti, kiṃ tumaṃ si evvaṃ|vādiṇī? pi'|âruho kkhu savvassa ajja|utto, visesado mama piasahīe.⌟

VĀSANTĪ:

«tvaṃ jīvitaṃ, tvam asi me hṛdayaṃ dvitīyaṃ,
tvaṃ kaumudī nayanayor, amṛtaṃ tvam aṅge,»
ity|ādibhiḥ priya|śatair anubadhya mugdhāṃ
tām eva... śāntam. atha vā kim ih' ôttareṇa? [27]

(iti muhyati)

TAMASĀ: sthāne khalu vākya|nivṛttir mohaś ca.

3.140 RĀMAḤ: sakhi, samāśvasihi, samāśvasihi.

VĀSANTĪ: *(samāśvasya)* tat kim idam a|kāryam anuṣṭhitaṃ devena?

SĪTĀ: ⌜sahi Vāsanti, virama, virama.⌟

RĀMAḤ: loko na mṛṣyat' îti.

VĀSANTĪ: tat kasya hetoḥ?

3.145 RĀMAḤ: sa eva jānāti kim api.

VASÁNTI: Ah my lord, why did you have to be so cruel, after all? 3.135

SITA: Vasánti my friend, how can you speak this way to him? My husband deserves kindness from everyone, not least from a dear friend of mine.

VASÁNTI:

> "You are my life, you are my second heart,
> moonlight to my eyes, nectar to my limbs,"
> and so on—with countless honeyed words you charmed* her,
> that simple girl... But enough, why bother saying more?

(falls faint)

TÁMASA: It's to be expected, after all, that she should fall speechless, even become delirious.

RAMA: Compose yourself, my friend, I beg you. 3.140

VASÁNTI: *(regaining her composure)* But why did my lord commit this unspeakable act?

SITA: Cease, my friend Vasánti, cease.

RAMA: Because of the people's censure.

VASÁNTI: And what was the cause of that?

RAMA: The people alone have some idea.* 3.145

TAMASĀ: cirād upālambhaḥ.

VĀSANTĪ:

ayi kaṭhora, yaśaḥ kila te priyaṃ.
kim a|yaśo nanu ghoram ataḥ param?
kim abhavad vipine hariṇī|dṛśaḥ?
kathaya, nātha, kathaṃ bata manyase? [28]

SĪTĀ: ⌜tumaṃ jevva, sahi Vāsanti, dāruṇā kaṭhorā a jā evvaṃ palittaṃ palīvesi.⌟

TAMASĀ: praṇaya evaṃ vyāharati śokaś ca.

3.150 RĀMAḤ: sakhi, kim atra mantavyam?

trast'|âika|hāyana|kuraṅga|vilola|dṛṣṭes
tasyāḥ parisphurita|garbha|bhar'|âlasāyāḥ
jyotsnāmay" îva mṛdu|mugdha|mṛṇāla|kalpā
kravyādbhir aṅga|latikā niyataṃ viluptā. [29]

SĪTĀ: ⌜ajja|utta, dharāmi esā dharāmi.⌟

RĀMAḤ: hā, priye Jānaki, kv' âsi?

SĪTĀ: ⌜haddhī, haddhī. ajja|utto vi pamukka|kaṇṭhaṃ paruṇṇo.⌟

TÁMASA: Too late for a reproach.*

VASÁNTI:

> Ah, heartless man, you prize your reputation,
> they say, but what ill repute is worse than this?
> What can have become of the fawn-eyed woman
> in the woods, do you suppose? Tell me, my master.

SITA: It's you, Vasánti my friend, who is cruel and heartless for inflaming a man already engulfed in flames.

TÁMASA: It's love speaking thus, and grief.

RAMA: My friend, what is one to suppose in such a case? 3.150

> No doubt her eyes would have rolled like those of
> a frightened yearling
> as she lay exhausted with the weight of the unborn
> kicking within
> while her delicate body, soft and tender as a lotus
> petal
> or a mass of moonbeams, was torn apart by savage
> beasts.

SITA: My husband, I am alive, here, alive.

RAMA: Oh my beloved Jánaki, where are you?

SITA: Dear god, even* my husband is crying out, at the top of his lungs.

3.155 TAMASĀ: vatse, sāmpratikam ev' âitat. kartavyāni duḥkhitair duḥkha|nirvāpaṇāni. yataḥ:

pūr'|ôtpīḍe taṭākasya
parīvāhaḥ pratikriyā.
śoka|kṣobhe ca hṛdayaṃ
pralāpair eva dhāryate. [30]

viśeṣato Rāma|bhadrasya bahutara|prakāra|kaṣṭo jīva|lokaḥ.

idaṃ viśvaṃ pālyaṃ
vidhivad abhiyuktena manasā.
priyā|śoko jīvaṃ
kusumam iva gharmaḥ klamayati.
svayaṃ kṛtvā tyāgaṃ
vilapana|vinodo 'py a|sulabhas
tad ady' âpy ucchvāso.
bhavati nanu lābho hi ruditam. [31]

RĀMAḤ: kaṣṭaṃ bhoḥ kaṣṭam.

3.160 dalati hṛdayaṃ gāḍh'|ôdvegaṃ,
dvidhā tu na bhidyate.
vahati vikalaḥ kāyo mohaṃ,
na muñcati cetanām.
jvalayati tanūm antar|dāhaḥ,
karoti na bhasmasāt.
praharati vidhir marma|cchedī,
na kṛntati jīvitam. [32]

TÁMASA: But my child, this is beneficial. Those who are sorrowful must try to expel their sorrow, for 3.155

When a flood puts pressure on a dam
one counteracts it by releasing water,
and it is weeping that helps the heart
hold out when it's overcome by grief.

And especially when for dear Rama this world has now become so awful in so many ways.

He must use his sharpest wits to protect
the whole earth according to law
while grief for his beloved withers his soul
as summer heat can wither a flower.
Since he himself is to blame for disowning her
no relief can be found in lamenting,
yet the breath of life stubbornly remains.*
So surely to weep is a blessing.

RAMA: How truly awful.

My heart breaks in sheer agony 3.160
but doesn't split apart,
my crippled body is delirious
but doesn't lose consciousness,
an inner fire enflames my limbs
but doesn't reduce them to ash.
Fate strikes me to the quick
but doesn't end my life.

SĪTĀ: ⌜evvaṃ edaṃ.⌟

RĀMAḤ: he bhavantaḥ paura|jānapadāḥ!

na kila bhavatāṃ sthānaṃ devyā
  gṛhe 'bhimataṃ, tatas
tṛṇam iva vane śūnye tyaktā,
  na c' âpy anuśocitā.
cira|paricitās tv ete bhāvāḥ
  paridravayanti mām.
idam a|śaraṇair ady' âpy evaṃ
  —prasīdata—rudyate. [33]

TAMASĀ: atigambhīram avagūraṇaṃ śoka|sāgarasya.

3.165 VĀSANTĪ: deva, atikrānte dhairyam avalambyatām.

RĀMAḤ: sakhi, kim atr' ôcyate «dhairyam» iti?

devyā śūnyasya jagato
  dvādaśaḥ parivatsaraḥ.
praṇaṣṭam iva nām' âpi.
  na ca Rāmo na jīvati. [34]

SĪTĀ: ⌜mohida mhi edehiṃ ajja|utta|vaaṇehiṃ.⌟

TAMASĀ: evaṃ, vatse.

3.170 n' âitāḥ priyatamā vācaḥ
  sneh'|ārdrāḥ śoka|dāruṇāḥ.
etās tā madhuno dhārāḥ
  ścyotanti sa|viṣās tvayi. [35]

SITA: Yes, it is so.

RAMA: You people of the city and countryside!

> You refused to allow the queen
> to continue living in my house,
> and so I left her in the empty forest
> unmourned, as if not worth a straw.
> But these long-familiar sights
> are utterly undoing me
> and hence this helpless—please forgive me—
> weeping of mine, even still.*

TÁMASA: How deep is the roar of the ocean of his grief.

VASÁNTI: Be strong, my lord, in the face of what is past. 3.165

RAMA: My friend, what do you mean by "strong"?

> This is the twelfth year of the world
> left empty by his queen—her name
> itself all but blotted out—
> yet Rama has not ceased to live.

SITA: My husband's words are tormenting me.

TÁMASA: Yes, my child.

> These are not a beloved's words, 3.170
> now gentle with love, now harsh with grief.
> They are streams of honey mixed
> with poison dripping in your ear.*

RĀMAḤ: ayi Vāsanti, mayā khalu

yathā tiraścīnam alāta|śalyaṃ
pratyuptam antaḥ sa|viṣaś ca daṃśaḥ
tath" âiva tīvro hṛdi śoka|śaṅkur
marmāṇi kṛntann api kiṃ na soḍhaḥ? [36]

SĪTĀ: ⌜evvaṃ mhi manda|bhāiṇī puṇo puṇo vi āāsa|āriṇī ajja|uttassa.⌟

RĀMAḤ: evam atinirutsukasya stambhit'|ântaḥ|karaṇasy' âpi mama saṃstuta|priya|vastu darśanād ady' âyam āvegaḥ. tathā hi:

3.175 hel'|ôllola|
kṣubhita|karuṇ'|ôjjṛmbhaṇa|stambhan'|ârthaṃ
yo yo yatnaḥ
katham api may" ādhīyate, taṃ tam antaḥ
bhittvā bhittvā
prasarati balāt ko 'pi ceto|vikāras
toyasy' êv' â|
pratihata|rayaḥ saikataṃ setum oghaḥ. [37]

SĪTĀ: ⌜ediṇā ajja|uttassa duv|vāra|dāruṇ'|ārambheṇa dukkha|saṅkhoheṇa pamusia|ṇia|dukkhaṃ via vevadi me hiaaṃ.⌟

VĀSANTĪ: *(sva|gatam)* kaṣṭam abhyāpanno devaḥ. tad ākṣipāmi tāvat. *(prakāśam)* cira|paricitān idānīṃ Janasthāna|bhāgān avalokayatu devaḥ.

RAMA: Ah Vasánti, have I, after all,

> Not borne the fiery goad of grief
> in my heart, though it jabs at my vitals,
> just like a heated arrowhead fixed
> athwart within, or a poisoned sting?*

SITA: So cursed am I that I am still making trouble for my husband.

RAMA: And though I have been broken and my heart rendered insensate, I have been stunned anew today by seeing these things, familiar things that she once loved.

> Every attempt I made with the greatest effort 3.175
> to control the intensification of pity*
> as it was stirred to the point of wild frenzy,
> was thwarted within, each and every one,
> by an indescribable transformation
> of consciousness that then poured out in full
> strength,
> as flood water surging unabated
> pours through a dam of sand it has destroyed.

SITA: The shock of my husband's sorrow, cruelly and implacably welling up, seems to have displaced the sorrow in my own heart, and left it throbbing uncontrollably.

VASÁNTI: *(aside)* My lord is in an awful state. Let me just try to divert him. *(aloud)* Would my lord now care to visit those regions of Jana·sthana that are familiar from long ago?

RĀMAḤ: evam astu.

utthāya parikrāmati.

3.180 SĪTĀ: ⌜sandīvaṇāiṃ jevva dukkhassa pia|sahī viṇodaṇ'|ôvāo tti maṇṇedi.⌟

VĀSANTĪ: *(sa|karuṇam)* deva, deva:

asminn eva latā|gṛhe tvam abhavas
 tan|mārga|datt'|ēkṣaṇaḥ.
sā haṃsaiḥ kṛta|kautukā ciram abhūd
 Godāvarī|saikate.
āyāntyā paridurmanāyitam iva
 tvāṃ vīkṣya baddhas tayā
kātaryād aravinda|kuḍmala|nibho
 mugdhaḥ praṇām'|âñjaliḥ. [38]

SĪTĀ: ⌜dāruṇ" âsi, Vāsanti, dāruṇ" âsi, jā edehiṃ hiaa|mamma|gūḍha|salla|ghaṭṭaṇehiṃ puṇo puṇo maṃ manda|bhāiṇiṃ ajja|uttaṃ sumarāvesi.⌟

RĀMAḤ: caṇḍi Jānaki, itas tato dṛśyasa iva. na c' ânukampase.

3.185 hā hā devi, sphuṭati hṛdayaṃ,
 dhvaṃsate deha|bandhaḥ.
śūnyaṃ manye jagad, a|virata|
 jvālam antar jvalāmi.
sīdann andhe tamasi vidhuro
 majjat' îv' ântar|ātmā.
viśvaṅ|mohaḥ sthagayati. kathaṃ
 manda|bhāgyaḥ karomi? [39]

RAMA: Yes, alright.

He stands up and walks around.

SITA: What my friend believes will be a means of distraction will instead inflame his sorrow. 3.180

VASÁNTI: *(with pity)* My lord, my lord:

It was in this bower of vines
you once stood watching the way back home
when she was delayed, enchanted
by the geese on the Godávari shore,
and on returning, seeing that you
looked cross, she anxiously paid reverence
by a simple cupping together
of hands like a lotus still unfolded.

SITA: You are cruel, Vasánti, so cruel, twisting the knife deeper into the heart's soft core to remind my husband over and over of me, cursed me.

RAMA: Hardhearted Jánaki, you show yourself in one place after another yet show me no compassion.

Oh my queen, my heart is breaking, 3.185
my body's bonds are coming undone,
the world is empty for me, and I burn
with an unrelenting fire within.
My very soul, submerged in blinding
darkness, is drowning helplessly,
utter* delirium envelopes me.
What am I, cursed I, to do?

(mūrchati)

SĪTĀ: ⌜haddhī, haddhī! puṇo vi pamūḍho ajja|utto.⌟

VĀSANTĪ: deva, samāśvasihi, samāśvasihi.

SĪTĀ: ⌜hā ajja|utta, maṃ manda|bhāiṇiṃ uddisia saala|jīa|loa|maṅgal'|ādhārassa de jamma|lāhassa vāraṃ vāraṃ saṃsaïda|jīa|dāruṇo dasā|pariṇāmo, tti hā hada mhi.⌟ *(mūrchati)*

3.190 TAMASĀ: vatse, samāśvasihi, samāśvasihi. punas tvat|pāṇi|sparśa eva sañjīvan'|ôpāyo Rāma|bhadrasya.

VĀSANTĪ: kaṣṭam, ady' âpi n' ôcchvasiti. hā priya|sakhi Sīte, kv' âsi? sambhāvay' ātmano jīvit'|ēśvaram.

SĪTĀ *sa|sambhramam upasṛtya hṛdi lalāṭe ca spṛśati.*

VĀSANTĪ: diṣṭyā pratyāpanna|cetano Rāma|bhadraḥ.

RĀMAḤ:

> ālimpann amṛtamayair iva pralepair
> antar vā bahir api vā śarīra|dhātūn
> saṃsparśaḥ punar api jīvayann a|kasmād
> ānandād apara|vidhaṃ tanoti moham. [40]

3.195 *(ānanda|nimīlit'|âkṣa eva)* sakhi Vāsanti, diṣṭyā vardhase.

(falls faint)

SITA: Dear god, my husband has fallen faint again!

VASÁNTI: Compose yourself, my lord, I beg you.

SITA: Oh my husband, you are the source of blessings to all the mortal world yet the gift of birth has turned into its opposite for you, brutalized by constant threats to your soul—and all because of cursed me. Oh I am lost. *(falls faint)*

TÁMASA: Compose yourself, my child, I beg you. The touch 3.190
of your hand is all it will take to revive dear Rama.

VASÁNTI: Alas, he still hasn't revived. Oh Sita, my beloved friend, where are you? Come comfort the lord of your life.

SITA *approaches in alarm, and touches him on the heart and forehead.*

VASÁNTI: How fortunate that dear Rama has regained consciousness.

RAMA:

Smoothing an almost ambrosial balm
over all my body's parts,* inside and out,
a touch has suddenly revived me and spread
a different—a blissful—delirium.

(his eyes still closed in bliss) Vasánti my friend, how fortunate 3.195
you are.

VĀSANTĪ: katham iva?

RĀMAḤ: sakhi, kim anyat? punaḥ prāptā Jānakī.

VĀSANTĪ: ayi deva Rāma|bhadra, kva sā?

RĀMAḤ: *(sparśa|sukham abhinīya)* paśya, nanv iyaṃ purata eva.

3.200 VĀSANTĪ: ayi, kim|iti marma|ccheda|dāruṇair atipralāpaiḥ priya|sakhī|duḥkha|dagdhām api punar manda|bhāginīṃ dahasi mām?

SĪTĀ: ⌜osariduṃ icchāmi. eso uṇa cira|sab|bhāva|somma|sīdaleṇa ajja|utta|pphaṃseṇa dīha|dāruṇaṃ pi sandāvaṃ jhatti ollavanteṇa vajja|lev'|ôvaṇaddho via sijjanta|ṇīsaha|vivalhattho vevadi a|vaso via me hattho.⌟

RĀMAḤ: sakhi, kutaḥ pralāpāḥ?

gṛhīto yaḥ pūrvaṃ
  pariṇaya|vidhau kaṅkaṇa|dharaś,
citaṃ sv'|êcchā|sparśair
  amṛta|śiśirair yaḥ paricitaḥ, [41ab]

SĪTĀ: ⌜ajja|utta, so evva. dāṇiṃ jāṇāsi.⌟

RĀMAḤ:

3.205 sa ev' âyaṃ tasyās
  tad|itara|kar'|āupamya|subhago
mayā labdhaḥ pāṇir
  lalita|lavalī|kandala|nibhaḥ. [41cd]

VASÁNTI: How so?

RAMA: My friend, what else can it mean but that Jánaki has returned?

VASÁNTI: But my lord, dear Rama, where is she then?

RAMA: *(miming the pleasure of her touch)* Look, here she is, right in front of us.

VASÁNTI: Oh, why burn me again, cursed as I am, with this cruel, utter nonsense that cuts me to the quick, when I have already been burned by the sorrow of my beloved friend?

SITA: I must leave, but my husband's touch—how gentle and cool his long and true affection has made it, how it eases* my cruel long-lasting pain—seems almost to have cemented my hand in place, so that it's perspiring, weary, agitated, trembling, and helpless all at once.

RAMA: My friend, why do you speak of "nonsense"?

The hand I held at the wedding ceremony
years ago when it bore the marriage bracelet,
a long-familiar hand I once could touch
whenever I desired, cool as ambrosia...

SITA: My husband, it is the very same. Now you know.*

RAMA:

this is the very same hand— her hand,
as graceful as a *lávali* stalk
and so beautiful it sets the standard
of comparison for all other hands.

(gṛhṇāti)

SĪTĀ: ⌜haddhī, haddhī. ajja|utta|pphaṃsa|mohidāe pamādo kkhu saṃvutto.⌟

RĀMAḤ: sakhi Vāsanti, ānanda|nimīlit'|êndriyaḥ sādhvasena paravān asmi. tat tvam api dhāray' âinām.

VĀSANTĪ: kaṣṭam, unmāda eva.

3.210 SĪTĀ *sa|sambhramam ākṣipy' âpasarpati.*

RĀMAḤ: hā dhik, pramādaḥ.

kara|pallavaḥ sa tasyāḥ
  sahas" âiva jaḍ'|ātmanaḥ paribhraṣṭaḥ
parikampinaḥ prakampī
  karān mama svidyataḥ svidyan. [42]

SĪTĀ: ⌜haddhī, haddhī. ajja vi aṇ|avatthida|tthimida|mūḍha|ghuṇṇanta|veaṇaṃ ṇa pajjavatthāvemi attāṇam.⌟

TAMASĀ: *(sa|sneham nirvarṇya)*

3.215 sa|sveda|rom'|âñcita|kampit'|âṅgī
  jātā priya|sparśa|vaśena bālā
marun|nav'|âmbhaḥ|pravidhūta|siktā
  kadamba|yaṣṭiḥ sphuṭa|korak" êva. [43]

SĪTĀ: *(sva|gatam)* ⌜ammahe, a|vaseṇa edeṇa attāṇaeṇa lajjāvida mhi bhaavadīe Tamasāe. kiṃ ti kila esā maṇṇissadi: «eso de pariccāo, eso ahisaṅgo» tti?⌟

(takes hold)

SITA: Dear god, the rapture of my husband's touch has led to a terrible blunder.

RAMA: Vasánti my friend, my senses are benumbed by bliss and I'm so agitated I don't trust myself. So please, touch her yourself.

VASÁNTI: Alas, this is sheer madness.

SITA *in alarm shakes his hand loose and steps back.* 3.210

RAMA: Oh god, what a blunder.

> I'm so dazed I suddenly let her petal-soft hand fall from mine
> that shook as her hand shook and sweated as hers sweated.

SITA: Dear god, I still can't get control* of myself, I'm restive, benumbed, and confused all at once, and the pain is overwhelming.

TÁMASA: *(gazing affectionately)*

> At your beloved's touch, poor girl, your limbs 3.215
> break out in sweat and goose bumps, and you shake
> like the trunk of a *kadámba* blown by the wind,
> drenched with fresh rain, and sprouting suddenly.

SITA: *(aside)* Oh dear, I have embarrassed myself before Támasa, by this unruly body of mine. She must be thinking, mustn't she, that though such was his disowning of me, such remains my infatuation?

RĀMAḤ: *(sarvato 'valokya)* hā, kathaṃ n' âsty eva? nanv a|karuṇe Vaidehi!

SĪTĀ: ⌜saccaṃ a|karuṇa mhi jā evvaṃ|vidhaṃ tumaṃ pekkhantī dharāmi jjeva jīvidaṃ.⌟

RĀMAḤ: kv' âsi devi? prasīda. na māṃ evaṃ|vidhaṃ parityaktum arhasi.

3.220 SĪTĀ: ⌜aï ajja|utta, vivarīdaṃ via.⌟

VĀSANTĪ: deva, prasīda prasīda. sven' âiva lok'|ôttareṇa dhairyeṇa saṃstambhay" âtibhūmi|gata|vipralambham ātmānam. kuto 'tra me priya|sakhī?

RĀMAḤ: vyaktaṃ n' âsti. katham anyathā Vāsanty api tāṃ na paśyet? api khalu svapna eṣa syāt... na c' âsmi suptaḥ—kuto Rāmasya nidrā? sarvathā sa ev' âiṣa bhagavān an|eka|vāra|parikalpanā|nirmito vipralambhaḥ punaḥ punar anubadhnāti mām.

SĪTĀ: ⌜mae jjevva dāruṇāe vippaladdho ajja|utto.⌟

VĀSANTĪ: deva, paśya,

3.225 Paulastyasya Jaṭāyuṣā vighaṭitaḥ
kārṣṇ'|āyaso 'yaṃ rathaḥ.
paśy', âite purataḥ piśāca|vadanāḥ
kaṅkāla|śeṣāḥ kharāḥ.
khaḍga|cchinna|Jaṭāyu|pakṣatir itaḥ
Sītāṃ jvalantīṃ vahann
antar|vyākula|vidyud|ambuda iva
dyām abhyudasthād ariḥ. [44]

---

[i] Rāvaṇa's.

RAMA: *(looking all around)* What, she's nowhere to be found? Please, pitiless Vaidéhi!

SITA: Pitiless indeed, that I can behold you in this state and still hold on to life.

RAMA: Where are you, my queen? Oh please don't abandon me in this state.

SITA: Ah, my husband, don't you have it backward? 3.220

VASÁNTI: Please, my lord, please, use your strength, a superhuman strength, to check this sheer delusion. How could my beloved friend be here?

RAMA: Clearly she's not. How otherwise would Vasánti herself not see her? Yes, it must have been a dream... But no, I wasn't dreaming—how could Rama ever again find sleep? No, it was surely that blessed mental delusion afflicting me once more, produced by my fantasies time and again.

SITA: No, it was cruel me who deluded my husband.

VASÁNTI: Look, my lord:

> There is Paulástya's[i] blackiron chariot 3.225
> destroyed by Jatáyus—
> look at the imp-faced mules out in front,
> now nothing but skeletons.
> And from here, when his sword had severed
> Jatáyus' wings, the enemy
> took refulgent Sita and mounted the sky
> like a lightning-wreathed cloud.

SĪTĀ: *(sa|bhayam)* ⌜ajja|utta, tādo vāvādīadi. ahaṃ pi ava-harīāmi. parittāāhi!⌟

RĀMAḤ: *(sa|vegam utthāya)* āḥ pāpa tāta|prāṇa|sīt'|âpahārin, kva yāsi?

VĀSANTĪ: ayi deva rākṣasa|kula|pralaya|dhūma|keto, ady' âpi te manyu|viṣayaḥ?

SĪTĀ: ⌜ammo, ummattia mhi saṃvuttā.⌟

3.230 RĀMAḤ: aye anya ev' âyam adhunā pralayo vartate.

upāyānāṃ bhāvād
 a|virata|vinoda|vyatikarair
vimardair vīrāṇāṃ
 jagati janit'|âtyadbhuta|rasaiḥ
viyogo mugdh'|âkṣyāḥ
 sa khalu ripu|ghāt'|âvadhir abhūt.
katus tūṣṇīṃ sahyo
 niravadhir ayaṃ tu pravilayaḥ. [45]

SĪTĀ: ⌜«ṇiravadhi!» tti hā hada mhi.⌟

---

[i] Jaṭāyus.

SITA: *(frightened)* My husband, father[i] has been put to death, and I myself am being abducted. Save me!

RAMA: *(rising with a start)* Ah evil creature, you who stole at once our father's life and Sita, where do you think you're going?

VASÁNTI: My lord, you were a blazing fire of destruction to the tribe of *rákshasas*: Is it possible some object of your rage still exists?

SITA: Dear me, I went quite mad for a moment.

RAMA: Alas, altogether different is the calamity befalling me 3.230
today:

> Because there were steps I then could take—
> with heroic battles providing
> continual distraction, their *rasa* of wonder
> flooding all the world—
> that first parting from my wife I knew
> would end—with the enemy's death.
> But how bitter a thing it is to bear
> in silence an endless parting.*

SITA: "Endless!" Oh, I am truly lost.

RĀMAḤ: hā kaṣṭam.

vyarthaṃ yatra kap'|îndra|sakhyam api me,
vīryaṃ harīṇāṃ vṛthā,
prajñā Jāmbavato 'pi yatra na gatiḥ,
putrasya Vāyor api,
mārgaṃ yatra na Viśvakarma|tanayaḥ
kartuṃ Nalo 'pi kṣamaḥ,
Saumitrer api patriṇām a|viṣaye
tatra, priye, kv' âsi me? [46]

3.235 SĪTĀ: ⌜bahu|maṇṇāvida mhi puvva|virahaṃ.⌟

RĀMAḤ: sakhi Vāsanti, duḥkhāy' âiva suhṛdām idānīṃ Rāma|darśanam. kiyac|ciraṃ tvāṃ rodayiṣyāmi? tad anujānīhi māṃ gamanāya.

SĪTĀ: *(s'|ôdvega|mohaṃ* TAMASĀM *ālambya)* ⌜bhaavadi Tamase, gacchadi ajja|utto!⌟

TAMASĀ: vatse, samāśvasihi, samāśvasihi. nanv āvām apy āyuṣmatoḥ Kuśa|Lavayor varṣa|vardhana|maṅgalāni sampādayituṃ Bhāgīrathī|pād'|ântikam eva gacchāvaḥ.

SĪTĀ: ⌜bhaavadi, pasīda. khaṇaṃ pi dāva dul|lahaṃ jaṇaṃ pekkhāmi.⌟

3.240 RĀMAḤ: asti c' êdānīm aśva|medha|saha|dharma|cāriṇī me...

---

[i] Sugrīva. [ii] Hanumān. [iii] "All-maker," the architect of the gods. [iv] Lakṣmaṇa.

RAMA: Alas,

> Where even friendship with the monkey king[i] is useless
> to me, and futile the monkeys' strength;
> where Jámbavan's wisdom no longer shows the way
> or even that of the wind god's son[ii];
> where even Nala, son of Vishva·karma,[iii]
> is unable to build a road—
> where can you be, my beloved, somewhere out of range
> of even the arrows of Saumítri?[iv]*

SITA: How deeply I now cherish my former separation. 3.235

RAMA: Vasánti my friend, the sight of Rama now can only bring his friends sorrow.* How long am I to make you weep? Permit me then to take my leave.

SITA: *(startled and delirious, clinging to* TÁMASA*)* Oh Támasa, my husband is leaving!

TÁMASA: My child, compose yourself, I beg you. At all events we must now make our way to Bhagi·rathi, to perform the birthday rites for Kusha and Lava (long may they live).

SITA: Blessed one, please, just one last glance, for just a moment, of this man I'll never see again.

RAMA: I now have another wife in *dharma* to assist in the Horse Sacrifice… 3.240

SĪTĀ: *(s'|ôtkampam)* ⌜ajja|utta, kā?⌟

RĀMAḤ: hiraṇmayī Sītā|pratikṛtiḥ.

SĪTĀ: *(s'|ôcchvāsam)* ⌜ajja|utto dāṇiṃ si tumaṃ. ammahe, ukkhāṇidaṃ dāṇiṃ me pariccāa|lajjā|sallaṃ ajja|utteṇa.⌟

RĀMAḤ: tatr' âpi tāvad bāṣpa|digdhaṃ cakṣur viṅodayāmi.

3.245 SĪTĀ: ⌜dhaṇṇā sā jā ajja|utteṇa bahu|maṇṇīadi, jā ajja|uttaṃ viṇodaantī āsā|ṇibandhaṇaṃ jādā jīa|loassa.⌟

TAMASĀ: *(sa|smita|sneh'|âsraṃ pariṣvajya)* ayi vatse, evam ātmā stūyate.

SĪTĀ: *(sa|lajjam adho|mukhī, sva|gatam)* ⌜parihasida mhi bhaavadīe.⌟

VĀSANTĪ: mahān ayaṃ vyatikaro 'smākaṃ prasādaḥ. gamanaṃ prati punar yathā kārya|hānir na bhavati, tath" âstu.

SĪTĀ: ⌜paḍiūlā dāṇiṃ me Vāsantī saṃvuttā.⌟

3.250 TAMASĀ: vatse, ehi, gacchāvaḥ.

SĪTĀ: *(sa|kaṣṭam)* ⌜evvaṃ karemha.⌟

TAMASĀ: kathaṃ vā gamyate yasyās tava

SITA: *(trembling)* My husband, who?

RAMA: A golden statue of Sita.

SITA: *(breathing a sigh of relief)* My husband... yes, now you really are. Yes, now at last my husband has extracted from me the sharp arrowhead of shame at being disowned.

RAMA: There at least my eyes can find distraction, bathed as they ever are in tears.

SITA: Fortunate the woman my husband so esteems for dis- 3.245
tracting him—which makes her the source of hope for this world.

TÁMASA: *(smiling, with affection and tears, and embracing her)* Ah my child, that is praise owed to yourself.

SITA: *(hanging her head in shame; aside)* The blessed one is mocking me.

VASÁNTI: What has been a source of great turmoil* to you has been a kindness to us. As for leaving, do as you must to fulfil your obligations.

SITA: Vasánti has become my implacable foe.

TÁMASA: Child, come, let us go. 3.250

SITA: *(despondently)* Yes, I suppose we must.

TÁMASA: But how in fact can you go when

pratyuptasy' âiva dayite
  tṛṣṇā|dīrghasya cakṣuṣaḥ
marma|ccheda|parair yatnair
  ākarṣo na samāpyate? [47]

SĪTĀ: ⌜ṇamo a|puvva|puṇṇa|jaṇida|daṃsaṇāṇaṃ ajja|utta|caraṇa|kamalāṇaṃ.⌟ *(mūrchati)*

3.255 TAMASĀ: vatse, samāśvasihi, samāśvasihi.

SĪTĀ: *(āśvasya)* ⌜kec|ciraṃ vā meh'|antareṇa puṇṇa|candassa daṃsaṇaṃ?⌟

TAMASĀ: aho saṃvidhānakam.

eko rasaḥ karuṇa eva nimitta|bhedād
  bhinnaḥ pṛthak pṛthag iv' āśrayate vivartān
āvarta|budbuda|taraṅgamayān vikārān
  ambho yathā, salilam eva tu tat samagram. [48]

RĀMAḤ: vimānā|rāja, ita itaḥ.

3.260 *sarva uttiṣṭhanti.*

TAMASĀ|VĀSANTYAU: SĪTĀ|RĀMAU *(prati)*

By no effort however painstaking you can tear away
your eyes, wide with longing, that are fixed upon
your love?

SITA: Homage to the lotus feet of my husband—it must have been incomparable good karma that allowed me to see them today. *(falls faint)*

TÁMASA: My child, compose yourself, I beg you. 3.255

SITA: *(regaining her composure)* For how long may one glimpse the full moon through the dark clouds?

TÁMASA: How complex a plot* this is.

There is only a single *rasa*—
pity—but it takes different forms
since it changes in response
to circumstances that are changing,
just the way that water forms
into whirlpool, bubble, or wave
though in the end it all remains
the same: nothing but water.*

RAMA: King of chariots, over here, at once.

All rise. 3.260

TÁMASA AND VASÁNTI: *(speaking to* SITA *and* RAMA *respectively)*

avanir amara|sindhuḥ sārdham asmad|vidhābhiḥ
sa ca kula|patir ādyaś chandasāṃ yaḥ prayoktā
sa ca munir anuyāt'|Ârundhatīko Vasiṣṭhas
tvayi vitaratu bhadraṃ bhūyase maṅgalāya. [49]

niṣkrāntāḥ sarve.

iti mahā/kavi/śrī/Bhavabhūti/praṇīta
Uttara/Rāma/carita/nāṭake
chāyā nāma tṛtīyo 'ṅkaḥ.

---

[i] Vālmīki.

May Earth and the river of the gods, and others like
us,
the teacher[i] who was the first to use metrical forms,
sage Vasíshtha and Arúndhati in his retinue—
may all these grant you blessings and everlasting
good fortune.*

Exeunt all.

End of Act III

mở đầu, khúc dạo

PRELUDE TO ACT IV

tataḥ praviśatas TĀPASAU.

EKAḤ: Saudhātake, dṛśyatām adya bhūyiṣṭha|sannidhāpit'|âtithi|janasya samadhik'|ārambha|ramaṇīyatā bhagavato Vālmīker āśrama|padasya. tathā hi:

nīvār'|âudana|maṇḍam uṣṇa|madhuraṃ
  sadyaḥ|prasūta|priyā|
pītād abhyadhikaṃ tapo|vana|mṛgaḥ
  paryāptam ācāmati.
gandhena sphuratā manāg anusṛto
  bhaktasya sarpiṣmataḥ
karkandhū|phala|miśra|śāka|pacan'|
  āmodaḥ paristīryate. [1]

SAUDHĀTAKIḤ: ⌜sāadaṃ aṇ|ajjhāa|kāraṇāṇaṃ visesado jiṇṇa|kucchāṇaṃ.⌟

4.5 EKAḤ: *(vihasya)* a|pūrvaḥ ko 'pi bahumāna|hetur guruṣu Saudhātake.

SAUDHĀTAKIḤ: ⌜bho Bhaṇḍāaṇa, kiṃ|ṇāmadheo eso dāṇiṃ mahantassa therī|satthassa agga|dhori|ddhao adidhī āado?⌟

BHĀṆḌĀYANAḤ: dhik prahasanam. nanv ayam Ṛṣyaśṛṅg'|āśramād Arundhatī|puraskṛtān mahā|rāja|Daśarathasya dārān adhiṣṭhāya bhagavān Vasiṣṭhaḥ prāptaḥ. tat kim evaṃ pralapasi?

Enter two ascetics.

THE FIRST: Saudhátaki, how beautiful Valmíki's hermitage looks with all the different decorations and the crowds of guests who have come. You see,

> The buck that lives in the ashram drinks
> to his heart's content
> the sweet warm cream of rice left over
> by his just-foaling mate.
> And the aroma of cooking greens spreads,
> mixed with jujube fruit,
> along with the just barely perceptible
> fragrance of buttered rice.*

SAUDHÁTAKI: A most hearty welcome to anyone—above all the graybeards*—whose arrival gives us a break from studying.

FIRST: *(laughing)* Altogether unprecedented, Saudhátaki, is this respect you show your elders. 4.5

SAUDHÁTAKI: Say, Bhandáyana, what's the name of the guest who's come at the head of this troupe of old crones?

BHANDÁYANA: No joking now. Surely you know it's Vasíshtha, who's arrived from Rishya·shringa's ashram, watching over the wives of the great king Dasha·ratha and giving the place of honor to Arúndhati. So why the silly question?

SAUDHĀTAKIḤ: ⌜huṃ, Vasiṭṭho?⌟

BHĀṆḌĀYANAḤ: atha kim?

4.10 SAUDHĀTAKIḤ: ⌜mae uṇa jāṇidaṃ vagdho vakko* vā eso tti.⌟

BHĀṆḌĀYANAḤ: āḥ, kim uktaṃ bhavati?

SAUDHĀTAKIḤ: ⌜jeṇa parāvaḍideṇa jjeva sā varāiā kallāṇiā maḍamaḍāvidā.⌟

BHĀṆḌĀYANAḤ: sa|māṃso madhu|parka ity āmnāyaṃ bahu|manyamānāḥ śrotriyāy' âbhyāgatāya vatsatarīṃ mah"|ôkṣaṃ vā mah"|âjaṃ vā nirvapanti gṛha|medhinaḥ. taṃ hi dharmaṃ dharma|sūtra|kārāḥ samāmananti.

SAUDHĀTAKIḤ: ⌜bho! ṇigihido si.⌟

4.15 BHĀṆḌĀYANAḤ: katham iva?

SAUDHĀTAKIḤ: ⌜jeṇa āadesu Vasiṭṭha|missesu vacchadarī visasidā. ajja jjeva paccā āadassa rā'|êsiṇo Jaṇaassa bhaavadā Vammīeṇa vi dahi|mahūhiṃ jevva ṇivattido madhu|vakko. vacchadarī uṇa visajjidā.⌟

BHĀṆḌĀYANAḤ: a|nivṛtta|māṃsānām evam ṛṣayo manyante. nivṛtta|māṃsas tu tatra|bhavāñ Janakaḥ.

SAUDHĀTAKIḤ: ⌜kiṃ|ṇimittaṃ?⌟

BHĀṆḌĀYANAḤ: sa tad" âiva devyāḥ Sītāyās tādṛśaṃ daiva|dur|vipākam upaśrutya vaikhānasaḥ saṃvṛttaḥ. tath" âsya katipaye saṃvatsarāś Candradvīpa|tapo|vane tapas tapyamānasya.

SAUDHÁTAKI: Hmm, Vasíshtha?

BHANDÁYANA: Yes, of course.

SAUDHÁTAKI: I thought for sure it was a tiger or a wolf.   4.10

BHANDÁYANA: Now what is that supposed to mean?

SAUDHÁTAKI: Well, my poor little calf was completely rat- *bối rối* *kích động* tled from the moment he arrived.

BHANDÁYANA: When a scholar of scripture visits, house- holders who honor the Vedic precept requiring a wel- come offering of meat will slaughter a yearling or bull or goat. This is *dharma*, according to the authors of the 'Sutras on Dharma.'

SAUDHÁTAKI: Aha! You're caught in a contradiction. *mâu thuẫn, trái ngược*

BHANDÁYANA: How so?   4.15

SAUDHÁTAKI: Although a yearling was slaughtered on the arrival of the honorable Vasíshtha, when subsequently, just today, the royal seer Jánaka arrived, Valmíki made the guest offering of nothing more than milk and yo- gurt. The yearling herself was set free.

BHANDÁYANA: The seers had in mind those who had not given up meat. Jánaka has done so.

SAUDHÁTAKI: Why's that?

BHANDÁYANA: He became a hermit the moment he got word of the fated turn of events for Queen Sita. And so for some years he has been practicing austerities in the Moon Island penance grove.

4.20 SAUDHĀTAKIḤ: ⌜tado kiṃ ti āado?⌟

BHĀṆḌĀYANAḤ: cirantana|priya|suhṛdaṃ Prācetasaṃ draṣṭum.

SAUDHĀTAKIḤ: ⌜avi ajja sambandhiṇīhiṃ samaṃ saṃvuttaṃ se daṃsaṇaṃ ṇa vetti?⌟

BHĀṆḌĀYANAḤ: sampraty eva bhagavatā Vasiṣṭhena devyāḥ Kausalyāyāḥ sakāśaṃ bhagavaty Arundhatī prahitā, «svayam upetya Vaideho draṣṭavya» iti.

SAUDHĀTAKIḤ: ⌜jadhā ede savve therā paropparaṃ milidā tadhā amhe vi vaḍuehiṃ samaṃ milia aṇ|ajjhāa|mah"|ûsavaṃ khelantā sambhāvemha.⌟

4.25 *parikrāmataḥ.*

BHĀṆḌĀYANAḤ: tad ayaṃ brahma|vādī purāṇa|rāja'|rṣir Janakaḥ Prācetasa|Vasiṣṭhāv upāsya sampraty āśrama|bahir|vṛkṣa|mūlam adhitiṣṭhati. ya eṣaḥ

hṛdi nity'|ânuṣaktena
  Sītā|śokena tapyate,
antaḥ|prasṛpta|dahano
  jarann iva vanas|patiḥ. [2]

niṣkrāntau.

viṣkambhakaḥ.

[i] Janaka.

SAUDHÁTAKI: So why has he come here? 4.20

BHANDÁYANA: To see his dear old friend, the son of Prachétas.

SAUDHÁTAKI: Has he already had a chance to meet with his kinswomen?

BHANDÁYANA: Just now Vasíshtha sent Arúndhati to Queen Kausálya to ask her to go pay a visit to the king of Vidéha.[i]

SAUDHÁTAKI: Like the old folks gathering we should gather with our schoolmates and celebrate our holiday with games.

The two walk around. 4.25

BHANDÁYANA: There's the ancient royal seer, the spiritual master Jánaka. He has done obeisance to Prachétas' son and Vasíshtha and now is seated at the foot of a tree outside the ashram—the one who

> Is burning with a sorrow over Sita
> that is ever-present in his heart
> like an old tree burning with a fire
> that eats away at it from within.

Exeunt both.

End of the Prelude

ACT IV
THE MEETING OF KAUSÁLYA AND JÁNAKA

4.30 *tataḥ praviśati* JANAKAḤ.

JANAKAḤ:

apatye yat tādṛg
duritam abhavat tena mahatā
viṣaktas tīvreṇa
vraṇita|hṛdayena vyathayatā
paṭur dhārāvāhī
nava iva ciren' âpi hi na me
nikṛntan marmāṇi
krakaca iva manyur viramati. [3]

kaṣṭam! evaṃ nāma jarasā duḥkhena ca dur|āsadena bhūyaḥ parāka|sāntapana|prabhṛtibhis tapobhir ātta|rasa|dhātur an|upaṣṭambhano 'dy' âpi na me dagdha|dehaḥ patati. «andha|tāmisrā hy a|sūryā nāma te lokāḥ. tebhyaḥ prati-vidhīyante ya ātma|ghātina,» ity evam ṛṣayo manyante. an|eka|saṃvatsar'|âtikrame 'pi pratikṣaṇa|paribhāvanā|spaṣṭa|nirbhāsaḥ pratyagra iva dāruṇo na me duḥkha|saṃvegaḥ praśāmyati. ayi mātar! yajana|vedi|sambhave Sīte, īdṛśas te nirmāṇa|bhāgaḥ pariṇato yena lajjayā sva|cchandam ākranditum api na śakyate. hā hā putri!

a|niyata|rudita|smitaṃ virājat|
katipaya|komala|danta|kuḍmal'|âgram
vadana|kamalakaṃ śiśoḥ smarāmi
skhalad|asamañjasa|mugdha|jalpitaṃ te. [4]

---

[i] A general exclamation.

Enter JÁNAKA. 4.30

JÁNAKA:

The crime* against my child—a monstrous and
heinous crime
that shattered me and pierced my heart—has
provoked
a fierce, cascading anger,* ever new however old,
that cuts me to the quick like a saw and does not
cease.

How awful! I cannot believe that this wretched body—from which old age and unimaginable sorrow have removed every means of support, and austerities of every kind, month-long fasts and mortifications have sucked every drop of pith and sap—that even today it refuses to die. But then, "Blinding dark and sunless are the worlds to which suicides are condemned"*— thus the seers have declared. Even after all these years the shock of my savage sorrow, made fully manifest by my constant worry,* seems fresh as ever and does not abate. Ah mother![i]* O Sita, you who were born at the ritual altar, that such should be your lot in life, a life so transformed that one is too ashamed even to weep to one's full. Oh my daughter!

How I remember your face when you were a child
and you would laugh and cry for no apparent
reason,
with your few baby teeth shining like jasmine buds
and your first words faltering and imprecise.

bhagavati Vasuṃdhare, satyam atidṛḍh" âsi.

4.35 tvaṃ, vahnir, munayo, Vasiṣṭha|gṛhiṇī,
Gaṅgā ca yasyā vidur
māhātmyaṃ, yadi vā Raghoḥ kula|gurur
devaḥ svayaṃ Bhāskaraḥ;
vidyāṃ vāg iva yām asūta bhavatī
tadvat tu yā daivataṃ,
tasyās tvaṃ duhitus tathā viśasanaṃ
kiṃ, dāruṇe, mṛṣyathāḥ? [5]

NEPATHYE: ita ito bhagavatī|mahā|devyau.

JANAKAḤ: *(dṛṣṭvā)* aye Gṛṣṭin" ôpadiśyamāna|mārgā bhagavaty Arundhatī. *(utthāya)* kāṃ punar «mahā|dev"» îty āha? *(nirūpya)* hā katham mahā|rāja|Daśarathasya dharma|dārāḥ priya|sakhī me Kausalyā? ka etat pratyeti, s" âiv' êyam iti?

āsīd iyaṃ Daśarathasya gṛhe yathā śrīḥ,
śrīr eva vā—kim upamāna|padena?—s" êṣā?
kaṣṭaṃ bat', ânyad iva daiva|vaśena jātā
duḥkh'|ātmakaṃ kim api bhūtam. aho vipākaḥ!
[6]

ayam aparaḥ pāpo daśā|viparyāsaḥ.

---

[i] The "senior" among the wives of the king, insofar as she is the one who participates in her husband's rituals.

O Earth, how true it is that you are hard as stone.

The woman whose greatness you yourself 4.35
should have acknowledged,* and likewise Fire, the
sages,
Vasíshtha 's wife, and Ganga, to say nothing
of the Sun god himself, Raghu's family guru;
a goddess you yourself gave birth to
just as language gives birth to true knowledge—
how can you, cruel Earth, have condoned
the murder of this woman, my one daughter?

OFFSTAGE: This way, blessed one, and Your Highness.

JÁNAKA: *(watching)* Ah, it's Arúndhati being shown the way by Grishti. *(standing)* Whom is he addressing by "Your Highness"? *(looking)* Oh, it can't be my beloved friend Kausálya, the wife in *dharma*[i] of King Dasha·ratha? Who would have believed it's her?

She who was like the goddess of royalty in
Dasha·ratha's palace
or rather—what need of simile?—was royalty
herself
has been changed by force of fate, alas, into something altogether other,
a rare creature of pure sorrow. Ah, what a turn of
events!

There is yet another dreadful reversal of my condition:

4.40 ya eva me janaḥ pūrvam
āsīn mūrto mah"|ôtsavaḥ,
kṣate kṣāram iv' â|sahyaṃ
jātaṃ tasy' âiva darśanam. [7]

tataḥ praviśaty ARUNDHATĪ KAUSALYĀ KAÑCUKĪ *ca.*

ARUNDHATĪ: nanu bravīmi, «draṣṭavyaḥ svayam upetya Vaideha,» ity eṣa vaḥ kula|guror ādeśaḥ. ata ev' âhaṃ preṣitā. tat ko 'yam pade pade mahān an|adhyavasāyaḥ?

KAÑCUKĪ: devi, saṃstabhy' ātmānam anurudhyasva bhagavato Vasiṣṭhasy' ādeśam iti vijñāpayāmi.

KAUSALYĀ: ⌜īdise kāle Mithil"|âdhivo daṭṭhavvo tti samaṃ jevva savva|dukkhāiṃ samubbhavanti. ṇa sakkaṇomi uvvattamāṇa|mūla|bandhaṇaṃ hiaaṃ vavatthāviduṃ.⌟

4.45 ARUNDHATĪ: atra kaḥ sandehaḥ?

santāna|vāhīny api mānuṣāṇāṃ
duḥkhāni sad|bandhu|viyoga|jāni
dṛṣṭe jane preyasi duḥ|sahāni
srotaḥ|sahasrair iva saṃplavante. [8]

KAUSALYĀ: ⌜kahaṃ ca vacchāe vadhūe evvaṃ gade tassa rā'|êsiṇo muhaṃ daṃsemha?⌟

---

i Addressed to Kausalyā.

People who in the past were like 4.40
festivity incarnate for me
are unbearable now even to see—
so much salt upon a wound.

Enter ARÚNDHATI, KAUSÁLYA, *and the* CHAMBERLAIN.

ARÚNDHATI: But I am telling you that it is at the bidding of the family priest you were to go see Vaidéha yourself, that is why I was sent to you. Why this crippling hesitation every step of the way?[i]

CHAMBERLAIN: Your Highness, I ask you to steady yourself and comply with Vasíshtha's order.

KAUSÁLYA: The mere thought of encountering the king of Míthila on this occasion brings every sorrow back to me, all at once. The very strings of my heart are breaking and I am unable to keep it still.

ARÚNDHATI: Undoubtedly. 4.45

A person's sorrows from the loss of a dear kinsman
may be flowing in spate but the very sight
of a beloved friend makes them unbearable
as if augmented by a thousand streams.

KAUSÁLYA: How are we to face the royal seer, when such a thing has happened to our dear daughter-in-law?

ARUNDHATĪ:

> eṣa vaḥ ślāghya|sambandhī
>   Janakānāṃ kul'|ôdvahaḥ
> Yājñavalkyo munir yasmai
>   Brahma|pārāyaṇaṃ jagau. [9]

KAUSALYĀ: ⌜eso so mahā|rāassa hia'|āṇando vacchāe vadhūe pidā rā' |êsī. haddhī, haddhī. sumārida mhi aṇuṭṭhida| mah"|ûsave diase. hā devva, savvaṃ jevva taṃ ṇatthi.⌟

4.50 JANAKAḤ: *(upasṛtya)* bhagavaty Arundhati, Vaidehaḥ Sīradhvajo 'bhivādayate.

> yayā pūtaṃ manyo
>   nidhir api pavitrasya mahasaḥ
> patis te pūrveṣām
>   api khalu gurūṇāṃ gurutamaḥ
> trilokī|māṅgalyām
>   avani|tala|lolena śirasā
> jagad|vandyāṃ devīm
>   Uṣasam iva vande bhagavatīm. [10]

ARUNDHATĪ: paraṃ te jyotiḥ prakāśatām. ayaṃ tvā punātu devaḥ paro|rajā ya eṣa tapati.

JANAKAḤ: ārya Gṛṣṭe, api kuśalam asyāḥ prajā|pālasya mātuḥ?

---

[i] Daśaratha. [ii] The wedding of Rāma and Sītā. [iii] Literally, "He whose standard is marked with a plow." [iv] The sun.

ARÚNDHATI:

> He is your esteemed kinsman, mainstay of the
> Jánaka dynasty
> to whom the wise Yajna·valkya once transmitted all
> spiritual wisdom.

KAUSÁLYA: There stands the man who was the heart's delight of the great king,[i] the father of our dear daughter-in-law, the royal seer. Dear god, it's all coming back to me, the day we performed the great festival[ii]—and now, dear lord, it's all gone.

JÁNAKA: *(approaching)* Arúndhati, the king of Vidéha, Sira·dhvaja,[iii] greets you. 4.50

> The woman thanks to whom alone her husband
> counts himself pure, though himself a treasure
> house
> of purifying power, and among all the gurus
> who have preceded him the guru supreme…
> I offer greetings to this blessed goddess,
> like Dawn herself, whom all the world greets
> with heads lowered to the ground, a woman
> who brings good fortune to all the universe.

ARÚNDHATI: May your ultimate light shine bright, and may the god[iv] who burns beyond the dust* purify you.

JÁNAKA: Grishti, I trust the mother of the people's protector is faring well?

KAÑCUKĪ: *(sva|gatam)* niravaśeṣam atiniṣṭhuram upālabdhāḥ smaḥ. *(prakāśam)* rāja'|rṣe, anen' âiva manyunā cira|parityakta|Rāmabhadra|mukha|candra|darśanām n' ârhasi duḥkhayitum atiduḥkhitām devīm. Rāma|bhadrasy' âpi daiva|duryogaḥ ko 'pi yat kila samantataḥ pravṛtta|bībhatsa|kiṃvadantīkāḥ paurāḥ. na c' âgni|śuddhim alpakāḥ pratiyant' îty ato dāruṇam anuṣṭhitam.

4.55 JANAKAḤ: āḥ ko 'yam agnir nām' âsmat|prasūti|pariśodhane? kaṣṭam, evaṃ|vādinā janena Rāma|bhadra|paribhūtā api vayaṃ punaḥ paribhūyāmahe!

ARUNDHATĪ: *(niśvasya)* evam etat. «agnir, agnir» iti vatsāṃ prati parilaghūny akṣarāṇi. Sīt" êty eva paryāptam. hā vatse,

śiśur vā śiṣyā vā
　　yad asi mama tat tiṣṭhatu tathā.
　viśuddher utkarṣas
　　tvayi tu mama bhaktiṃ janayati.
śiśutvaṃ straiṇaṃ vā
　　bhavatu, nanu vandy" âsi jagatāṃ.
　guṇāḥ pūjā|sthānaṃ
　　guṇiṣu, na ca liṅgaṃ na ca vayaḥ. [11]

KAUSALYĀ: ⌜ammo, ummīlanti veaṇāo.⌟ *(mūrchati)*

CHAMBERLAIN: *(aside)* This is meant as a taunt to us, a pure and biting taunt. *(aloud)*. Royal seer, the queen is already deeply sorrowed by missing the sight of dear Rama's moonlike face for so long,* and you should take care not to increase her sorrow by this anger of yours. A dreadful fate befell Rama, too—malicious gossip was said to have been circulating among the townsmen, and with the petty-minded not believing in the purification by fire, he had to take radical measures.

JÁNAKA: Why, who in the name of heaven is this god of 4.55
fire to presume to purify my daughter? How dare anyone speak like this and insult us more when Rama has already insulted us enough!

ARÚNDHATI: *(sighing)* It's perfectly true. The word "fire" is a mere string of empty sounds next to our child; being Sita suffices.* Oh my child,

> Whether you were child of mine
> or pupil is really of no account,
> it was your high degree of purity
> that engenders this affection in me.
> Being child or woman does not matter—
> you have won the whole world's praise.
> What should be honored in the virtuous
> is virtue, and not gender or age.

KAUSÁLYA: Ah, my wounds are opening up again. *(falls faint)*

JANAKAḤ: hā, kim etat?

4.60 ARUNDHATĪ: rāja'|rṣe, kim anyat?

sa rājā, tat saukhyam,
  sa ca śiśu|janas, te ca divasāḥ
smṛtāv āvirbhūtaṃ
  tvayi suhṛdi dṛṣṭe tad akhilam.
vipāke ghore 'smin
  nanu khalu vimūḍhā tava sakhī.
purandhrīṇāṃ cetaḥ
  kusuma|sukumāraṃ hi bhavati. [12]

JANAKAḤ: hanta hanta, sarvathā nṛ|śaṃso 'smi yaś cirasya dṛṣṭān priya|suhṛdaḥ priyān dārān na snigdhaṃ paśyāmi.

sa sambandhī ślāghyaḥ,
  priya|suhṛd asau, tac ca hṛdayaṃ,
sa c' ānandaḥ sākṣād,
  api ca nikhilaṃ jīvita|phalam,
śarīraṃ jīvo vā
  yad adhikam ato vā priyataraṃ
mahā|rājaḥ śrīmān
  kim iva mama n' āsīd Daśarathaḥ? [13]

kaṣṭam, iyam eva sā Kausalyā?

JÁNAKA: Oh dear, what is it now?

ARÚNDHATI: Royal seer, what else can it be? 4.60

That king, that happiness, that pride
of children, those by-gone days—
the memory of it all returned when she
caught sight of you, her friend.
Surely you see she is distraught
at this dreadful event:
an aged mother's heart can be
as tender as a flower.

JÁNAKA: What an utter scoundrel I've been that I have not looked kindly on my dear friend's dear wife, when it's been so long since I've seen her.

Esteemed kinsman, dear friend, my very heart,
my joy incarnate, the whole point of existence,
my body and soul and whatever else is dearer—
what wasn't he to me, glorious king Dasha·ratha?

Alas, can this really be Kausálya?

4.65 yad asyāḥ patyur vā
rahasi parimantūyitam abhūd,
abhūvaṃ dampatyoḥ
pṛthag aham upālambha|viṣayaḥ.
prasāde kope vā
tad anu mad|adhīno vidhir abhūd...
alaṃ vā tat smṛtvā,
dahati yad avaskandya hṛdayam. [14]

ARUNDHATĪ: hā kaṣṭam, cira|niruddha|niśvāsa|niṣṭhuraṃ hṛdayam asyāḥ.

JANAKAḤ: hā priya|sakhi. *(kamaṇḍal'|ûdakena siñcati)*

KAÑCUKĪ:

suhṛd iva prakaṭayya sukha|pradaḥ
prathamam eka|rasām anukūlatām
punar a|kāṇḍa|vivartana|dāruṇaḥ
praviśinaṣṭi vidhir manaso rujam. [15]

KAUSALYĀ: *(saṃjñāṃ labdhvā)* ⌜hā vacche Jāṇaï, kahiṃ si? sumarāmi de vivāha|lacchī|pariggah'|ekka|maṅgalaṃ upphulla|suddha|hasidaṃ muddha|muha|puṇḍarīaṃ. apphuranta|canda|candiā|sundarehiṃ aṅgehiṃ puṇo vi me jāde ujjoehi ucchaṅgaṃ. savvadā mahā|rāo bhaṇādi, «esā Rahu|ula|mahattarāṇaṃ vadhū. amhāṇaṃ tu Jaṇaa|sambandheṇa duhidiā jevva.»⌟

If ever husband and wife had some argument in private, 4.65
apart from the couple I alone was privy to their complaint,
and on me depended what to do next, anger or forgiveness...
But enough of such memories. They assault and burn my heart.

ARÚNDHATI: How awful that her heart has been hardened* by sighs too long kept within.

JÁNAKA: Oh my dear friend. *(sprinkling her from his ascetic's cup)*

CHAMBERLAIN:

At first, fate was like a congenial friend
that went along with her every whim;
then without warning the cruel transformation
arrived, and left her with nothing but heartache.

KAUSÁLYA: *(regaining consciousness)* Oh my daughter Jánaki, where can you be? How well I remember your innocent lotus-like face adorned with nothing but the glow from the wedding, with your pure smile blossoming. Oh my child, brighten my lap once again with those limbs of yours beautiful as first moonlight. The great king always used to say, "This is the daughter-in-law of the head of the Raghu clan. But my kinship with Jánaka makes her my own little daughter."*

4.70 KAÑCUKĪ: yath" āha devī.

pañca|prasūter api rājña āsīt
  priyo viśeṣeṇa Subāhu|śatruḥ.
vadhū|catuṣke 'pi yathā hi Śāntā
  priyā tanūj" âsya tath" âiva Sītā. [16]

JANAKAḤ: hā priya|sakha mahā|rāja Daśaratha, evam asi sarva|prakāra|hṛdayaṃ|gamaḥ. kathaṃ vismaryase?

kanyāyāḥ kila pūjayanti pitaro
  jāmātur āptaṃ janaṃ.
 sambandhe viparītam eva tad abhūd
  ārādhanaṃ te mayi.
tvaṃ kālena tathā|vidho 'sy apahṛtaḥ,
  sambandha|bījaṃ ca tad.
 ghore 'smin mama jīva|loka|narake
  pāpasya dhig jīvitam. [17]

KAUSALYĀ: ⌜jāde Jāṇaï, kiṃ karomi? diḍha|vajja|leva|paḍibandha|ṇiccalaṃ hada|jīvidaṃ maṃ manda|bhāiṇiṃ ṇa pariccaadi.⌟

4.75 ARUNDHATĪ: āśvasihi, rāja|putri. bāṣpa|viśrāmo 'py antareṣu kartavya eva. anyac ca, kiṃ na smarasi yad avocad Ṛṣyaśṛṅg'|āśrame yuṣmākaṃ kula|guruḥ: «tath" êty upajñātam eva. kin tu kalyāṇ'|ôdarkaṃ bhaviṣyat'» îti?

---

[i] Rāma, who slew the demon Subāhu. [ii] Rāma's sister. [iii] Vasiṣṭha.

CHAMBERLAIN: It is just as the queen says: 4.70

> Although the king had five children
> his favorite was Subáhu's foe,[i]
> and although four daughters-in-law,
> no less a daughter than Shanta[ii] was Sita.

JÁNAKA: Oh my dear friend, King Dasha·ratha. This is why you were congenial to me in every way. How could I ever forget you?

> It is for the father of the bride, they say,
> to honor the son-in-law's kith and kin,
> but it was just the reverse in our kinship
> for you were the one who propitiated me.
> That someone such as you and the very seed
> of our kinship could both be taken by fate...
> a curse on me, evil as I must be
> for surviving in this dreadful hell of a world.

KAUSÁLYA: Jánaki my child, what am I to do? This wretched life of mine seems permanently fixed in place by some unyielding cement and will not leave me, cursed as I am.

ARÚNDHATI: Compose yourself, you are the daughter of a king. You must try as best you can in the interim to control your sobbing. And there is something else. Don't you recall what your family guru[iii] said in Rishya·shri·nga's ashram? He affirmed that what had happened had to happen, but that it would all turn out well in the end. 4.75

KAUSALYĀ: ⌜kudo adikkante maṇo|radhe?⌟

ARUNDHATĪ: tat kiṃ manyase, rāja|putri, mṛṣ" ôdyaṃ tad iti? na h' îdaṃ, su|kṣatriye, 'nyathā mantavyam. bhavitavyam eva tena.

āvirbhūta|jyotiṣāṃ brāhmaṇānāṃ
ye vyāhārās teṣu mā saṃśayo bhūt.
bhadrā hy eṣāṃ vāci Lakṣmīr niṣaktā.
n' âite vācaṃ viplutāṃ vyāharanti. [18]

nepathye kalakalaḥ. sarva ākarṇayanti.

4.80 JANAKAḤ: adya śiṣṭ'|ân|adhyayanam iti khelatāṃ baṭūnām ayaṃ kalakalaḥ.

KAUSALYĀ: ⌜su | laha | sokkhaṃ dāṇiṃ bālattaṇaṃ bhodi.⌟ *(nirūpya)* ⌜ammahe, edāṇaṃ majjhe ko eso Rāma|bhadda|lacchī|parisohidehiṃ s'|âvaṭṭambha|muddha|lalidehiṃ aṅgehiṃ amhāṇaṃ pi loaṇaṃ sīdalāvedi?⌟

ARUNDHATĪ: *(apavārya, sa|harṣa|bāṣpam)* idaṃ nāma tad Bhāgīrathī | niveditaṃ rahasyaṃ karṇ' | âmṛtam. na tv evaṃ vidmaḥ kataro 'yam āyuṣmatoḥ Kuśa|Lavayor iti.

KAUSÁLYA: How can that be so when all my dreams have been shattered?

ARÚNDHATI: So then, do you think he lied? You are the daughter of a king and the mother of strong Kshatriyas: don't think otherwise—this had to happen.

> Never doubt the utterances of Brahmans to whom
> the light has been revealed.
> Gracious Lakshmi inhabits their speech: no word
> of theirs is false.

A commotion offstage. All listen.

JÁNAKA: Today there is a break from studying*—that commotion must be coming from the boys playing. 4.80

KAUSÁLYA: How easy to find happiness when you are a child. *(looking)* My, who is the one in their midst who can soothe even my eyes with his limbs of such remarkable* grace and delicacy, adorned with the beauty of dear Rama himself?

ARÚNDHATI: *(aside; with tears of joy)* Here indeed is the secret—or rather, nectar—that Bhagi·rathi revealed. The one thing I don't know is which of the two, Kusha or Lava (long may they live), this one might be.

JANAKAḤ:

kuvalaya|dala|snigdha|śyāmaḥ
śikhaṇḍaka|maṇḍalo,
baṭu|pariṣadaṃ puṇya|śrīkaḥ
śriy" êva sabhājayan,
punar iva śiśur bhūtvā vatsaḥ
sa me Raghu|nandano
jhaṭiti kurute dṛṣṭaḥ ko 'yaṃ
dṛśor amṛt'|âñjanam? [19]

KAÑCUKĪ: nūnaṃ kṣatriya|brahmacārī dārako 'yam iti manye.

4.85 JANAKAḤ: evam etat. asya hi

cūḍā|cumbita|kaṅka|patram abhitas
tūṇī|dvayaṃ pṛṣṭhato.
bhasma|stoma|pavitra|lāñchanam uro
dhatte tvacaṃ rauravīm.
maurvyā mekhalayā niyantritam adho|
vāsaś ca māñjiṣṭhakaṃ.
pāṇau kārmukam akṣa|sūtra|valayaṃ
daṇḍo 'pare paippalaḥ. [20]

bhagavaty Arundhati, kim utprekṣase, kutastyo 'yam iti?

ARUNDHATĪ: ady' âiv' āgatā vayam.

JANAKAḤ: ārya Gṛṣṭe, at'|îva me kautukaṃ vartate. tad bhagavantaṃ Vālmīkim eva gatvā pṛccha, imaṃ ca dārakaṃ brūhi, «ke 'py ete pravayasas tvāṃ didṛkṣava» iti.

JÁNAKA:

With a dark sheen like a blue lotus petal,*
his head crowned by lovely locks,
beautified by goodness, his beauty
almost ennobling the crowd of boys,
he looks like Raghu·nándana,
my dear boy become a child again.
Who can this be, whose very sight
is a salve of nectar to my eyes?*

CHAMBERLAIN: I assume this boy is a Kshatriya seminarian.

JÁNAKA: That must be so, for he 4.85

Carries on his back two quivers
whose arrows kiss his top knot,
his chest bears a coat of arms—the holy
sign of ash—and a black buck's skin,
his lower garment is reddened with madder
and tied with a rope of *murva* grass,
in one hand a bow and a rosary,
in the other* a staff of peepul wood.

Arúndhati, where do you imagine this boy comes from?

ARÚNDHATI: But I am a new arrival here myself.

JÁNAKA: Grishti, my curiosity knows no bounds. Please go straightway to Valmíki and ask him. And tell the boy that some elders wish to see him.

4.90 KAÑCUKĪ: yath" ājñāpayasi. *(niṣkrāntaḥ)*

KAUSALYĀ: ⌜kiṃ maṇṇadha, evvaṃ bhaṇido āgamissadi tti?⌟

ARUNDHATĪ: bhidyeta vā sad|vṛttam īdṛśasya nirmāṇasya?

KAUSALYĀ: *(nirūpya)* ⌜kadhaṃ sa|viṇaaṃ ṇisāmida|Giṭṭhi|vaaṇo visajjia isi|dārae etto|muhaṃ pasarido jjevva so vaccho?⌟

JANAKAḤ: *(ciraṃ nirvarṇya)* bhoḥ kim apy etat?

4.95 mahimnām etasmin
vinaya|śiśiro maugdhya|masṛṇo
vidagdhair nirgrāhyo
na punar a|vidagdhair atiśayaḥ.
mano me sammoha|
sthiram api haraty eva balavān
ayo|dhātuṃ yadvat
parilaghur ayas|kānta|śakalaḥ. [21]

LAVAḤ: *(praviśya)* a|jñāta|nāma|kram'|ābhijātyān pūjyān api sataḥ katham abhivādayiṣye? *(vicintya)* ayaṃ punar a|viruddhaḥ prakāra iti vṛddhebyaḥ śrūyate. *(sa|vinayam upasṛtya)* eṣa vo Lavasya śirasā praṇāma|paryāyaḥ.

ARUNDHATĪ|JANAKAU: kalyāṇin, āyuṣmān bhūyāḥ.

KAUSALYĀ: ⌜jāda, ciraṃ jīva.⌟

CHAMBERLAIN: As you wish. *(exit)* 4.90

KAUSÁLYA: What makes you think he will come if asked?

ARÚNDHATI: Would his manners belie the figure he cuts?

KAUSÁLYA: *(looking)* How now? After listening politely to Grishti's words the child has sent away the seer's* other pupils and is making his way here.

JÁNAKA: *(gazing for a long time)* What can be happening to me now?

> The true extent of his powers, cooled now 4.95
> by courtesy and softened by innocence,
> can only be grasped by those with true
> perception, and by no one else.
> The boy has the strength to move my heart,
> immovable though despair has made it,
> just the way a trifling* fragment
> of magnet can move a lump of iron.

Enter LAVA: How am I to greet these eminent people without knowing their names and stations? *(reflecting)* There is one procedure I've learned from the elders that is beyond reproach. *(approaching deferentially)* This is Lava who bows his head successively* before you.

ARÚNDHATI *(and)* JÁNAKA: Good boy, long may you live.

KAUSÁLYA: Child, live long.

ARUNDHATĪ: ehi, vatsa. (LAVAM *utsaṅge gṛhītvā, apavārya*) diṣṭyā na kevalam utsaṅgaś cirān mano|ratho 'pi me sampūrṇaḥ.

4.100 KAUSALYĀ: ⌈jāda, ido vi dāva ehi.⌋ *(utsaṅge gṛhītvā)* ⌈ammahe, ṇa kevalaṃ dara|vippaṭṭa|kandoṭṭa|sāmal'|ujjaleṇa deha|bandheṇa, kavalid'|âravinda|kesara|kasāa|kaṇṭha|kala|haṃsa|ghosa|ghagghara|ṇiṇāda|dīhareṇa a sareṇa Rāma|bhaddassa aṇuharadi. ṇaṃ kaṭhora|kamala|gabbha|pamhalo sarīra|pphaṃso vi tādiso jjevva. jāda, pekkhāmi dāva de muhaṃ.⌋ *(cibukam unnamayya nirūpya ca, sa|bāṣp'|ākūtam)* ⌈rā'|esi, kiṃ ṇa pekkhasi? ṇiuṇaṃ ṇirūvijjanto vacchāe vadhūe muha|candeṇa saṃvadadi jjeva.⌋

JANAKAḤ: paśyāmi, sakhi, paśyāmi.

KAUSALYĀ: ⌈ammo, ummattī|bhūdaṃ via me hiaaṃ kiṃ pi cintaantīe bahu vippalavadi.⌋

JANAKAḤ:

vatsāyāś ca Ragh'|ûdvahasya ca śiśāv
asminn abhivyajyate
sampūrṇa|pratibimbik" êva nikhilā
s" âiv' ākṛtiḥ, sā dyutiḥ,
sā vāṇī, vinayaḥ sa eva saha|jaḥ,
puṇy'|ânubhāvo 'py asau.
hā hā daiva kim utpathair mama manaḥ
pāriplavaṃ dhāvati? [22]

ARÚNDHATI: Come, child. *(taking* LAVA *onto her lap; aside*)* How fortunate that not only is my lap full but at long last my dreams are fulfilled as well.

KAUSÁLYA: Child, come to me a moment too. *(taking him* 4.100
onto her lap) My, he resembles dear Rama not only in his physique, with its dark gleam of a blue lotus just blossoming, but in his voice, too, its drawn-out murmur like a swan's when its throat is painted by the lotus filaments it has eaten. And surely the body is the same to the touch, it's as downy as the inside of a full-blown lotus. Child, let me just look at your face. *(lifting his chin, and looking; with tears and curiosity)* Royal seer, can't you see? Take a good look, doesn't it exactly match the moon face of your child, our daughter-in-law?

JÁNAKA: Yes, I see, my friend, I do.

KAUSÁLYA: Oh dear, my heart is so confused I'm just rambling on amidst my scattered thoughts.

JÁNAKA:

In this child the exact same form
of my child and Rama, Raghu's heir
is made manifest, the spitting image
as it were: the radiance,
the voice, the same innate comportment,
even that pure majesty…
Oh fate, why is my agitated mind
chasing after this will-o'-the-wisp?

KAUSALYĀ: ⌜jāda, atthi de mādā? sumarasi vā tādaṃ?⌟

4.105 LAVAḤ: na hi.

KAUSALYĀ: ⌜tado kassa tumaṃ?⌟

LAVAḤ: bhagavato Vālmīkeḥ.

KAUSALYĀ: ⌜aï jāda, kadhidavvaṃ kadhehi.⌟

LAVAḤ: etāvad eva jānāmi.

4.110 NEPATHYE: bho bhoḥ sainikāḥ! eṣa khalu kumāra|Candraketur ājñāpayati: «na kena cid āśram'|âbhyarṇa|bhūmir ākramitavy"» êti.

ARUNDHATĪ|JANAKAU: aye, medhy'|âśva|rakṣā|prasaṅgād upāgato vatsaś Candraketur adya draṣṭavya, ity aho su|divasaḥ.

KAUSALYĀ: ⌜vaccha|Lakkhaṇassa puttako «āṇavedi» tti amida|bindu|sundarāiṃ akkharāiṃ suṇīanti.⌟

LAVAḤ: ārya, ka eṣa Candraketur nāma?

JANAKAḤ: jānāsi Rāma|Lakṣmaṇau Dāśarathī?

4.115 LAVAḤ: etāv eva Rāmāyaṇa|kathā|puruṣau.

KAUSÁLYA: Child, is your mother alive? Do you have any memory of your father?

LAVA: No, I don't. 4.105

KAUSÁLYA: Who takes care of you?

LAVA: The blessed Valmíki.

KAUSÁLYA: Come now, my child, you have a story here that needs telling.

LAVA: That is all I know.

OFFSTAGE: You there, soldiers! This is Prince Chandra·ketu 4.110
ordering that no one is to trespass upon the grounds of the ashram.

ARÚNDHATI AND JÁNAKA: Why, the young Chandra·ketu has arrived in connection with guarding the sacrificial horse, and we shall see him soon. What a lucky day.

KAUSÁLYA: The little son of dear Lákshmana is "ordering" —syllables as pleasing as drops of nectar to my ears.

LAVA: Sir, who is this person named Chandra·ketu?

JÁNAKA: You have heard of Rama and Lákshmana, sons of Dasha·ratha?

LAVA: They are the two heroes of the 'Ramáyana.' 4.115

JANAKAḤ: atha kim?

LAVAḤ: tat kathaṃ na jānāmi?

JANAKAḤ: tasya Lakṣmaṇasy' âyam ātmajaś Candraketuḥ.

LAVAḤ: Ūrmilā|putras tarhi, Maithilasya rāja'|rṣer dauhitraḥ.

4.120 ARUNDHATĪ: *(vihasya)* āviṣkṛtaṃ kathā|prāvīṇyaṃ vatsena.

JANAKAḤ: yadi tvam īdṛśaḥ kathāyām abhijñas, tad brūhi tāvat, pṛcchāmaḥ: teṣāṃ Daśarath'|ātmajānāṃ kiṃ|nāmadheyāny apatyāni keṣu dāreṣu prasūtāni?

LAVAḤ: n' âyaṃ kathā|pravibhāgo 'smābhir, anyena vā, śruta|pūrvaḥ.

JANAKAḤ: kiṃ na praṇītaḥ kavinā?

LAVAḤ: praṇīto, na tu prakāśitaḥ. tasy' âiva ko 'py eka|deśaḥ sandarbh'|ântareṇa rasavān abhiney'|ârthaḥ kṛtaḥ. taṃ ca sva|hasta|likhitaṃ munir bhagavān vyasṛjad Bharatasya munes taurya|trika|sūtra|kārasya.

4.125 JANAKAḤ: kim|artham?

LAVAḤ: sa kila bhagavān Bharatas tam apsarobhiḥ prayojayiṣyat' îti.

JANAKAḤ: sarvam idam asmākam ākūta|karam.

---

[i] Divine courtesans.

JÁNAKA: To be sure.

LAVA: Then how should I not have heard of them?

JÁNAKA: This Chandra·ketu is the son of Lákshmana.

LAVA: So he must be the son of Úrmila and grandson of the king of Míthila.

ARÚNDHATI: *(laughing)* It's clear the child's well versed in the story. 4.120

JÁNAKA: If you are so knowledgeable about the story then answer a few of my questions: What are the names of the children of Dasha·ratha's other* sons, and to which of the wives were they born?

LAVA: We haven't heard this portion of the story nor has anyone else.

JÁNAKA: Hasn't the poet composed it?

LAVA: Yes, but it isn't published yet. A portion of it, its *rasa* heightened by its new form, is meant for performance. The sage wrote out the manuscript in his own hand and sent it to Bharata, author of the 'Sutras on the Triad of Music.'

JÁNAKA: What for? 4.125

LAVA: So Bharata could have the *ápsaras*es[i] stage it, or so it's said.

JÁNAKA: All this piques our curiosity.

LAVAḤ: mahatī punas tasmin bhagavato Vālmīker āsthā, yato yeṣām ante|vāsināṃ hastena tat pustakaṃ Bharat'|āśramam preṣitaṃ teṣām ānuyātrikaś cāpa|pāṇiḥ pramād'|âpanodan'|ârtham asmad|bhrātā preṣitaḥ.

KAUSALYĀ: ⌈bhādā vi de atthi?⌋

4.130 LAVAḤ: asty āryaḥ Kuśo nāma.

KAUSALYĀ: ⌈jeṭṭho tti bhaṇidaṃ bhodi.⌋

LAVAḤ: evam etat. prasava|krameṇa sa kila jyāyān.

JANAKAḤ: kiṃ yama|jāv āyuṣmantau?

LAVAḤ: atha kim?

4.135 JANAKAḤ: kathaya: kathā|prabandhasya kīdṛśaḥ paryantaḥ?

LAVAḤ: alīka|paura|pravād'|ôdvignena rājñā nirvāsitāṃ deva|yajana|sambhavāṃ Sītā|devīm āsanna|prasava|vedanām ekākinīm araṇye parityajya Lakṣmaṇaḥ pratinivṛtta iti.

KAUSALYĀ: ⌈hā vacche muddha|canda|muhi, ko dāṇiṃ de sarīra|kusumassa jhatti devva|duvvilāsa|pariṇāmo ekkaliāe ṇivaḍido?⌋

JANAKAḤ: hā vatse,

> nūnaṃ tvayā paribhavaṃ ca vanaṃ ca ghoraṃ
> tāṃ ca vyathāṃ prasava|kāla|kṛtām avāpya
> kravyād|gaṇeṣu paritaḥ parivārayatsu
> santrastayā śaraṇam ity a|sakṛt smṛto 'smi. [23]

LAVA: Valmíki is very concerned about it, since he sent my brother armed with his bow to accompany the students hand-delivering the manuscript to Bharata's ashram, to make sure there were no missteps.

KAUSÁLYA: You have a brother, too?

LAVA: I have a noble brother named Kusha. 4.130

KAUSÁLYA: You mean he is older.

LAVA: Quite so. By birth order he is my elder.

JÁNAKA: What, are the two of you twins?

LAVA: To be sure.

JÁNAKA: Tell me, how does the main story end? 4.135

LAVA: The king, upset over the townsmen's malicious rumors, exiled Sita, the queen who was born at a sacred rite. Lákshmana returned after leaving her in the wilderness all alone, with the birth pangs coming on.

KAUSÁLYA: Oh my innocent moonfaced daughter, what perverse reversal of fortune has now befallen your flower of a body, all of a sudden, and all alone?

JÁNAKA: Oh child.

Surely when you had to confront all at once
disgrace, the dreadful forest, and labor pains,
and the packs of flesh-eating beasts encircled
you
your thoughts were fixed on me, your last refuge,
in your terror.

4.140 LAVAḤ: (ARUNDHATĪṂ *prati)* ārye, kāv etau?

ARUNDHATĪ: iyaṃ Kausalyā, ayaṃ Janakaḥ.

LAVAḤ *sa|bahumāna|kheda|kautukaṃ paśyati.*

JANAKAḤ: aho dur|maryādatā paurāṇām, aho Rāmasya rājñaḥ kṣipra|kāritā.

etad vaiśasa|ghora|vajra|patanaṃ
  śaśvan mam' ôtpaśyataḥ
krodhasya jvalituṃ dhagity avasaraś
  cāpena śāpena vā. [24]

4.145 KAUSALYĀ: *(sa|bhayam)* ⌜bhaavadi, parittāāhi, parittāāhi! prasādehi kuvidaṃ rā'|esiṃ.⌟

LAVAḤ:

etadd hi paribhūtānāṃ
  prāyaś|cittaṃ manasvinām. [25]

ARUNDHATĪ:

rājann, apatyaṃ Rāmas te,
  pālyāś ca kṛpaṇāḥ prajāḥ. [26]

JANAKAḤ:

śāntaṃ vā Raghu|nandane tad ubhayaṃ,
  tat putra|bhāṇḍaṃ hi me,
bhūyiṣṭha|dvija|bāla|vṛddha|vikala|
  straiṇaś ca pauro janaḥ. [27]

---

[i] Janaka's bow or his anger.

LAVA: *(to* ARÚNDHATI*)* Who are these two noble persons? 4.140

ARÚNDHATI: She is Kausálya, and he is Jánaka.

LAVA *looks with respect, concern, and curiosity.*

JÁNAKA: Oh, how perverse of the townsmen, how impulsive of King Rama.

As I brood on the terrible crash
of this thunderbolt calamity,
the time has come for my bow
or my curse to ignite my rage.

KAUSÁLYA: *(afraid)* Help, Arúndhati, help! Please try to calm the angry king. 4.145

LAVA: *

This is the only form of redress
for a self-respecting man disgraced.

ARÚNDHATI:

But, Your Majesty, Rama is your son,
and the unfortunate townsmen deserve protection.

JÁNAKA:

Then let neither[i] threaten Raghu·nándana—
he is a treasure of a son to me, after all,
and many of the townsmen are aged and infirm,
Brahmans, children, and womenfolk.

BAṬAVAḤ: *(sambhrāntāḥ, praviśya)* kumāra, kumāra! aśvo, 'śva iti ko 'pi bhūta|viśeṣo jana|padeṣu śrūyate. so 'yam adhun" âsmābhiḥ pratyakṣī|kṛtaḥ.

4.150 LAVAḤ: aśva iti tatra paśu|samāmnāye sāṅgrāmike ca paṭhyate. tad brūta, kīdṛśaḥ?

BAṬAVAḤ: are, śrūyatām.

paścāt puccham vahati vipulaṃ,
tac ca dhūnoty ajasram.
dīrgha|grīvaḥ sa bhavati, khurās
tasya catvāra eva.
śaṣpāṇy atti, prakirati śakṛt|
piṇḍakān āmra|mātrān.
kiṃ vyākhyātair? vrajati sa punar
dūram. ehy ehi, yāmaḥ! [28]

upasṛty' âjine hastayoś c' ākarṣanti.

LAVAḤ: *(sa|kautuk'|ôparodha|vinayam)* āryāḥ paśyata, ebhir nīto 'smi.

4.155 *tvaritaṃ parikrāmati.*

ARUNDHATĪ|JANAKAU: pūrayatu kautukaṃ vatsaḥ

KAUSALYĀ: ⌜bhaavadi, jāṇāmi, edaṃ aṇ|avekkhantī vañcidā via. tā ido aṇṇado bhavia pekkhamha dāva gacchamāṇaṃ dīh'|āuṃ.⌟

Enter SCHOOLBOYS *in a commotion* Young sir!* We've heard tell across the countryside of the appearance of an amazing creature called a horse, and now we've actually seen one for ourselves.

LAVA: "Horse" is mentioned both in texts that treat of sacrificial victims and in texts that treat of war. Tell me, which is it? 4.150

BOYS: Why, just listen:

> It has a large tail behind
> that it constantly flicks,
> and a long neck, and it has
> four hooves, not more, not less,
> and it eats grass and drops dung
> the size of mangoes... But enough
> commentary. He's getting away,
> hurry up, let's go!*

They approach LAVA *and pull him by the hands and his ascetic's hide.*

LAVA: *(with curiosity, reluctance, and courtesy)* My elders can see that I'm being dragged away.

He walks around hurriedly. 4.155

ARÚNDHATI AND JÁNAKA: Go ahead, child, and satisfy your curiosity.

KAUSÁLYA: Blessed one, I feel cheated* if I don't get to see him (long may he live). Let's find another spot to watch him as he makes his way.

ARUNDHATĪ: atijavena dūram atikrāntaḥ sa capalaḥ kathaṃ dṛśyate?

KAÑCUKĪ: *(praviśya)* bhagavān Vālmīkir āha: jñātavyam etad avasare bhavadbhiḥ.

4.160 JANAKAḤ: atigambhīram etat kim api bhaviṣyati. bhagavaty Arundhati, sakhi Kausalye, ārya Gṛṣṭe, svayam eva gatvā bhagavantaṃ Prācetasaṃ paśyāmaḥ.

niṣkrānto VṚDDHA*|vargaḥ.*

praviśya

BAṬAVAḤ: paśyatu kumāras tad āścaryam.

LAVAḤ: dṛṣṭam avagataṃ ca. nūnam āśvamedhiko 'yam aśvaḥ.

4.165 BAṬAVAḤ: kathaṃ jñāyate?

LAVAḤ: nanu mūrkhāḥ, paṭhitam eva yuṣmābhis tat kāṇḍam. kiṃ na paśyatha? pratyekaṃ śata|saṅkhyāḥ kavacino daṇḍino niṣaṅgiṇāś ca rakṣitāraḥ. tat|prāyam eva balam idaṃ dṛśyate. yadi ha na pratyayas, tat pṛcchata.

BAṬAVAḤ: bho bhoḥ, kim|prayojano 'yam aśvaḥ parivṛtaḥ paryaṭati?

LAVAḤ: *(sa|spṛham, ātma|gatam)* aśva|medha iti viśva|vijayināṃ kṣatriyāṇām ūrjasvalaḥ sarva|kṣatriya|paribhāvī mahān utkarṣa|nikaṣaḥ.

ARÚNDHATI: The little rascal has gone so far so fast that he is almost out of sight.

Enter the CHAMBERLAIN: Valmíki has replied saying that you will come to know the answer to your question in due course.

JÁNAKA: It must be something very important. Arúndhati, 4.160
Kausálya, my friend, Grishti, let us go and see Prachétas's son ourselves.

Exit group of ELDERS.

Enter SCHOOLBOYS

BOYS: Look at this miraculous thing, young sir.

LAVA: I've understood at first sight: this is a horse meant for the Horse Sacrifice.

BOYS: How can you tell? 4.165

LAVA: You dolts, you've already studied that section of the Veda and you still can't see? There have to be guards, with armor, clubs, or arrows, each contingent numbering a hundred. Such is almost exactly the army you see here. If you don't believe me go ask them.

BOYS: You there, what's the reason this horse is wandering about under guard?

LAVA: *(enviously, aside)* The Horse Sacrifice is the ultimate test of a world-conquering Kshatriya's preeminence, for it's meant to bring all other Kshatriyas into disgrace.

NEPATHYE:

yo 'yam aśvaḥ, patāk" êyam,
  atha vā vīra|ghoṣaṇā
sapta|lok'|âika|vīrasya
  Daśakaṇṭha|kula|dviṣaḥ. [29]

4.170 LAVAḤ: *(sa|vyatham iva)* aho, sandīpanāny akṣarāṇi!

BAṬAVAḤ: kim ucyate? prājñaḥ khalu kumāraḥ.

LAVAḤ: bho bhoḥ, kim a|kṣatriyā pṛthivī yad evam udghuṣyate?

NEPATHYE: are, mahā|rājaṃ prati kutaḥ kṣatriyāḥ?

LAVAḤ: dhik, jālmāḥ!

4.175 yadi te santi, santv eva.
  k" êyam adya vibhīṣikā?
kim uktaiḥ? sannipaty' âiṣa
  tāṃ patākāṃ harāmi vaḥ. [30]

bho baṭavaḥ, parivṛtya loṣṭair apaghnantaḥ parāvartayat' âinam aśvam. eṣa rohitānāṃ madhye varākaś caratu.

PURUṢAḤ: *(praviśya, sa|krodha|darpaḥ)* dhik, capala, kim uktavān asi? tīkṣṇa|nīrasā hy āyudhīya|śreṇayaḥ śiśor api dṛptāṃ vācaṃ na sahante. rāja|putraś Candraketur ari|vimardanaḥ so py apūrv'|âraṇya|darśana|kutūhal'|ākṣipta|hṛdayo na yāvad āyāti tāvat tvaritam anena taru|gahanen' âpasarpata.

---

[i] Rāvaṇa's.

OFFSTAGE:

> This is not so much a horse
> as a banner or war cry announcing
> the one true hero in the seven worlds,
> the enemy of Ten-Neck's[i] tribe.

LAVA: *(as if perturbed)* Ah, fighting words! 4.170

BOYS: What can we say? Young sir is well informed indeed.

LAVA: You there, you think no Kshatriyas are left on earth that you can shoot off your mouth like this?

OFFSTAGE: Come now, what are other Kshatriyas to the emperor?

LAVA: Damn, you scoundrels!*

> If there be Kshatriyas then Kshatriyas 4.175
> indeed they are. Who are you trying to scare?
> But the time for talk is past: I am going
> to attack and carry that banner away.

You there, boys: Surround them and bombard them with clumps of dirt and lead the horse back here. Let the poor thing wander free among the ashram's deer.

Enter an angry and arrogant OFFICER: Damn, you rascal, what did you say? The king's regiments are ruthless and hard-hearted, and they won't stand for arrogant talk even from a child. Before Prince Chandra·ketu, crusher of enemies, reaches this celebrated* wilderness to tour it as he is heartily eager to do, you all had better hurry and leave by way of this thicket of trees.

BAṬAVAḤ: kumāra, kṛtam anen' âśvena. tarjayanti visphurita|śastrāḥ kumāram āyudhīya|śreṇayaḥ; dūre c' āśrama|padam itaḥ. tad ehi. hariṇa|plutaiḥ palāyāmahe.

LAVAḤ: *(vihasya)* kiṃ nāma visphuranti śastrāṇi? *(dhanur āropayan)*

4.180 jyā|jihvayā valayit'|ôtkaṭa|koṭi|daṃṣṭram
udgāri|ghora|ghana|ghargharа|ghoṣam etat
grāsa|prasakta|hasad|Antaka|vaktra|yantra|
jṛmbhā|viḍambi vikaṭ'|ôdaram astu cāpam. [31]

yath''|ôcitaṃ parikramya niṣkrāntāḥ sarve.

iti mahā|kavi|śrī|Bhavabhūti|praṇīta
Uttara|Rāma|carita|nāṭake
Kausalyā|Janaka|yogo nāma
caturtho 'ṅkaḥ.

BOYS: Young sir, forget about the horse. The regiments are coming, brandishing their weapons and threatening you, and the ashram is far away. So come on, let's high-tail it out of here!

LAVA: *(laughing)* What do I care about their brandishing weapons? *(stringing his bow)*

My dreadful bow is ready to yawn—no weapon 4.180
but the laughing maw of Death greedily feeding,
rumbling with a wild, dull, thundercloud-like roar,
its tips sharp fangs licked by its bowstring tongue.

Walking about as befitting them, exeunt all.

End of Act IV

ACT V
THE YOUNG MAN'S* VALOR

NEPATHYE: bho bhoḥ, sainikāḥ! jātaṃ jātam avalambanam asmākam.

nanv eṣa tvarita|Sumantra|nudyamāna|
vyāvalgat|prajavana|vājinā rathena
utkhāta|pracalita|kovidāra|ketuḥ
śrutvā naḥ pradhanam upaiti Candraketuḥ. [1]

tataḥ praviśati SUMANTRA*|sārathinā rathena dhanuṣ|pāṇiḥ s'|âdbhuta|harṣa|sambhramaś* CANDRAKETUḤ.

CANDRAKETUḤ: ārya Sumantra, paśya paśya:

5.5 kirati kalita|kiñcit|kopa|rajyan|mukha|śrīr
an|avarata|niguñjat|koṭinā kārmukeṇa
samara|śirasi cañcat|pañca|cūḍaś camūnām
upari śara|tuṣāraṃ ko 'py ayaṃ vīra|potaḥ. [2]

āścaryam.

muni|jana|śiśur ekaḥ saṃvṛttaḥ sainya|saṅgaiḥ
nava iva Raghu|vaṃśasy' â|prasiddhaḥ prarohaḥ
dalita|kari|kapola|granthi|ṭaṅkāra|ghora|
jvalita|śara|sahasraḥ kautukaṃ me karoti. [3]

SUMANTRAḤ: āyuṣman,

OFFSTAGE: You there, soldiers! Finally reinforcements for us.

That must be—on a chariot with speeding horses
galloping, urged on by a rushing Sumántra,
a *kovidára** banner fluttering where it's been
hoisted—
Chandra·ketu coming at the news of our fight.

Enter, on a chariot driven by SUMÁNTRA, CHANDRA·KETU *bow in hand and filled with wonder, joy, and alarm.*

CHANDRA·KETU: Look, Sumántra, look.

There is some child hero at the forefront of battle, 5.5
unleashing a blizzard of arrows upon the army,
his five topknots* waving, his bow ever
twanging, his beautiful face reddened with anger.

It's a miracle.

That a single child, reared by sages,
surrounded by so many troops,
a new and unfamiliar sprout
of Raghu's family, it seems,
should shoot a thousand flaming arrows
from a dreadfully twanging bow,
splitting the war elephants' temples,
fires my curiosity.*

SUMÁNTRA: Young sir (long may you live),

atiśayita|sur'|âsura|prabhāvaṃ
śiśum avalokya tath" âiva tulya|rūpam
Kuśika|suta|makha|dviṣāṃ pramāthe
dhṛta|dhanuṣaṃ Raghu|nandanaṃ smarāmi. [4]

5.10 CANDRAKETUḤ: imam ekam uddiśya bhūyasām ārambha iti hṛdayam apatrapate.

ayaṃ hi śiśur ekakaḥ samabhareṇa bhūri|sphurat|
karāla|kara|kandalī|jaṭila|śastra|jālair balaiḥ
kvaṇat|kanaka|kiṅkiṇī|jhaṇajhaṇāyita|syandanair
a|manda|mada|durdina|dvirada|vāridair āvṛtaḥ. [5]

SUMANTRAḤ: vatsa, ebhiḥ samastair api kim asya? kiṃ punar vyastaiḥ?

CANDRAKETUḤ: ārya, tvaryatāṃ tvaryatām! anena hi mahān āśrita|jana|pramātho 'smākam ārabdhaḥ. tathā hi:

āgarjad|giri|kuñja|kuñjara|ghaṭā|
vistīrṇa|karṇa|jvaraṃ
jyā|nirghoṣam a|manda|dundubhi|ravair
ādhmātam ujjṛmbhayan
vellad|bhairava|ruṇḍa|khaṇḍa|nikarair
vīro vidhatte bhuvas
tṛpyat|Kāla|karāla|vaktra|vighasa|
vyākīryamāṇā iva. [6]

---

[i] Literally, "Kuśika's son." See 1.76 [17].

As I watch this child—his power exceeds at once
the gods' and antigods', and his form is the same*
as well—
I am reminded of Rama wielding his bow
to crush the foes of Vishva·mitra's rite.[i]

CHANDRA·KETU: My heart recoils to see so many attacking one all alone. 5.10

He is a child and all on his own,
while vast forces—with a latticework
of weapons tangled in hands that are huge
as palm trees, bristling with battle gear,*
advancing on chariots that make a jangle
with ringing golden bells, on cloud-like
war elephants that stir up a storm
with torrents of musk—are surrounding him.

SUMÁNTRA: My child, they're no match for him all together let alone singly.

CHANDRA·KETU: Hurry, sir, hurry! He's started a wholesale slaughter of our retainers. For

While raising a twanging sound from his bow
that's amplified by the deep roar of war drums—
a cacophony vaster than elephant herds
trumpeting in mountain caves—
the hero bedecks the earth with mounds
of grisly twitching headless bodies
as if with scraps of food that have dropped
from the gruesome mouth of a sated Death.

5.15 SUMANTRAḤ: *(sva|gatam)* katham īdṛśena saha vatsasya Candraketor dvandva|saṃprahāram anujānīyām? *(vicintya)* atha vā, Ikṣvāku|kula|vṛddhāḥ khalu vayam. pratyupasthite ca kā gatiḥ?

CANDRAKETUḤ: *(sa|vismaya|lajjā|sambhramam)* dhik, apacitāni sarvataḥ sainyāni mama!

SUMANTRAḤ: *(ratha|vegam abhinīya)* āyuṣman, eṣa vāg|viṣayī|bhūtaḥ sa te vīraḥ.

CANDRAKETUḤ: *(vismṛtim abhinīya)* ārya, kiṃ nāma|dheyam ākhyātam āhvāyakaiḥ?

SUMANTRAḤ: «Lava» iti.

CANDRAKETUḤ:

5.20 bho bho Lava mahā|bāho,
kim ebhis tava sainikaiḥ?
eṣo 'ham. ehi mām eva.
tejas tejasi śāmyatu. [7]

SUMANTRAḤ: kumāra, paśya paśya.

vyapavartata eṣa bāla|vīraḥ
pṛtanā|nirmathanāt tvay" ôpahūtaḥ
stanayitnu|ravād ibh'|āvalīnām
avamardād iva dṛpta|siṃha|śāvaḥ. [8]

tataḥ praviśati tvarit'|ôddhata|parikramo LAVAḤ.

SUMÁNTRA: *(aside)* How could I possibly permit a duel to take place between the young Chandra·ketu and such a being as this? *(reflecting)* But then, we are elders of the Ikshváku clan, after all.* And what other recourse is there in the present circumstances? 5.15

CHANDRA·KETU: *(with astonishment, shame, and alarm)* Why, my troops are losing ground everywhere!

SUMÁNTRA: *(miming a speeding chariot)* My child (long may you live), the hero is now within shouting range.

CHANDRA·KETU: *(miming forgetfulness)* Sir, what was the name the messengers mentioned?

SUMÁNTRA: Lava.

CHANDRA·KETU:

You there, Lava, what are such soldiers to someone 5.20
as strong as you?
Here I am, come get me one on one:
One should fight fire with fire.

SUMÁNTRA: Look, young sir, look:

At your challenge the boy hero
leaves off annihilating the army,
as a bold lion cub at a stormcloud's roar
leaves off slaughtering an elephant herd.

Enter LAVA *walking swiftly and boldly.*

LAVAḤ: sādhu rāja|putra, sādhu! satyam Aikṣvākaḥ khalv asi. tad ayaṃ parāgata ev' âsmi.

5.25 *nepathye mahān kalakalaḥ.*

LAVAḤ: *(s'|āvegaṃ parāvṛtya)* āḥ katham idānīṃ bhagnā api pratinivṛtya pṛṣṭh'|ânusāriṇaḥ paryavaṣṭabhnanti māṃ camū|patayaḥ? dhig jālmān!

> ayaṃ śail'|āghāta|
> kṣubhita|vaḍavā|vaktra|hutabhuk|
> pracaṇḍa|krodh'|ârcir|
> nicaya|kavalatvaṃ vrajatu me
> samantād utsarpan
> ghana|tumula|helā|kalakalaḥ
> payo|rāśer oghaḥ
> pralaya|pavan'|āsphālita iva. [9]

s'|āvegaṃ parikrāmati.

CANDRAKETUḤ: bho bhoḥ kumāra!

5.30
> atyadbhutād asi guṇ'|âtiśayāt priyo me.
> tasmāt sakhā tvam asi. yan mama tat tav' âiva.
> tat kiṃ nije parijane kadanaṃ karoṣi?
> nanv eṣa darpa|nikaṣas tava Candraketuḥ. [10]

LAVAḤ: *(sa|harṣa|sambhramaṃ parāvṛtya)* aho, mah"|ânubhāvasya prasanna|karkaśā vīra|vacana|prayuktir vikartana|kula|kumārasya. tat kim ebhiḥ? enam eva tāvat sambhāvayāmi.

LAVA: Bravo, prince, bravo! You really are in truth an Aikshváka. So here I am, returned to you.

Offstage a great tumult. 5.25

LAVA: *(turning around abruptly)* What, are the battalion commanders, though once defeated, returning to encircle me and attack me from the rear?* The scoundrels!

> Let their flood—like the ocean's flood
> when battered by the doomsday winds,
> with a terrifying earsplitting noise
> and swelling to its highest tide—
> become a morsel to feed the blazing
> bonfire of my anger, as hot
> as the fire in the mouth of Vádava*
> whipped up by blows from the mountains.

He walks about excitedly.

CHANDRA·KETU: You there, young sir!

> Your truly wondrous virtues have endeared you 5.30
> to me. You're now my friend, what's mine is yours.
> Why then slaughter your own people? Surely
> Chandra·ketu here is the touchstone for your pride.

LAVA: *(turning back in excitement and alarm)* Ah, a clever show of words, brave words, smooth and rough at once, on the part of the majestic scion of the Solar dynasty. Why should I bother with these fellows then? Let me first pay my respects to him.

punar nepathye kalakalaḥ.

LAVAḤ: *(sa|krodha|nirvedam)* āḥ, kadarthito 'ham ebhir vīra|saṃvāda|vighna|kāribhiḥ pāpaiḥ.

tad|abhimukhaṃ parikrāmati.

5.35 CANDRAKETUḤ: ārya, dṛśyatāṃ draṣṭavyam.

darpeṇa kautukavatā mayi baddha|lakṣyaḥ
paścād balair anusṛto 'yam udīrṇa|dhanvā
dvedhā samuddhata|marut|taralasya dhatte
meghasya Māghavata|cāpa|dharasya lakṣmīm.
[11]

SUMANTRAḤ: kumāra ev' âinaṃ draṣṭum api jānāti. kevalaṃ tu paravanto vayaṃ vismayena.

CANDRAKETUḤ: bho bho rājānaḥ,

saṃkhy"|âtītair dvirada|turaga|
syandana|sthaiḥ padātāv
atr' âikasmin kavaca|nicitair
medhya|carm'|ôttarīye
kāla|jyeṣṭhair a|carama|vayaḥ|
kāmya|kāye bhavadbhir
yo 'yaṃ baddho yudhi samabharas,
tena vo dhig dhig asmān. [12]

Still offstage a great tumult.

LAVA: *(with anger and disgust)* Ah, what disrespectful treatment I'm shown by these curs: They've interrupted a conversation between heroes.

He walks about in the direction of CHANDRA·KETU.

CHANDRA·KETU: Look, sir, look, here's something worth 5.35
seeing:

> At once confident and curious, brandishing his bow
> he has fixed his aim on me while hounded by forces
> at the rear,
> looking for all the world like a rainbow-bearing
> stormcloud
> driven in opposite directions by the gusting wind.

SUMÁNTRA: Even to look at him—well, young sir alone is capable of doing so. We ourselves are simply overcome with astonishment.

CHANDRA·KETU: You there, nobles,

> Your forces are past counting, while he
> is all alone. You come on chariots,
> elephants, and horses—and he's on foot.
> You are protected by armor, he wears
> an ascetic's hide. You are adults
> while his body glows with youth's first bloom.
> Readying arms like this for battle
> will only bring shame on you and me.

5.40 LAVAḤ: *(s'|ônmātham)* katham, anukampate nāma? *(vicintya)* bhavatu. kāla|haraṇa|pratiṣedhāya Jṛmbhak'|âstreṇa tāvat sainyāni saṃstambhayāmi. *(dhyānaṃ nāṭayati)*

SUMANTRAḤ: tat kim a|kasmād asmat|sainya|ghoṣaḥ praśāmyati?

LAVAḤ: paśyāmy enam adhunā sa|pragalbham.

SUMANTRAḤ: *(sa|sambhramam)* vatsa, manye kumārakeṇ' ânena Jṛmbhak'|âstram āmantritam.

CANDRAKETUḤ: atra kaḥ sandehaḥ?

5.45 vyatikara iva bhīmas tāmaso vaidyutaś ca
pranihitam api cakṣur grasta|muktaṃ hinasti.
atha likhitam iv' âitat sainyam a|spandam āste.
niyatam a|jita|vīryaṃ jṛmbhate Jṛmbhak'|âstram.
[13]

āścaryam, āścaryam!

pātāl'|ôdara|kuñja|puñjita|tamaḥ|
śyāmair nabho Jṛmbhakair
uttapta|sphurad|ārakūṭa|kapila|
jyotir|jvalad|dīptibhiḥ
kalp'|ākṣepa|kaṭhora|bhairava|marud|
vyastair avastīryate
mīlan|megha|taḍit|kaḍāra|kuharair
Vindhy'|âdri|kūṭair iva. [14]

LAVA: *(with consternation)** What the devil, is he moved to compassion? *(reflecting)* Well, I'll waste no more time but simply paralyze the troops with my magic Jrímbhaka weapons. *(miming concentration)* 5.40

SUMÁNTRA: Now, why has the ruckus among our troops suddenly died down?

LAVA: So I behold the impudent fellow at last.

SUMÁNTRA: *(with alarm)* My child, I believe the youngster has invoked the Jrímbhaka weapons.

CHANDRA·KETU: There can be no doubt:

An awesome combination, like that of darkness and lightning, 5.45
first blinding then dazzling* assails even the steady eye.
Our troops are stock-still, as if painted in a picture.
the invincible Jrímbhaka weapons must have been deployed.

It's a miracle, a sheer miracle!

Black as the darkness massed in the womb
of hell, agleam with the red radiance
of heated glowing brass the Jrímbhakas
blanket the sky like Vindhya's peaks
torn off by the awesome howling winds
that announce the end of a cosmic age,
their caverns tawny within from lightning
that shoots from the gathering bank of clouds.

SUMANTRAḤ: kutaḥ punar asya Jṛmbhakāṇām āgamaḥ syāt?

CANDRAKETUḤ: bhagavataḥ Prācetasād iti manyāmahe.

5.50 SUMANTRAḤ: vatsa, n' âitad evam astreṣu, viśeṣato Jṛmbhakeṣu. yataḥ,

Kṛśāśva|tanayā hy ete,
  Kṛśāśvāt Kauśikaṃ gatāḥ,
atha tat|sampradāyena
  Rāmabhadre sthitā iti. [15]

CANDRAKETUḤ: apare 'pi pracīyamāna|sattva|prakāśāḥ svayaṃ hi mantra|dṛśaḥ paśyanti.

SUMANTRAḤ: vatsa, s' | âvadhāno bhava. parāgataḥ prativīraḥ.

KUMĀRAU: *(anyonyam uddiśya)* aho priya | daraśanaḥ kumāraḥ. *(sa|sneh'|ânurāgaṃ nirvarṇya)*

5.55 yadṛcchā|saṃvādaḥ
  kim u? kim u guṇānām atiśayaḥ?
purāṇo vā janm'|â-
  ntara|nibiḍa|bandhaḥ paricayaḥ?
nijo vā sambandhaḥ
  kim u vidhi|vaśāt ko 'py a|vidito?
mam' âitasmin dṛṣṭe
  hṛdayam avadhānaṃ racayati. [16]

---

[i] Viśvāmitra.

SUMÁNTRA: But how could he have acquired the Jrímbhakas?

CHANDRA·KETU: From the son of Prachétas, I suppose.

SUMÁNTRA: My child, that is not how it works with such weapons, especially the Jrímbhakas. For 5.50

These are the offspring of Krisháshva,
and passed from him to Káushika,[i]
who transmitted them to dear Rama,
where ever since they've come to reside.

CHANDRA·KETU: But others have beheld them, men who have gained illumination by their purity and had visions of mantras on their own.

SUMÁNTRA: Child, pay heed: Your adversary* has returned.

THE TWO YOUNG MEN: *(each in reference to the other)* The young man is so kind looking. *(gazing with affection and love)*

Is it some chance meeting of minds? 5.55
His many virtues? An ancient friendship
fast formed in some previous birth?
A relative of mine kept hidden
by fate, that my heart should be rapt in attention
at the very sight of him?

SUMANTRAḤ: bhūyasā jīvi|dharma eṣa yat sva|rasamayī kasya cit kva cit prītiḥ. yatra laukikānām upacāras «tārā| maitrakaṃ», «cakṣū|rāga» iti, tam a|pratisaṃkhyeyam a|nibandhanaṃ pramāṇam āmananti.

a|hetuḥ pakṣa|pāto yas
tasya n' âsti pratikriyā,
sa hi sneh'|ātmakas tantur
antar|bhūtāni sīvyati. [17]

KUMĀRAU: *(anyonyam uddiśya)*

etasmin masṛṇita|rāja|paṭṭa|kānte
moktavyāḥ katham iha sāyakāḥ śarīre
yat|prāptau mama parirambhaṇ'|âbhilāṣād
unmīlat|pulaka|kadambam aṅgam āste? [18]

5.60 kin tv ākrānta|kaṭhora|tejasi gatiḥ
kā nāma śastraṃ vinā?
śastreṇ' âpi hi tena kiṃ na viṣayo
jāyeta yasy' êdṛśaḥ?
kiṃ vakṣyaty ayam eva yuddha|vimukhaṃ
mām udyate 'py āyudhe?
vīrāṇāṃ samayo hi dāruṇa|rasaḥ
sneha|kramaṃ bādhate. [19]

SUMANTRAḤ: *(LAVAṂ nirvarṇya, s'|âsram, ātma|gatam)* hṛdaya, kim anyathā pariplavase?

SUMÁNTRA: It is a common characteristic of the soul that a given person should feel a natural affection for another given person. Worldly men have a figurative expression for this, "Being starry-eyed"* or "Love at first sight." And therefore it's written that this is something real, however unfounded and inexplicable it may appear to be.

There is no way to counteract
a predilection that has no cause.
There is some thread of affection that knits
living things* together deep within.

THE TWO YOUNG MEN: *(each in reference to the other)*

How could I shoot my arrows into this body
adorned by the soft* fillet of royalty
when no sooner having met than my limbs
began to tremble, longing to hold him close?

But then, what recourse can there be but arms 5.60
when faced with such an overwhelming force?*
And yet what use are arms when he is such
as far exceeds the scope of their power?
What would he say of me were I to turn
away from battle after swords were drawn?
The *rasa** of the hero's way is cruel
and blocks the normal course of affection.

SUMÁNTRA: *(gazing at* LAVA*; tearfully, aside)* My heart, why are you running riot?

mano|rathasya yad bījaṃ
tad daiven' ādito hṛtam.
latāyāṃ pūrva|lūnāyāṃ
prasavasy' āgamaḥ kutaḥ? [20]

CANDRAKETUḤ: avatarāmy, ārya Sumantra, syandanāt.

SUMANTRAḤ: tat kasya hetoḥ?

5.65 CANDRAKETUḤ: yatas tāvad ayaṃ vīra|puruṣaḥ pūjito bhavati. api ca khalv, ārya, kṣātra|dharmaḥ samanugato bhavati. na rathinaḥ pāda|cāram abhiyodhayant' îti śāstra|vidaḥ paribhāṣante.

SUMANTRAḤ: *(sva|gatam)* kaṣṭaṃ bat', ânuprasanno 'smi.

kathaṃ nyāyyam anuṣṭhānaṃ
mādṛśaḥ pratiṣedhatu?
kathaṃ v" âbhyanujānātu
sāhas'|âika|rasāṃ kriyām? [21]

CANDRAKETUḤ: yadā tāta|miśrā api pituḥ priyaṃ sakhāyaṃ dharm'|ârtha|saṃśayeṣv āryam eva pṛcchanti, tat kim āryo vimṛśati?

SUMANTRAḤ: āyuṣmann, evaṃ yathā|dharmam abhimanyase.

5.70 eṣa sāṅgrāmiko nyāya,
eṣa dharmaḥ sanātanaḥ,
iyaṃ hi Raghu|siṃhānāṃ
vīra|cāritra|paddhatiḥ. [22]

CANDRAKETUḤ: a|pratirūpaṃ vacanam āryasya.

The one seed of our hope was stolen away by fate.
Once the vine is cut how is any shoot to grow?

CHANDRA·KETU: Sumántra, I want to get off the chariot.

SUMÁNTRA: Why so?

CHANDRA·KETU: For one thing, this is the way to show respect to a hero. For another, it's following Kshatriya custom, as you are aware, sir. According to the interpretation of those who know the Shastra, one riding a chariot should never give battle to another who is on foot. 5.65

SUMÁNTRA: *(aside)* I am facing a terrible dilemma here.

How can such a one as I forbid the proper act
or give assent to a deed whose *rasa** is sheer
recklessness?

CHANDRA·KETU: My honored father addresses every question of *dharma* or statecraft to you, his own father's dear friend. Why then your vacillation?

SUMÁNTRA: My child (long may you live), your thinking is in accordance with *dharma*.

This is the proper conduct in war, the age-old way of *dharma*, 5.70
the course of action for heroes that the Raghu lions have followed.

CHANDRA·KETU: Your words are without peer.

itihāsaṃ purāṇaṃ ca,
  dharma|pravacanāni ca
bhavanta eva jānanti,
  Raghūṇāṃ ca kula|sthitim. [23]

SUMANTRAḤ: *(sa|sneh'|âsraṃ pariṣvajya)*

jātasya te pitur ap' Îndrajito vijetur
  vatsasya, vatsa, kati nāma dināny amūni?
tasy' âpy apatyam anugacchati vīra|vṛttaṃ.
  diṣṭyā gataṃ Daśarathasya kulaṃ pratiṣṭhām.
[24]

5.75 CANDRAKETUḤ: *(sa|kaṣṭam)*

«a|pratiṣṭhe Raghu|jyeṣṭhe
  kā pratiṣṭhā kulasya naḥ?»
iti duḥkhena tapyante
  trayo naḥ pitaro 'pare. [25]

SUMANTRAḤ: ahaha, hṛdaya|marma|dāraṇāny etāni Candraketor vacanāni.

LAVAḤ: hanta, miśrī|kṛto rasa|kramo vartate.

yath" êndāv ānandaṃ
    vrajati samupoḍhe kumudinī
  tath" âiv' âsmin dṛṣṭir.
    mama kalaha|kāmaḥ punar ayam
jhaṇat|kāra|krūra|
    kvaṇita|guṇa|guñjad|guru|dhanur|
  dhṛta|premā bāhur
    vikaca|vikarāla|vraṇa|mukhaḥ. [26]

---

[i] Son of Rāvaṇa. [ii] That is, has found a son to continue the line. [iii] Lakṣmaṇa, Bharata, Śatrughna. [iv] I.e., blossom.

The histories and legends, the discourses of *dharma*,
the family customs of the Raghus—all are known
to you alone.

SUMÁNTRA: *(embracing him with tears of affection)*

My dear child, how many days can possibly have passed
since your dear father, conqueror of Índrajit,[i] was born?
And here is his own son following the hero's path.
What good fortune Dasha·ratha's clan has found fulfillment.[ii]

CHANDRA·KETU: *(despondently)* 5.75

So long as the eldest Raghu is unfulfilled
how could our clan find fulfillment?
This is the single thought that makes our fathers,
our three other fathers,[iii] burn with sorrow.

SUMÁNTRA: Ah, Chandra·ketu's words tear at my heart's soft core.

LAVA: Well really, the development of the *rasa* here is all muddled.

Night-blooming lotuses rejoice[iv] when the moon begins to rise
and so do my eyes when I see him. And yet my arm—
its ghastly wounds agape, throbbing with love for the heavy bow
and its string twanging so cruelly and loud—is hankering for battle.

5.80 CANDRAKETUḤ: *(avataraṇaṃ rūpayan)* ārya, Sāvitraś Candraketur abhivādayate.

SUMANTRAḤ:

> a|jitaṃ puṇyam ūrjasvi
> Kakutsthasy' êva te mahaḥ
> śreyase śāśvato devo
> Varāhaḥ parikalpatām. [27]

api ca

> devas tvāṃ Savitā dhinotu samare
> gotrasya yas te pitā.
> tvāṃ Maitrāvaruṇo 'bhinandatu gurur
> yas te gurūṇām api.
> Aindrā|Vaiṣṇavam Āgni|Mārutam atho
> Sauparṇam ojo 'stu te.
> deyād eva ca Rāma|Lakṣmaṇa|dhanur|
> jyā|ghoṣa|mantro jayam. [28]

LAVAḤ: kumāra, ati hi nāma śobhase rathastha eva. kṛtaṃ kṛtam atyādareṇa.

5.85 CANDRAKETUḤ: tarhi mahā|bhāgo 'py anyaṃ ratham alaṅ|karotu.

LAVAḤ: ārya, pratyāropaya rath'|ôpari rāja|putram.

---

[i] An ancestor of the Raghu dynasty. [ii] In the Boar incarnation Viṣṇu rescued the world from the depths of the ocean. [iii] Vasiṣṭha, descendant of the gods Mitra and Varuṇa. [iv] Garuḍa, the divine bird that is Viṣṇu's vehicle.

CHANDRA·KETU: *(imitating climbing down from the chariot)* 5.80
Sir, Chandra·ketu of the Solar dynasty greets you.

SUMÁNTRA:

Grandeur indomitable, pristine, imposing as
Kakútstha's[i]
may the Boar,[ii] the everlasting god, grant you
eternal welfare.

Moreover:

May the Sun, the father of your clan, impel* you in
battle.
May Maitra·váruna,[iii] your
gurus' guru and your own, rejoice in you.
May you have the strength of Indra, Vishnu, Fire,
the Storm gods, Supárna.[iv]
May the loud mantra of Rama and Lákshmana's
bowstring bestow success.

LAVA: Young sir, you look quite grand aboard the chariot. No need whatever for such a show of deference.

CHANDRA·KETU: Then let the well-favored young man adorn a chariot of his own. 5.85

LAVA: Sir, have the prince board the chariot once again.

SUMANTRAḤ: tvam apy anurudhyasva vatsyasya Candraketor vacanam.

LAVAḤ: ko vicāraḥ sveṣ' ûpakaraṇeṣu? kin tv araṇya|sado vayam an|abhyasta|ratha|caryāḥ.

SUMANTRAḤ: jānāsi, vatsa, darpa|saujanyayor yath"|ôcitam. yadi punar īdṛśaṃ tvām Aikṣvāko rājā Rāmaḥ paśyet, tad" âsya snehena hṛdayam abhiṣyandeta.

5.90 LAVAḤ: manye su|janaḥ sa rāja'|rṣiḥ śrūyate. *(sa|lajjam iva)*

vayam api na khalv evaṃ|prāyāḥ
kratuṣv api matsarāḥ.
ka iva ca guṇais taṃ rājānaṃ
na vā bahu manyate?
tad api khalu me sa vyāhāras
turaṅgama|rakṣiṇāṃ
vikṛtim akhila|kṣatr'|ākṣepa|
pracaṇḍatay" âkarot. [29]

CANDRAKETUḤ: *(sa|smitam)* kiṃ nu bhavatas tāta|pratāp'|ôtkarṣe 'py a|marṣaḥ?

LAVAḤ: astv a|marṣo, mā bhūd vā. etat tu pṛcchāmi: dāntaṃ hi Rāghavaṃ rājānam anuśuśruma. sa kila n' ātmanā dṛpyati, n' âsya prajāyāṃ dṛptatvaṃ jāyate. tat kiṃ manuṣyās tasya rākṣasīṃ vācam udīrayanti?

---

[i] See Act 5.30 [10]. [ii] Act 4.169 [29]. [iii] An elder paternal uncle was also called *tāta*, father.

SUMÁNTRA: Then please comply, for your part, with young Chandra·ketu's request.

LAVA: One wouldn't hesitate to use equipment of one's own.[i] But we who live in the wilderness are unpracticed in chariot riding.

SUMÁNTRA: You are mindful, my child, of the claims* of pride and magnanimity both. Were the Aikshváka king Rama to witness this behavior of yours, his heart would gush with affection.

LAVA: That royal seer himself, I think, is the one who is truly 5.90
magnanimous—or so one hears. *(half ashamed)*

As for me, you know, I don't as a rule
begrudge* such rituals,
and who in the world could fail to respect
the king for his many virtues?
Still, you know, it was because of the challenge[ii]
from the guardians of the horse—
a provocation to all Kshatriyas—
this change came over me.

CHANDRA·KETU: *(smiling)* Are you also resentful of the grandeur of my father's[iii] power?

LAVA: Whether I am or not doesn't matter; let me just ask this: We have heard that Rághava is a reserved man; they say he's not arrogant himself nor is there any arrogance among his subjects. So why do his men give voice to words fit for a *rákshasa*?

ṛṣayo «rākṣasīm» āhur
  vācam unmatta|dṛptayoḥ.
«sā yoniḥ sarva|vairāṇāṃ.
  sā hi lokasya nirṛtiḥ,» [30]

5.95 iti ha sma tāṃ nindanti. ath' êtarām abhiṣṭuvanti.

kāmān dugdhe viprakarṣaty a|lakṣmīṃ
  kīrtiṃ sūte duṣkṛtaṃ yā hinasti
tāṃ c' âpy etāṃ mātaraṃ maṅgalānāṃ
  dhenuṃ dhīrāḥ sūnṛtāṃ vācam āhuḥ. [31]

SUMANTRAḤ: paripūta|sva|bhāvo 'yaṃ kumāraḥ Prācetas'|ânte|vāsī vadaty abhisampannam ārṣeṇa saṃskāreṇa.

LAVAḤ: yat punaś, Candraketo, vadasi, «kiṃ nu bhavatas tāta|pratāp'|ôtkarṣe 'py a|marṣaḥ?» iti, tat pṛcchāmi: kiṃ vyavasthita|viṣayāḥ kṣātra|dharmāḥ?

SUMANTRAḤ: n' âiva khalu jānāsi devam Aikṣvākam. tad virama, viram' âtiprasaṅgāt.

5.100 sainikānāṃ pramāthena
  satyam ojāyitaṃ tvayā.
Jāmadagnyasya damane
  na hi nirbandham arhasi. [32]

[i] The son of Jamadagni, Paraśurāma, a powerful Brahman warrior defeated by Rāma.

A "*rákshasa* word," the seers say, is one fit only for
the mad or arrogant.
"It is the source of all enmity, the very bane of the
world,"

is how people have condemned it. By contrast, they extol 5.95
its opposite:

A goodly word, the wise declare, is a veritable magic
cow:
It milks out anything one desires, dispels privation,
gives birth to fame, and expunges all bad karma.
It is the very mother of the richest of blessings.

SUMÁNTRA: How good-natured is this young student of Valmíki; what he says is infused with the very disposition of a seer.

LAVA: As for what you just said, Chandra·ketu—"Are you also resentful of the grandeur of my father's power?"—let me just ask: Are the *dharma*s of Kshatriyas limited in their application?*

SUMÁNTRA: You really have no idea of the Aikshváka lord. Please, no more of this obstinacy.

True enough, you've shown your strength in 5.100
decimating the soldiers
but it's better not to vie* with the conqueror of
Jamadágnya.[i]

LAVAḤ: *(sa|hāsam)* ārya, Jāmadagnyasya damanaḥ sa rāj" êti. ko 'yam uccair|vādaḥ?

siddhaṃ hy etad vāci vīryaṃ dvijānāṃ.
bāhvor vīryaṃ yat tu tat kṣatriyāṇām.
śastra|grāhī brāhmaṇo Jāmadagnyas.
tasmin dānte kā stutis tasya rājñaḥ? [33]

CANDRAKETUḤ: *(s'|ônmātham iva)* ārya, ārya, kṛtam uttar'|ôttareṇa.

ko 'py eṣa samprati navaḥ puruṣ'|âvatāro
vīro na yasya bhagavān Bhṛgu|nandano 'pi
paryāpta|sapta|bhuvan'|âbhaya|dakṣiṇāni
puṇyāni tāta|caritāni ca yo na veda. [34]

5.105 LAVAḤ: ko hi Raghu|pateś caritaṃ mahimānaṃ ca na jānāti? yadi nāma kiṃ cid vaktavyam asti... atha vā śāntam.

---

[i] An ancestor of Paraśurāma.

LAVA: *(with a laugh)* Sir, why broadcast the fact that the king conquered Jamadágnya?

> It's an established fact that the power of Brahmans lies in their speech
> while the power that Kshatriyas possess lies in their arms.
> Jamadágnya was a Brahman who took up the sword—
> what glory is conferred on a king for conquering a man like that?

CHANDRA·KETU: *(with some consternation)* Sir, enough of this repartee.

> This fellow must be some new avatar of the Primal Being*
> if even the son of Bhrigu[i] is no rival in his eyes,
> if he won't acknowledge how father Rama's holy acts
> could guarantee security for all the seven worlds.

LAVA: Who doesn't acknowledge Rama's acts and greatness? 5.105
On the other hand there is room for criticism... But enough.

Sunda|strī|damane 'py a|khaṇḍa|yaśaso
loke mahānto hi te.
yāni trīṇy a|kuto|mukhāny api padāny
āsan Khar'|āyodhane,
yad vā kauśalam Indra|sūnu|nidhane
tatr' âpy abhijño janaḥ. [35]

CANDRAKETUḤ: āḥ, tāt'|âpavāda|bhinna|maryāda, ati hi nāma pragalbhase.

LAVAḤ: aye, mayy eva bhru|kuṭī|dharaḥ saṃvṛttaḥ?

SUMANTRAḤ: sphuritam anayoḥ krodhena. tathā hi:

5.110 cūḍā|maṇḍala|bandhanaṃ taralayaty
ākūta|jo vepathuḥ.
kiṃ cit kokanada|cchadasya sadṛśe
netre svayaṃ rajyataḥ.
dhatte kāntim a|kāṇḍa|tāṇḍavitayor
bhaṅgena vaktraṃ bhruvoś
candrasy' ôtkaṭa|lāñchanasya kamalasy'
ôdbhrānta|bhṛṅgasya ca. [36]

KUMĀRAU: tad ito vimarda|kṣamāṃ bhūmim avatarāvaḥ!

niṣkrāntāḥ sarve.

iti mahā|kavi|śrī|Bhavabhūti|praṇīta
Uttara|Rāma|carita|nāṭake
Kumāra|vikramo nāma
pañcamo 'ṅkaḥ.

He's old, there's no need to second-guess his acts—
let them be, why bother rehashing* them now?
His reputation wasn't stained even by conquering
Sunda's wife—he's still great in the eyes of the world.
And as for those three backward steps he took*
in the battle he had with Khara, or the finesse
that he displayed in slaying the son of Indra...
why, people are fully aware of all these things.*

CHANDRA·KETU: No, now you're out of bounds in disparaging father Rama, your audacity has gone too far.

LAVA: What, are you making a face at me?

SUMÁNTRA: I can see their anger is flaring up, for

As they catch each other's drift they begin 5.110
to shake so much their topknots come undone,
and their eyes, by nature like the petals
of a pink lotus, naturally turn crimson,
and their brows that furrow while beginning
their sudden* wild dance lend their faces
the look of the dark mark on the full moon,
or wild black bees on a white lotus in bloom.

THE TWO YOUNG MEN: Let's go and find somewhere more suitable for battle!

Exeunt all.

End of Act V

PRELUDE TO ACT VI

tataḥ praviśati vimānen' ôjjvalaṃ VIDYĀ|DHARA/*mithunam.*

VIDYĀ|DHARAḤ: aho nu khalv anayor Vikartana|kula|kumārayor a|kāṇḍa|kalaha|pracaṇḍayor uddyotita|kṣātra|lakṣmīkāṇy adbhut'|ôdbhrānta|dev'|âsurāṇi vikrānta|caritāni. tathā hi, priye, paśya paśya:

jhaṇajjhaṇita|kaṅkaṇa|
kvaṇita|kiṅkiṇīkaṃ dhanur
dhvanad|guru|guṇ'|âṭanī
kṛta|karāla|kolāhalam
vitatya kiratoḥ śarān
a|virata|sphurac|cūḍayor
vicitram abhivardhate
bhuvana|bhīmam āyodhanam. [1]

vijṛmbhitaṃ ca divyasya
maṅgalāya dvayor api
stanayitnor iv' āmandraṃ
dundubher dundumāyitam. [2]

6.5 tat pravartyatām anayoḥ pravīrayor an|avaratam a|virala|lulita|vikaca|kanaka|kamala|kamanīya|saṃhatir amara|taru|taruṇa|maṇi|mukula|nikara|makaranda|sundaraḥ puṣpa|nipātaḥ.

VIDYĀ|DHARĪ: ⌜tā kiṃ ti uṇa a|aṇḍa|taṇḍavid'|uddaṇḍa|taralida|taḍic|chaṭā|kaḍāraṃ via ambaraṃ jhatti saṃvuttaṃ?⌟

i A class of demigods.

The scene opens on a VIDYA·DHARA[i] *couple in a flying chariot.*

VIDYA·DHARA: My, what acts of valor on the part of these two young men of the Solar dynasty, heatedly engaged in their unexpected combat. The beauty of Kshatriya power has been lent new luster, and the gods and anti-gods themselves are struck dumb* with wonder. Just take a look, my beloved:

They bend the bows that sound with ringing
golden bells and raise an awful
ruckus from their heavy strings
twanging at their tips, all the while
showering down arrows as their topknots
swing constantly and the battle
rages with dramatic intensity,
bringing terror to all the world.

And for the welfare of both the war drums
of heaven boom as deeply*as stormclouds.

So let an endless stream of flowers rain down on these two 6.5
proven heroes, laden with blooming golden lotuses and densely packed together, flowing with sap from the tender jewel-like* buds from the trees that belong to the deathless gods .

VIDYA·DHARA WOMAN: But why out of the blue has the sky turned so tawny with terrible flashes of lightning suddenly starting their *tándava* dance?

VIDYĀ|DHARAḤ: tat kiṃ nu khalv adya

Tvāṣṭra|yantra|bhrami|bhrānta|
  Mārtaṇḍa|jyotir ujjvalaḥ
puṭa|bhedo lalāṭa|stha|
  nīla|lohita|cakṣuṣaḥ? [3]

(vicintya) āṃ, jñātam. vatsena Candraketunā prayuktam astram Āgneyaṃ yasy' âyam agni|cchaṭā|sampātaḥ. samprati hi

6.10 avadagdha|karburita|ketu|cāmarair
  apayātam eva hi vimāna|maṇḍalaiḥ.
dadhati dhvaj'|âṃśuka|paṭ'|âñcaleṣv imāḥ
  kṣaṇa|kuṅkuma|cchuraṇa|vibhramaṃ śikhāḥ. [4]

āścaryam! pravṛtta ev' âyam uccaṇḍa|vajra|khaṇḍ'|âvasphoṭa|paṭu|raṭac|caṭula|sphuliṅga|nirgatir uttāla|tumula|lelihāna|jvālā|sambhāra|bhairavo bhagavān Uṣarbudhaḥ. pracaṇḍaś c' âsya sarvataḥ santāpaḥ. tat priyām aṅgen' ācchādya dūram apasarāmi. *(tathā karoti)*

VIDYĀ|DHARĪ: ⌜diṭṭhiā edeṇa vimala|muttā|phala|sīdala|siṇiddha|masiṇa|maṃsaleṇa ṇādha|deha|pphaṃseṇa āṇanda|manda|muulida|ghummanta|loaṇāe antarido jjevva me sandāvo.⌟

VIDYĀ|DHARAḤ: ayi, kim atra mayā kṛtam? atha vā

a|kiṃcid api kurvāṇaḥ
  saukhyair duḥkhāny apohati.
tat tasya kim api dravyaṃ
  yo hi yasya priyo janaḥ. [5]

---

[i] Rudra/Śiva [ii] The celestial craftsman, who reduced the brilliance of the sun to please his daughter, the wife of the Sun god.

VIDYA·DHARA: What indeed is happening now?

> Has the third eye of the black-red god[i] opened wide,
> to blaze like the light of the sun when twirling on Tvashtri's[ii] lathe?

(reflecting) Ah, I see. Young Chandra·ketu has launched the Fire weapon, its flames spreading far and wide. For now

> The other celestial chariots have all fled, 6.10
> their yak tail banners scorched and iridescent,
> while the flames upon our standard's pennants
> make them look for a moment as if dyed with saffron.

A miracle! The god of fire has appeared, emitting sparks that explode with the crash of lightning flashes—how awesomely its flames leap up, licking wildly. The heat it sends out everywhere is ferocious. I had better shield my beloved with my body and move to a safe distance. *(does so)*

VIDYA·DHARA WOMAN: How fortunate the heat has been blocked by the touch of my husband's body—so cool and smooth, like the purest pearls, so soft and full that my eyes roll back and close in bliss.*

VIDYA·DHARA: Come now, what have I done here? But then,

> The person need do nothing at all,
> the mere joy of being together
> dispels sorrow. What a gift it is,
> to have someone who loves you.

6.15 VIDYĀ|DHARĪ: ⌜kahaṃ a|virala|vilola|gholanta|vijjul|ladā|vilāsa|maṇḍidehiṃ matta|mora|kaṇṭha|sāmalehiṃ ottharīadi ṇaho|'ṅgaṇaṃ jala|harehiṃ?⌟

VIDYĀ|DHARAḤ: ayi kumāra|Lava|prayukta|Vāruṇ'|âstra|prabhāvaḥ khalv eṣaḥ. katham? a|virala|pravṛtta|vāri|dhārā|sahasra|sampātaiḥ praśāntam eva Pāvak'|âstram.

VIDYĀ|DHARĪ: ⌜piaṃ me, piaṃ me!⌟

VIDYĀ|DHARAḤ: hanta bhoḥ. sarvam atimātraṃ doṣāya, yat pralaya|vāt'|āvali|kṣobha|gambhīra|gulagulāyamāna|megha|medurit'|ândhakāra|nīrandhra|nibaddham eka|vāra|viśva|grasana|vikaca|vikarāla|Kāla|kaṇṭha|kandara|vivartamānam iva yug'|ânta|yoga|nidrā|niruddha|sarva|dvāra|Nārāyaṇ'|ôdara|niviṣṭam iva bhūta|jātaṃ pravepate. sādhu, vatsa Candraketo, sādhu! sthāne Vāyavy'|âstram īritam. yataḥ:

vidyā|kalpena marutā
  meghānāṃ bhūyasām api
brahmaṇ' îva vivartānāṃ
  kv' âpi vipralayaḥ kṛtaḥ. [6]

6.20 VIDYĀ|DHARĪ: ⌜ṇādha, ko dāṇiṃ eso sa|sambhaṃ|ukkhitta|kara|bbhamida|pot'|añcalo dūrado evva madhura|vaaṇa|paḍisiddha|juddha|vvāvāro edāṇaṃ kumārāṇaṃ antare vimāṇa|varaṃ odarāvedi?⌟

---

i Literally, Varuṇa weapon, named for the god of the ocean, from which clouds are said to arise. ii Viṣṇu.

VIDYA·DHARA WOMAN: Why has the sky suddenly darkened over with clouds, floating rolling masses adorned with darting lightning, and dark as the throat of a wild peacock? 6.15

VIDYA·DHARA: This must be an effect of the Water[i] weapon launched by the young Lava. What's this? The Fire weapon has been quenched by the thousands of massing clouds.

VIDYA·DHARA WOMAN: How I love it!

VIDYA·DHARA: But alas, all excess leads to trouble: now the world is shivering with cold, enveloped in a deep darkness thickened by clouds roaring with the sound of doomsday winds; as if it were floundering in the cave-like maw of Time, hideous and gaping wide to swallow the universe at a single gulp; as if entered into the belly of Naráyana,[ii] all his orifices closed in the yoga sleep that he sleeps at the end of a cosmic age. Bravo, young Chandra·ketu, bravo! Now is the right time to unleash the Wind weapon, as he must have done, since

The wind has dispelled the billowing clouds
as knowledge dispels illusions into *brahma.*

VIDYA·DHARA WOMAN: My husband, who is that landing his heavenly chariot in alarm between the two young men and waving the hem of his garment* in upraised hands, trying desperately to stop the fighting by addressing them gently from afar? 6.20

VIDYĀ|DHARAḤ: *(dṛṣṭvā)* eṣa Śambūka|vadhāt pratinivṛtto Raghu|patiḥ.

> śabdaṃ mahā|puruṣa|saṃvihitaṃ niśamya
> tad|gauravāt samupasaṃhṛta|samprahāraḥ
> śānto Lavaḥ, praṇata eva ca Candraketuḥ.
> kalyāṇam astu suta|saṅgamanena rājñaḥ. [7]

tad itas tāvat.

niṣkrāntau.

6.25 *viṣkambhakaḥ*

---

[i] Though a nephew Candraketu is regarded by Rāma as his son.

VIDYA·DHARA: *(looking)* This is the lord of the Raghus returning from slaying Shambúka.

Hearing the words the great man has spoken
they stop their fighting out of respect for him.
Lava falls silent, and Chandra·ketu bows low.
May good come from the king's meeting with his sons.[i]

Away then for now.

Exeunt both.

End of the Prelude 6.25

ACT VI
THE RECOGNITION OF THE YOUNG MEN

tataḥ praviśati RĀMO, LAVAḤ, *praṇataś* CANDRAKETUŚ *ca.*

RĀMAḤ: *(Puṣpakād avataran)*

dinakara|kula|candra Candraketo
sa|rabhasam ehi, dṛḍhaṃ pariṣvajasva.
tuhina|śakala|śītalais tav' âṅgaiḥ
śamam upayātu mam' âpi citta|dāhaḥ. [8]

(utthāpya, sa|sneh'|âsraṃ pariṣvajya) api nāma kuśalaṃ tava divy'|âstra|dhara|dehasya?

6.30 CANDRAKETUḤ: kuśalam atyadbhuta | kriyasya priya | darśanasya Lavasya lābh' | âbhyudayena. tad vijñāpayāmi: mām iva viśeṣeṇa vā mattaḥ śivena cakṣuṣā paśyatv amuṃ mahā|vīra|prakāṇḍaṃ tātaḥ.

RĀMAḤ: (LAVAṂ *nirūpya)* diṣṭy" âtigambhīra | kalyāṇ' | ākṛtir ayaṃ vayasyo vatsasya.

trātuṃ lokān iva pariṇataḥ
kāyavān astra|vedaḥ,
kṣātro dharmaḥ śrita iva tanuṃ
Brahma|kośasya guptyai,
sāmarthyānām iva samudayaḥ
sañcayo vā guṇānām,
āvirbhūya sthita iva jagat|
puṇya|nirmāṇa|rāśiḥ. [9]

---

[i] The name means literally "He whose flag bears the moon."

The scene opens on RAMA, LAVA, *and the bowing* CHANDRA·KETU.

RAMA: *(climbing down from Púshpaka)*

> Moon of the Solar dynasty, Chandra·ketu,[i]
> come to me straightway and hug me tight.
> Your limbs are cool as chips of ice and able
> to soothe the burning even in a heart like mine.*

(having him rise, and embracing him with tears of affection) All is well with you, I trust, and the divine weapons your body bears?

CHANDRA·KETU: All is well because of the good fortune of 6.30
meeting Lava, this handsome youngster of wondrous deeds. I would ask Father to look with a kindly eye upon this preeminent great hero, just as he would look upon me, or even more so.

RAMA: *(looking at* LAVA*)* How fortunate my child has acquired a new friend. He has an air about him at once inscrutable and benign.

> As if the science of weapons were transmuted
> into bodily form to save the worlds,
> as if Kshatriya *dharma* were embodied
> to guard the treasure house of Brahma,*
> as if capabilities were in full flower,
> all virtues conglomerated,
> all the world's good karma aggregated
> and present, fully manifest.

LAVAḤ: *(sva|gatam)* aho, puṇy'|ânubhāva|darśano 'yaṃ ma-hā|puruṣaḥ.

āśvāsa|sneha|bhaktīnām
ekam ālambanaṃ mahat,
prakṛṣṭasy' êva dharmasya
prasādo mūrti|sañcaraḥ. [10]

6.35 āścaryam:

virodho viśrāntaḥ,
prasarati raso nirvṛti|ghanas,
tad auddhatyaṃ kv' âpi
vrajati, vinayaḥ prahvayati mām,
jhaṭity asmin dṛṣṭe.
kim iti paravān asmi? yadi|vā
mah"|ārghas tīrthānām
iva hi mahatāṃ ko 'py atiśayaḥ. [11]

RĀMAḤ: tat kim ayam eka|pada eva duḥkha|viśrāmaṃ dadāty, upasnehayati ca kuto 'pi nimittād antar|ātmānam? atha vā snehaś ca nimitta|sa|vyapekṣaś c' êti vipratiṣiddham etat.

vyatiṣajati pad'|ârthān āntaraḥ ko 'pi hetur.
na khalu bahir|upādhīn prītayaḥ saṃśrayante.
vikasati hi pataṅgasy' ôdaye puṇḍarīkaṃ,
dravati ca hima|raśmāv udgate candra|kāntaḥ. [12]

LAVA: *(aside)* Ah, what a great man, pure majesty in appearance.*

> The one great resting place of trust, affection, and devotion,
> the graciousness of ultimate *dharma* in physical form.

It's miraculous: 6.35

> Enmity has ceased, and *rasa* rich with joy flows forth;
> my brashness is somehow gone, deference overwhelms me;
> at the mere sight of him I'm under his power—why so? But then,
> like holy places the great have some greatly precious potency.

RAMA:* How is it he all of a sudden affords me respite from sorrow, and for some reason excites affection in my innermost soul? Then again, to say that affection needs a reason is a contradiction in terms.

> There is some inner cause that accounts for mutual attraction;
> feelings of love do not in the least depend on external factors.
> Why should the white lotus open when the sun comes up
> or the moonstone start to ooze with the rising of the moon?*

LAVAḤ: Candraketo, ka ete?

6.40 CANDRAKETUḤ: priya|vayasya, nanu tāta|pādāḥ.

LAVAḤ: mam' âpi tarhi dharmatas tath" âiva, yataḥ «priya| vayasy'» êty āttha. kin tu catvāraḥ kila bhavatām evaṃ| vyapadeśa|bhāginas tatra|bhavanto Rāmāyaṇa|kathā| puruṣāḥ. tad viśeṣaṃ brūhi.

CANDRAKETUḤ: nanu jyeṣṭha|tāta|pādā ity avehi.

LAVAḤ: *(s'|ôllāsam)* kathaṃ, Raghu|nātha eva? diṣṭyā su|prabhātam adya yad ayaṃ devo dṛṣṭaḥ. *(sa|vinaya|kautukaṃ nirvarṇya)* tāta, Prācetas'|ânte|vāsī Lavo 'bhivādayate.

RĀMAḤ: āyuṣmann, ehy ehi. *(sa|sneham āśliṣya)* ayi vatsa, kṛtaṃ, kṛtam ativinayena. an|eka|vāram a|pariślathaṃ māṃ pariṣvajasva.

6.45 pariṇata|kaṭhora|puṣkara|
garbha|cchada|pīna|masṛṇa|sukumāraḥ
nandayati candra|candana|
niṣyanda|jaḍas tava sparśaḥ. [13]

LAVAḤ: *(sva|gatam)* idṛśo māṃ praty amīṣām a|kāraṇa|snehaḥ. mayā punar ebhya ev' âbhidugdham a|jñena yad āyudha|parigrahaṃ yāvad adhyārūḍho dur|yogaḥ. *(prakāśam)* mṛṣyantv idānīṃ Lavasya bāliśatāṃ tāta|pādāḥ.

LAVA: Chandra·ketu, who is this?

CHANDRA·KETU: Why, my dear friend, it's my honored father. 6.40

LAVA: Then by rights he's mine too since you've called me your dear friend. But there are four men in the 'Ramáyana' that you refer to by this designation. Tell me which is he.

CHANDRA·KETU: Why, this is my eldest father.

LAVA: *(joyfully)* You mean this is the lord of the Raghus? What good fortune the day dawned to bring me the sight of the lord. *(gazing with courtesy and curiosity)* Father, Lava, a student of the son of Prachétas, greets you.

RAMA: My child (long may you live), do come to me. *(embracing him affectionately)* Ah, enough, enough of this formality. Come hug me tightly again and again.

> Your touch is soft and smooth yet firm 6.45
> like the inner leaves of a hard ripe lotus,
> and has a coolness that refreshes
> like extract of sandalwood or moonbeams.*

LAVA: *(aside)* That such should be his unprompted affection for me and that I should have ignorantly done him such wrong, him of all people, to the point of taking up weapons and mounting an attack.* *(aloud)* May my respected father please forgive Lava's childishness today.

RĀMAḤ: kim aparāddhaṃ vatsena?

CANDRAKETUḤ: aśv'|ānuyātrikebhyas tāta|pratāp'|āviṣkaraṇam upaśrutya vīrāyitam anena.

RĀMAḤ: nanv ayam alaṅkāraḥ kṣatrasya.

6.50 na tejas tejasvī prasṛtam apareṣāṃ hi sahate.
sa tasya svo bhāvaḥ prakṛti|niyatatvād a|kṛtakaḥ.
mayūkhair a|śrāntaṃ tapati yadi devo dina|karaḥ,
kim āgneyo grāvā nikṛta iva tejāṃsi vamati? [14]

CANDRAKETUḤ: a|marṣo 'py asy' âiva śobhate vīrasya. paśyatu hi tātaḥ priya|vayasya|vinirmukta|Jṛmbhak'|âstra|niṣkampa|stambhitāni sarva|sainyāni.

RĀMAḤ: *(vilokya)* vatsa Lava, saṃhriyatām astram. tvam api, Candraketo, nirvyāpāra|vilakṣitāni sāntvaya balāni.

LAVAḤ *praṇidhānaṃ nāṭayati.*

CANDRAKETUḤ: yath" ādiṣṭam. *(niṣkrāntaḥ)*

6.55 LAVAḤ: praśāntam astram.

RĀMAḤ: vatsa, sa|rahasya|prayoga|saṃharaṇāny astrāṇy āmnāyavanti.

RAMA: What has my child done wrong?

CHANDRA·KETU: He wanted to play the hero when he overheard talk of father's display of power from those accompanying the horse.

RAMA: But surely that ornaments a Kshatriya.

> A mighty man cannot bear it when others show their might— 6.50
> that is his true temper, fixed by nature and not contrived.
> If the god that makes the day heats the sunstone tirelessly
> with its beams, will it not spit out fire as if insulted?

CHANDRA·KETU: Even his indignation is remarkable. Father should see how this hero, my dear friend, unleashed the Jrímbhaka weapons and completely paralyzed the soldiers.

RAMA: *(looking)* Lava, my child, withdraw the weapon. And you, too, Chandra·ketu, go and calm the soldiers who have been incapacitated and humbled.

LAVA *mimes meditating.*

CHANDRA·KETU: As ordered. *(exit)*

LAVA: The weapon has been stilled. 6.55

RAMA: My child, the discharge and withdrawal of these weapons along with their secret invocations are imparted by tradition:

Brahm'|ādayo brahma|hitāya taptvā
paraḥ|sahasrāḥ śaradas tapāṃsi
etāny apaśyan guravaḥ purāṇāḥ
svāny eva tejāṃsi tapomayāni. [15]

ath' âitan|mantra|pārāyaṇ'|ôpaniṣadaṃ bhagavān Kṛśāśvaḥ paraḥ|sahasra|parivatsar'|ântevāsine Kauśikāya Viśvāmitrāya provāca, sa tu bhagavān mahyam. ity eṣa pūrv'|ânukramaḥ. kumārasya tu kutaḥ sampradāya? iti pṛcchāmi.

LAVAḤ: svataḥ|prakāśāny āvayor astrāṇi.

6.60 RĀMAḤ: *(vicintya)* kiṃ na sambhāvyate? prakṛṣṭa|puṇya|paripāk'|ôpādānaḥ ko 'pi mahimā syāt. dvi|vacanaṃ tu katham?

LAVAḤ: Bhrātarāv āvāṃ yama|jau.

RĀMAḤ: sa tarhi dvitīyaḥ kva?

NEPATHYE: Bhāṇḍāyana, Bhāṇḍāyana!

Brahma and the other gods, for the good of the Vedic way of life,
undertook ascetic acts for a thousand years and more,
and what those ancient gurus then were able to behold
were these very weapons, their own ascetic energies.

Thereupon Krisháshva imparted the esoteric doctrine of their mantras in its totality to a student who had lived with him for a thousand years and more, Vishva·mitra, descendent of Kusha. And that blessed one imparted it to me. Such was the earlier succession. How, may I ask, did the tradition reach the young sir?

LAVA: The weapons revealed themselves of their own accord to the two of us.

RAMA: *(reflecting)* Why shouldn't it be possible? There might be some such capacity resulting from the ripening of exceptionally good karma in the past... But why do you use the dual? 6.60

LAVA: We are two brothers, twins.

RAMA: Where then is the other one?

OFFSTAGE: Bhandáyana, Bhandáyana!

āyuṣmataḥ kila Lavasya nar'|êndra|sainyair
  āyodhanaṃ nanu kim āttha, sakhe, tath" êti?
ady' âstam etu bhuvaneṣv adhirāja|śabdaḥ.
  kṣatrasya śastra|śikhinaḥ śamam adya yāntu. [16]

RĀMAḤ:

6.65 atha ko 'yam indra|maṇi|mecaka|cchavir
  dhvanin" âiva datta|pulakaṃ karoti mām
nava|nīla|nīradhara|dhīra|garjita|
  kṣaṇa|baddha|kuḍmala|kadamba|ḍambaram? [17]

LAVAḤ: ayam asau mama jyāyān āryaḥ Kuśo nāma Bharat'|āśramāt pratinivṛttaḥ.

RĀMAḤ: *(sa|kautukam)* vatsa, ita āhvay' âinam āyuṣmantam.

LAVAḤ: evam.

parikrāmati.

6.70 *tataḥ praviśati* KUŚAḤ.

KUŚAḤ: *(sa|krodh'|ākūta|harṣa|dhairyaṃ dhanur āsphālayan)*

---

[i] The author of the 'Sutras on the Triad of Music,' to whom Kuśa had delivered Vālmīki's play.

My dear friend, are you telling me
that soldiers of the king have launched
so vicious an attack as that*
against Lava (long may he live)?
Why, then the sun-like title
"king" will set across the worlds
and the fire of Kshatriya weapons
is soon to be extinguished.

RAMA:

Now who is this, his complexion dark as sapphire,
his voice making goosebumps rise on my skin
the way a *kadámba* buds the very moment
a new black stormcloud starts its low rumble?

LAVA: That is my elder brother Kusha returning from Bharata's[i] ashram.

RAMA: *(with curiosity)* My child, call your brother (long may he live).

LAVA: I will.

He walks about.

Enter KUSHA.

KUSHA: *(twanging his bow with anger, curiosity, eagerness, and firmness)*

datt'|Êndr'|âbhaya|dakṣiṇair bhagavato
Vaivasvatād ā Manor
dṛptānāṃ dahanāya dīpita|nija|
kṣatra|pratāp'|âgnibhiḥ
Ādityair yadi vigraho nṛpatibhir,
dhanyaṃ mam' âitat tato
dīpt'|âstra|sphurad|ugra|dīdhiti|śikhā|
nīrājita|jyaṃ dhanuḥ. [18]

vikaṭaṃ parikrāmati.

RĀMAḤ: ko 'py asmin kṣatriya|potake pauruṣ'|âtirekaḥ.

6.75 dṛṣṭis tṛṇī|kṛta|jagat|traya|sattva|sārā.
dhīr'|ôddhatā namayat' îva gatir dharitrīm.
kaumārake 'pi girivad gurutāṃ dadhāno
vīro rasaḥ kim ayam aity uta darpa eva? [19]

LAVAḤ: *(upasṛtya)* jayatv āryaḥ.

KUŚAḤ: nanv āyuṣman, kim iyaṃ vārtā, «yuddhaṃ, yuddham» iti?

LAVAḤ: yat kiñ cid etat. āryo 'smin dṛpta|bhāvam utsṛjya vinayena vartatām.

KUŚAḤ: kim|artham?

---

[i] The sun.

From the days of Manu son of Vivásvan[i]
they have granted the gift of security
to Indra himself, and stoked the blazing fires
of their Kshatriya power to burn the proud.
Should I now be given the chance to fight
with a king of this Solar dynasty,
then how blessed my bow, its string lustrated
in the dread flames of my gleaming magic weapons.

He walks about with long strides.

RAMA: What remarkable manliness in this Kshatriya boy.

His glance shows he doesn't care a straw 6.75
for any creature in the universe;
he moves with impetuosity
and causes earth itself to bow.
Although still in his youth he bears
a weightiness like a mountain's.
Is this the heroic *rasa* approaching
or is it Pride incarnate?

LAVA: *(approaching)* Victory to my elder brother.

KUSHA: What is this report, my brother (long may you live), about a battle?

LAVA: It was nothing. Brother, swallow your pride before this man, and act politely.

KUSHA: What for?

6.80 LAVAḤ: atra devo Raghu|patis tiṣṭhati. sa ca snihyaty āvayoḥ. utkaṇṭhate ca yuṣmat|sannikarṣasya.

KUŚAḤ: *(sa|tarkam)* sa Rāmāyaṇa|kathā|nāyako Brahma|kośasya gopāyitā?

LAVAḤ: atha kim?

KUŚAḤ: āśaṃsanīya|puṇya|darśanaḥ sa mah"|ātmā. kin tu katham asmābhir upagantavya, iti na sampradhārayāmi.

LAVAḤ: yath" âiva gurus tath" ôpasadanena.

6.85 KUŚAḤ: ayi, kathaṃ nām' âitat?

LAVAḤ: atyudāttaś Candraketur Aurmileyaḥ «priya|vayasy'» êti sakhyena mām upatiṣṭhate. tena tat|sambandhena dharma|tāta ev' âyaṃ rāja'|rṣiḥ.

KUŚAḤ: sampraty a|vacanīyo rājanye 'pi praśrayaḥ.

ubhau parikrāmataḥ.

LAVAḤ: paśyatv enam ākār'|ânubhāva|gāmbhīrya|sambhāvyamāna|vividha|lok'|ôttara|carit'|âtiśayam āryo mahā|puruṣam.

6.90 KUŚAḤ: *(nirvarṇya)*

[i] I.e., a Kshatriya. For one Kshatriya to bow before another was to acknowledge his superiority.

LAVA: The man standing there is Lord Raghu·pati. He has 6.80
affection for the two of us, and is keen to have you in his presence.

KUSHA: *(reasoning)* Isn't he the hero of the 'Ramáyana' story and guardian of the treasure house of Brahma?

LAVA: Yes of course.

KUSHA: He is a great man, and the sight of him is pure and devoutly to be wished for. But I can't imagine how I am supposed to approach him.

LAVA: The way one draws near to a parent.

KUSHA: And why in the world should that be the case? 6.85

LAVA: Chandra·ketu, son of Úrmila and a very high-minded fellow, treats me as a friend, calling me his dear companion. Because of this kinship with him the royal seer here has become a father by *dharma* to us.

KUSHA: Then no blame will attach to our bowing before him, royalty[i] though he be.

Both walk about.

LAVA: Behold the great man, brother. His supernatural deeds in all their grandeur can be read from the majesty and profundity of his bearing.

KUSHA: *(gazing)* 6.90

aho prāsādikaṃ rūpam
anubhāvaś ca pāvanaḥ.
sthāne Rāmāyaṇa|kavir
devīṃ vācaṃ vyavīvṛtat. [20]

(upasṛtya) tāta, Prācetas'|ânte|vāsī Kuśo 'bhivādayate.

RĀMAḤ: ehy ehy, āyuṣman.

amṛt'|ādhmāta|jīmūta|
snigdha|saṃhananasya te
pariṣvaṅgāya vātsalyād
ayam utkaṇṭhate janaḥ. [21]

6.95 *(pariṣvajya, sva|gatam)* tat kim ity ayaṃ dārakaḥ

aṅgād aṅgāt sruta iva nijaḥ sneha|jo deha|sāraḥ
prādur|bhūya sthita iva bahiś cetanā|dhātur ekaḥ
sāndr'|ānanda|kṣubhita|hṛdaya|prasraveṇ' êva sikto
gātr'|āśleṣe yad amṛta|rasa|srotasā siñcat' îva? [22]

LAVAḤ: tāta, lalāṭaṃ|tapo gharma|dīdhitiḥ. tad atra sāla|pracchāye muhūrtam āsana|parigrahaṃ karotu tātaḥ.

RĀMAḤ: yad abhirucitaṃ vatsāya.

parikramya yath"|ôcitam upaviśanti.

Ah, his physical form breathes serenity,
his majesty is purifying.
How fitting the 'Ramáyana' poet
should have transfigured the goddess Language .

(approaching) Father, Kusha, a student of the son of Prachétas, greets you.

RAMA: Come to me, do come—long may you live.

Your body is soft as a cloud swollen with ambrosial water,
and this person longs to hug you with fatherly affection.

(embracing; aside) But why should it be that this boy*— 6.95

As if my body's very essence, poured out
limb for limb because of my affection;
as if my consciousness, prime element,
were standing there, manifest outside me—
should be drenched by the flow from my own heart
shaken by these deep feelings of bliss, and then
drench me in return when I embrace his limbs
with a true flood of nectar-like *rasa*?

LAVA: Father, the sunshine is burning my forehead. Can father pause to sit for a moment in the shade of the *sal* tree here?

RAMA: Whatever my child wishes.

Walking around all sit in the proper order.

6.100 RĀMAḤ: *(sva|gatam)*

aho praśraya|yoge 'pi
gati|sthity|āsan'|ādayaḥ
sāmrājya|śaṃsino bhāvāḥ
Kuśasya ca Lavasya ca. [23]

vapur|a|viyuta|siddhā eva lakṣmī|vilāsāḥ
pratikala|kamanīyāṃ kāntim udbhedayanti,
a|malinam iva candraṃraśmayaḥ sve yathā vā,
vikasitam aravindaṃ bindavo mākarandāḥ. [24]

Bhūyiṣṭhaṃ ca Raghu|kula|kaumārakam anayoḥ paśyāmi.

kaṭhora|pārāvata|kaṇṭha|mecakaṃ
vapur vṛṣa|skandha|subandhur'|âṃsayoḥ,
prasanna|siṃha|stimitaṃ ca vīkṣitaṃ,
dhvaniś ca māṅgalya|mṛdaṅga|māṃsalaḥ. [25]

6.105 *(sūkṣmaṃ nirūpya)* aye, na kevalam asmad|vaṃśa|saṃvādiny ākṛtiḥ,

api Janaka|sutāyās tac ca tac c' ânurūpaṃ
sphuṭam iha śiśu|yugme naipuṇ'|ônneyam asti.
nanu punar iva tan me gocarī|bhūtam akṣnor
abhinava|śata|patra|śrīmad|āsyaṃ priyāyāḥ. [26]

śukl'|âccha|danta|cchavi|sundar" êyaṃ,
s" âiv' oṣṭha|mudrā, sa ca karṇa|pāśaḥ.
netre punar yady api rakta|nīle,
tath" âpi saubhāgya|guṇaḥ sa eva. [27]

[i] The corners are red, the pupils black (said to be a sign of virility).

RAMA: *(aside)* 6.100

Ah, the way they walk and stand
and sit, though deferential,
hints that Kusha and Lava both
are emperors to be.

A royal grace inherent in their bodies
enhances a beauty charming in every part,
just as its rays enhance the spotless moon
or its drops of sap the full blown lotus.*

And there are yet further signs I see that these two are young men of Raghu's family.

Bodies blue-black as the neck of a full-grown* dove,
shoulders tapered like the shoulders of a bull,*
glances steady like a lion's at ease,
voices deep and rich as festival drums.

(looking closely) Why, it's not only my family they take after 6.105
in their looks,

But in each and every feature the two boys clearly resemble
Jánaka's daughter—one can infer it on close inspection.
It is really as if once more the face of my beloved
has come back into view, beautiful as the freshest lotus.

The very same mouth* made lovely by the gleam
of flawless white teeth; the same charming* ears;
and although their eyes are red and black[i]
they have the same trait of comeliness.

(vicintya) tad etat Prācetas'|âdhyuṣitam araṇyaṃ yatra kila devī parityaktā. iyaṃ c' ânayor ākṛtir vayo 'nubhāvaś ca. yad api svataḥ|prakāśāny astrāṇ' îti tatra vimṛśāmi. api khalu tac citra|darśana|prāsaṅgikam astr'|âbhyanujñānam udbhūtaṃ syāt? na hy a|sāmpradāyikāny astrāṇi pūrveṣām apy anuśuśruma. ayaṃ ca samplavamānam ātmānaṃ sukha|duḥkh'|âtiśayo hṛdayasya me visrambhayate. bhūyiṣṭhaṃ ca mayā dvidhā pratipanno devyā garbhiṇī|bhāva āsīt. *(s'|âsram)*

purā rūḍhe snehe
paricaya|vikāsād upacite
raho visrabdhāyā
api sahaja|lajjā|jaḍa|dṛśaḥ
may" âiv' ādau jñātaḥ
kara|tala|parāmarśa|kalayā
dvidhā garbha|granthis
tad anu divasaiḥ kair api tayā. [28]

6.110 *(ruditvā)* tat kim etau pṛcchāmi ken' âpy upāyena?

LAVAḤ: tāta, kim etat?

bāṣpa|varṣeṇa nītaṃ vo
jagan|maṅgalam ānanam
avaśyāy'|âvasiktasya
puṇḍarīkasya cārutām. [29]

(reflecting) This is the very wilderness, inhabited by the son of Prachétas, where I'm told the queen was abandoned. Then there's their looks, their age, their majesty. I am also struck by the fact that the magic weapons revealed themselves of their own accord: Is it possible the charge laid on the weapons on the occasion of viewing the paintings has taken effect?* For we have heard that even the ancients had no access to the weapons without the traditional transmission. Then there is this boundless joy and sorrow, both at once, in my heart that convinces my wavering soul. And most of all I understood the queen was pregnant with twins. *(tearfully)*

When long ago our affection began to grow
and strengthen as familiarity blossomed
and she became more confident in private,
though her look was constrained by natural
  bashfulness,
I was the one who first came to discover,
by the technique of feeling with my palm,
that the knot of the embryo was double—
and she herself only some days later.

(weeping) Shall I find some way to ask them? 6.110

LAVA: Father, what is it?

This rain of tears has made your face—
the source of blessings to the world—
take on the look of a waterlily
sprinkled by the morning dew.

KUŚAḤ: ayi vatsa,

vinā Sītā|devyā
kim iva hi na duḥkhaṃ Raghu|pateḥ?
priyā|nāśe kṛtsnaṃ
kila jagad araṇyaṃ hi bhavati.
sa ca snehas tāvān
ayam api viyogo niravadhiḥ…
kim ity evaṃ pṛcchasy
an|adhigata|Rāmāyaṇa iva? [30]

6.115 RĀMAḤ: *(sva|gatam)* aye, taṭa|sthita ālāpaḥ. kṛtaṃ praśnena. dagdha|hṛdaya, ko 'yam ākasmikas te pāriplavo vikāraḥ? evaṃ nirbhinna|hṛday'|āvegaḥ śiśu|janen' âpy anukampito 'smi. bhavatu, tāvad antarayāmi. *(prakāśam)* vatsau, Rāmāyaṇam iti śrūyate bhagavato Vālmīkeḥ Sarasvatī| niṣyandaḥ, praśastir Āditya|vaṃśasya. tatra kautūhalena yat kiñ cic chrotum icchāmi.

KUŚAḤ: sa kṛtsna eva sandarbho 'smābhir āvṛttaḥ. smṛty| upasthitau tāvad imau Bāla|caritasy' ântye 'dhyāye ślokau.

RĀMAḤ: udīrayatu vatsaḥ.

KUŚAḤ:

prakṛty" âiva priyā Sītā
Rāmasy' āsīn mah"|ātmanaḥ.
priya|bhāvaḥ sa tu tayā
sva|guṇair abhivardhitaḥ. [31]

KUSHA: Why, you child,

> Without Queen Sita what is not
> a source of sorrow to the Raghus' lord?
> When one's beloved is gone they say
> the whole world becomes a wilderness.
> Such was their affection,
> and this separation of theirs endless…
> how can you ask such a question
> as if ignorant of the 'Ramáyana'?

RAMA: *(aside)* Alas, this way of talking shows they're just by- 6.115
standers. I won't ask them then. Foolish heart, why this sudden, mad transformation of yours? That I should let the shock to my heart show in such a way that even children must feel compassion to me. Well, I had better just change the subject. *(aloud)* Children, one has heard tell of a 'Ramáyana,' a pure effusion* of Sarásvati, Goddess of language, by way of the blessed Valmíki, and a eulogy to the Solar dynasty. I am very curious to hear some of it.

KUSHA: We have gone over the composition in its entirety. Offhand there are two verses from the last chapter* of the "Boyhood" section that immediately come to mind.

RAMA: Recite them, my child.

KUSHA:

> Sita was naturally beloved of the great Rama
> but she made that love increase by all her virtues.

tath" âiva Rāmaḥ Sītāyāḥ
prāṇebhyo 'pi priyo 'bhavat.
hṛdayaṃ tv eva jānāti
prīti|yogaṃ parasparam. [32]

6.120 RĀMAḤ: kaṣṭam! atidāruṇo hṛdaya|marm'|ôdghātaḥ. hā devi, evaṃ kila tad āsīt. aho niranvaya|viparyāsa|virasa|vṛttayo vipralambha|paryavasāyinas tāpayanti saṃsāra|vṛttāntāḥ.

kva tāvān ānando
niratiśaya|visrambha|bahulaḥ?
kva te 'nyonyaṃ yatnāḥ?
kva ca nu gahanāḥ kautuka|rasāḥ?
sukhe vā duḥkhe vā
kva nu khalu tad aikyaṃ hṛdayayos?
tath" âpy eṣa prāṇaḥ
sphurati na tu pāpo viramati. [33]

bhoḥ kaṣṭam!

priyā|guṇa|sahasrāṇām
ek'|ônmīlana|peśalaḥ
ya eva duḥsmaraḥ kālas,
tam eva smāritā vayam. [34]

---

[i] Sītā's youth (indicated by verses 31–32 on their marriage).

In the same way Rama was more beloved of Sita
than life itself.
Their hearts knew full well the extent of their
mutual affection.

RAMA: How awful! Another savage blow to my heart's soft 6.120
core. Oh my queen, this is how it really was. Alas for the affairs of life, their incoherent, upside-down events, that lack all *rasa*, that end in frustrated love, that bring only burning pain.*

Where again will I ever find such bliss
and the perfect trust that enhanced it,
such concern on each other's behalf,
such deep-flowing *rasas* of wonder,
such unanimity of two hearts
in sorrow no less than joy?
And yet this evil life breath of mine
lingers and won't depart.

Ah, how truly awful!

They have reminded me of the single most
painful time to remember,
the one where, all at once, my beloved's
countless virtues were on display:[i]

yadā kiṃ cit kiṃ cit
kṛta|padam ahobhiḥ katipayais
tad īṣad vistāri
stana|mukulam āsīn mṛga|dṛśaḥ;
vayaḥ|sneh'|ākūta|
vyatikara|ghano yatra madanaḥ
pragalbha|vyāpāraḥ
sphurati hṛdi mugdhaś ca vapuṣi. [35]

6.125 LAVAḤ: ayaṃ tu Citrakūṭa|Mandākinī|vana|vihāre Sītā|devīm uddiśya Raghu|pateḥ ślokaḥ.

tvad|artham iva vinyastaḥ
śilā|paṭṭo 'yam agrataḥ,
yasy' âyam abhitaḥ puṣpaiḥ
pravṛṣṭa iva kesaraḥ. [36]

RĀMAḤ: *(sa/lajjā/smita/sneha/karuṇam)* ati nāma mugdhaḥ śiśu|janaḥ, viśeṣatas tv araṇya|caraḥ. hā devi, smarasi vā tasya tat|samaya|visrambh'|âtiprasaṅgasya? bhoḥ kaṣṭam!

śram'|âmbu|śiśirī|bhavat
prasṛta|manda|Mandākinī|
marut|taralit'|âlak'|ā-
kula|lalāṭa|candra|dyuti
a|kuṅkuma|kalaṅkit'|ô-
jjvala|kapolam utprekṣyate
nirābharaṇa|sundara|
śravaṇa|pāśa|saumyaṃ mukham. [37]

---

[i] Typically worn on the forehead by married women.

When the bud-like breasts of the girl had just begun
to sprout
and within a very few days had developed a little
more;
when passion, deepened by youth, love, curiosity
all combined,
was bold in action within her heart but shy upon
her body.

LAVA: Well, here then is a verse addressed by the Raghus' lord to Sita once when they were relaxing in the Mandákini woods by Mount Chitra·kuta: 6.125

It's almost as if the rock ledge ahead
were set in place for you alone,
and the *késara* tree rained down
flowers all around it.

RAMA: *(with an embarrassed smile, affection, and pity)** How incredibly innocent children can be, especially when growing up in the wilderness. Oh my queen, do you remember our intimate conversations* on that occasion? How truly awful it is!

In my mind's eye I see your face,
the forehead lustrous as the moon
with hair blowing in the Mandákini's
slow breeze, cooled by beads of sweat,
unmarked by a saffron mark,[i] with blooming
cheeks, and the most charming ears
all the more lovely without earrings.

(stambhita iva sthitvā, sa|karuṇam) aho nu khalu bhoḥ!

6.130 ciraṃ dhyātvā dhyātvā
nihita iva nirmāya purataḥ
pravāse 'py āśvāsaṃ
na khalu na karoti priya|janaḥ.
jagaj jīrṇ'|âraṇyaṃ
bhavati hi vikalpa|vyuparame
kukūlānāṃ rāśau
tad anu hṛdayaṃ pacyata iva. [38]

NEPATHYE:

Vasiṣṭho, Vālmīkir,
Daśaratha|mahiṣyo, 'tha Janakaḥ,
sah' âiv' Ârundhatyā
śiśu|kalaham ākarṇya sa|bhayāḥ
jarā|grastair aṅgair
atha khalu vidūr'|āśramatayā
cireṇ' āgacchanti
tvarita|manaso 'pi śrama|jaḍāḥ. [39]

RĀMAḤ: kathaṃ, bhagavantāv Arundhatī|Vasiṣṭhāv, ambā, Janakaś c' âtr' âiva? kaṣṭam, kathaṃ khalv ete draṣṭavyāḥ? *(sa|karuṇaṃ vilokya)* Ahaha, tāta|Janako 'py atr' âiv' āyāta iti vajreṇ' êva tāḍito 'smi manda|bhāgyaḥ.

(standing as if paralyzed; with pity) Oh dear god!

The people we love even when parted 6.130
never fail to bring some consolation
since we think so long and hard of them
we create them right before our eyes.
But when this option* too is removed
the world is a desolate wilderness
and the heart then feels as if it's baking
on a slow burning fire of chaff.

OFFSTAGE:

Vasíshtha, Valmíki, the queens of Dasha·ratha,
and Jánaka
along with Arúndhati, frightened to hear the
  children were fighting
are coming at last. Their legs are gripped by old age,
  and the ashram is far,
but if their bodies are slowed by exhaustion, their
  minds are racing ahead.

RAMA: What, are Arúndhati, Vasíshtha, my mothers, and Jánaka here? It's too awful for me to think of setting eyes on them. *(glancing with pity)* Oh no, father Jánaka himself is headed right this way—a bolt of lightning, it seems, to strike me, cursed as I am.

sambandha|spṛhaṇīyatā|pramuditair
juṣṭe Vasiṣṭh'|ādibhir
dṛṣṭv" âpatya|vivāha|maṅgala|mahe
tat tātayoḥ saṅgatam
paśyann īdṛśam īdṛśe pitṛ|sakhaṃ
vṛtte mahā|vaiśase
dīrye kiṃ na sahasradh" âham? atha vā
Rāmeṇa kiṃ duṣkaram? [40]

NEPATHYE: kaṣṭam,

6.135 anubhāva|mātra|samavasthita|śriyaṃ
sahas" âiva vīkṣya Raghu|nātham īdṛśam
prathama|pramūḍha|Janaka|prabodhanād
vidhurāḥ pramoham upayānti mātaraḥ. [41]

RĀMAḤ: hā tāta, hā mātaraḥ,

Janakānāṃ Raghūṇāṃ ca
yat kṛtsnaṃ gotra|maṅgalam,
tasyāṃ a|karuṇe pāpe
vṛthā vaḥ karuṇā mayi. [42]

yāvat sambhāvayāmi. *(uttiṣṭhati)*

KUŚA|LAVAU: ita itas tātaḥ.

6.140 *sa|karuṇ'|ākulaṃ parikramya niṣkrāntāḥ sarve.*

iti mahā|kavi|śrī|Bhavabhūti|praṇīta
Uttara|Rāma|carita|nāṭake
Kumāra|pratyabhijñāno
nāma ṣaṣṭho 'ṅkaḥ.

Having once beheld my two fathers meeting
at their children's marriage ceremony
with Vasíshtha and the others in attendance
delighted at the desirability of the match,
how can I now, when such devastation
has occurred, behold such a friend of father's
and not break apart into a thousand pieces?—
Then again, what's too hard for Rama to do?

OFFSTAGE: Alas,

No sooner did they glimpse the Raghus' lord— 6.135
his beauty preserved in his majesty alone—
than his mothers, already distraught from rousing
the fainting Jánaka, have fallen faint themselves.

RAMA: Oh father, oh mothers,

Waste no pity on me, an evil man who showed no pity
to her, the good fortune entire of the Jánaka and Raghu clans.

I had better go pay my respects. *(rises)*

KUSHA AND LAVA: This way, father.

Walking about overcome with pity exeunt all. 6.140

End of Act VI

ACT VII
REUNION

tataḥ praviśati LAKṢMAṆAḤ.

LAKṢMAṆAḤ: bhoḥ, kiṃ nu khalu bhagavatā Vālmīkinā sa|brahma|kṣatra|paura|jānapadāḥ prajāḥ sah' âsmābhir āhūya kṛtsna eva marty'|âmartya|dev'|âsura|nara|nārī|tiryaṅ|nikāyaḥ sāntarā|bhava|cara|sthāvaro bhūta|grāmaḥ sva|prabhāvena sannidhāpitaḥ? ādiṣṭaś c' âham āryeṇa: «vatsa Lakṣmaṇa, bhagavatā Vālmīkinā sva|kṛtim apsarobhiḥ prayujyamānāṃ draṣṭum upanimantritāḥ smaḥ. tad Gaṅgā|tīram ātodya|sthānam upagamya kriyatāṃ samāja|sanniveśa» iti. kṛtaś ca marty'|âmartyasya bhūta|grāmasya samucita|sthāna|sargo mayā. ayaṃ tu

rājy'|āśrama|nivāse 'pi
  prāpta|kaṣṭa|muni|vrataḥ
Vālmīki|gauravād ārya
  ita ev' âbhivartate. [1]

tataḥ praviśati RĀMAḤ.

7.5 RĀMAḤ: vatsa Lakṣmaṇa, api sthitā raṅga|prāśnikāḥ?

LAKṢMAṆAḤ: atha kim.

RĀMAḤ: imau punar vatsau Kuśa|Lavau kumāra|Candraketu|sadṛśīṃ sthāna|pratipattiṃ lambhayitavyau.

Enter LÁKSHMANA.

LÁKSHMANA: My goodness, has Valmíki used his spiritual power to assemble the entire world of living things—the whole host of mortals and immortals, gods and antigods, men and women and animals, along with the beings of the middle space both moving and unmoving*—summoning along with us all the Brahmans, Kshatriyas, and people of the city and countryside?* My elder brother has given me an order, too, saying, "Dear Lákshmana, we've been invited by Valmíki to watch the *ápsaras*es perform his dramatic composition. So go down to the theater on the bank of the Ganga and see to it the audience is properly seated." I've already arranged seating appropriate for everyone, mortals and immortals alike. Now there,

My elder brother is headed this way
out of respect for Valmíki,
for though he still remains the king
he's taken a strict ascetic's vow.

Enter RAMA.

RAMA: Dear brother Lákshmana, are the drama critics in place? 7.5

LÁKSHMANA: To be sure.

RAMA: These two children, Kusha and Lava, are to be accorded a seat of honor, just like prince Chandra·ketu.

LAKṢMAṆAḤ: prabhu | sneha | pratyayāt tath" âiva kṛtam. idaṃ tv āstīrṇaṃ rāj'|āsanam.

upaviśati.

7.10 RĀMAḤ: prastūyatāṃ, bhoḥ.

SŪTRA|DHĀRAḤ: *(praviśya)* bhagavān bhūt'|ârtha|vādī Prācetasaḥ sa | jaṅgama | sthāvaraṃ jagad ājñāpayati. «yad idam asmābhir ārṣeṇa cakṣuṣā samudvīkṣya pāvanaṃ ca karuṇ'|âdbhuta|rasaṃ ca kiṃ cid upanibaddhaṃ, tatra kārya|gauravād avadhātavyam» iti.

RĀMAḤ: etad uktaṃ bhavati. sākṣāt|kṛta|dharmāṇa ṛṣayaḥ. teṣām ṛtam|bharāṇi bhagavatāṃ paro|rajāṃsi prajñānāni na kva cid vyāhanyanta ity an|abhiśaṅkanīyāni.

NEPATHYE: ⌈hā ajja | utta, hā kumāra Lakkhaṇa, eāiṇiṃ a | saraṇaṃ araṇṇe āsaṇṇa | ppasava | veaṇaṃ had' | āsā sāvadā maṃ abhilasanti. sā dāṇiṃ manda|bhāiṇī Mandāiṇīe attāṇaaṃ ṇikkhivissaṃ.⌋

LAKṢMAṆAḤ: *(ātma|gatam)* kaṣṭaṃ bat', ânyad eva kim api.

LÁKSHMANA: I've done so, aware of my lord's affection for them. Here, the royal lodge has been arranged.

*He takes his seat.**

RAMA: Let the show begin. 7.10

DIRECTOR: The son of Prachétas, who tells things as they truly are, has the following request to make of everyone here, moving and unmoving beings alike: "Through deep insight made possible by a seer's vision we have produced a brief composition at once purifying and filled with *rasa*, the *rasa*s of pity and wonder. In light of the gravity of its subject matter please give us your undivided attention."

RAMA: What he means is that seers have direct vision of *dharma*. The insights of the blessed ones are "truth-bearing," "beyond the dust* of untruth," never found to be contradicted—and hence never to be doubted.

OFFSTAGE: Oh my husband, oh Prince Lákshmana, I am all alone in the wilderness and without refuge, the pangs of childbirth have started, and awful* wild beasts are thristing for me. Cursed as I am I have no choice but to hurl myself into the Mandákini.

LÁKSHMANA: *(aside)* What an awful situation, something far worse than I thought.

SŪTRA|DHĀRAḤ:

7.15 Viśvambhar"|ātmajā devī
rājñā tyaktā mahā|vane
prāpta|prasavam ātmānaṃ
Gaṅgā|devyāṃ vimuñcati. [2]

niṣkrāntaḥ.

RĀMAḤ: *(s'|āvegam)* devi devi, lakṣmaṇam avekṣasva!

LAKṢMAṆAḤ: ārya, nāṭakam idam.

RĀMAḤ: hā devi Daṇḍak"|âraṇya|priya|sakhi, eṣa te Rāmād vipākaḥ.

7.20 LAKṢMAṆAḤ: ārya, dṛśyatāṃ tāvat prabandh'|ârthaḥ.

RĀMAḤ: eṣa sajjo 'smi vajramayaḥ.

tataḥ praviśaty utsaṅgit'|âik'|âika|dārakābhyāṃ PṚTHIVĪ/JĀHNAVĪBHYĀM *avalambitā pramugdhā* SĪTĀ.

RĀMAḤ: vatsa, a|saṃvijñāta|pada|nibandhanaṃ tama iva praviśāmi. dhāraya mām!

DEVYAU:

samāśvasihi, kalyāṇi.
diṣṭyā, Vaidéhi, vardhase.
antar|jalaṃ prasūt" âsi
Raghu|vaṃśa|dharau sutau. [3]

DIRECTOR:

The daughter of all-sustaining Earth, 7.15
the queen left in the great forest
by the king, as her labor begins
casts herself into goddess Ganga.

Exit.

RAMA: *(shocked)* My queen, my queen, look, Lákshmana is here!*

LÁKSHMANA: But brother, this is only a play.

RAMA: Oh my queen, dear companion in the Dándaka wilderness. This turn of events* befell you because of Rama.

LÁKSHMANA: Brother, let's just watch the story. 7.20

RAMA: I've steeled myself, I'm ready.

Enter SITA *in a daze and supported by the* EARTH *and* GANGA, *each of them holding one of* SITA*'s sons.*

RAMA: Dear brother, I am entering a realm of darkness where neither cause nor cure* can be perceived. Hold me up!

THE TWO GODDESSES:

Compose yourself, beautiful Vaidéhi;
by good fortune you've achieved success:
for in the river you have given birth
to two sons who will uphold the Raghu clan.

7.25 SĪTĀ: *(samāśvasya)* ⌜diṭṭhiā dārake pasūda mhi. hā ajja|utta!⌟ *(mūrchati)*

LAKṢMAṆAḤ: *(pādayor nipatya)* ārya, ārya, diṣṭyā vardhāmahe. kalyāṇa|praroho Raghu|vaṃśaḥ. *(vilokya)* hā katham, kṣubhita|bāsp'|ôtpīḍa|nirbharaḥ pramugdha ev' āryaḥ. *(vījayati)*

DEVYAU: vatse, samāśvasihi, samāśvasihi.

SĪTĀ: *(āśvasya)* ⌜bhaavadi, kā tumaṃ? tumaṃ ca?⌟

PṚTHIVĪ: iyaṃ te śvaśura|kula|devatā Bhāgīrathī.

7.30 SĪTĀ: ⌜bhaavadi, ṇamo de.⌟

BHĀGĪRATHĪ: cāritr'|ôcitāṃ kalyāṇa|sampadam adhigaccha.

LAKṢMAṆAḤ: anugṛhītāḥ smaḥ.

BHĀGĪRATHĪ: iyaṃ tu jananī te bhagavatī Vasundharā.

SĪTĀ: ⌜hā amba, īdisī ahaṃ tae diṭṭhā.⌟

7.35 PṚTHIVĪ: ehi vatse, ehi putri. *(*SĪTĀM *āliṅgya mūrchati)*

LAKṢMAṆAḤ: *(sa|harṣam)* kathaṃ, Pṛthvī|Bhāgīrathībhyām abhyupapann" āryā.

SITA: *(having composed herself)* How fortunate I've given 7.25
birth to sons... Oh my husband! *(falls faint)*

LÁKSHMANA: *(falling at his feet)* Brother, dear brother, what good fortune that we've achieved success. The Raghu family tree has produced a splendid new branch. *(glancing)* Why, my brother is in a state of shock, overwhelmed by a gushing flood of tears. *(fans him)*

THE TWO GODDESSES: Child, compose yourself, we beg you.

SITA: *(regaining her composure)* Who are you, blessed one? And you?

EARTH: This is Bhagi·rathi, your father-in-law's family deity.

SITA: Blessed one, homage to you. 7.30

BHAGI·RATHI: May you attain the full measure of good fortune in keeping with your chastity.

LÁKSHMANA: We have been shown great favor.*

BHAGI·RATHI: And this is your mother, blessed Earth.

SITA: Ah mother, that you should see me in such a state.

EARTH: Come, my child, come, little daughter. *(falls faint* 7.35
holding SITA *in her embrace)*

LÁKSHMANA: *(excitedly)* Why, Earth and Ganga together have come to the aid of sister-in-law.

RĀMAḤ: *(avalokya)* diṣṭyā khalv etat. karuṇataraṃ tu vartate.

BHĀGĪRATHĪ: Viśvambhar" âpi nāma vyathata iti jitam apatya|snehena. yad vā sarva|sādhāraṇo hy eṣa moha|granthir antaś|caraś cetanāvatām upaplavaḥ saṃsāra|tantuḥ. vatse Vaidehi, devi bhūta|dhātri, samāśvasihi, samāśvasihi.

PṚTHIVĪ: *(āśvasya)* devi, Sītāṃ prasūya katham āśvasimi?

7.40 ekaś ciraṃ rākṣasa|madhyavāsas,
tyāgo dvitīyaś ca su|duḥ|śravo 'syāḥ [4ab]

BHĀGĪRATHĪ:

ko nāma pāk'|âbhimukhasya jantur
dvārāṇi daivasya pidhātum īṣṭe? [4cd]

PṚTHIVĪ: Bhāgīrathi, yuktaṃ. sadṛśam etad vā Rāma|bhadrasya?

na pramāṇī|kṛtaḥ pāṇir
bālye bālena pīḍitaḥ,
n' âhaṃ, na Janako, n' âgnir,
n' ânuvṛttir, na saṃtatiḥ. [5]

SĪTĀ: ⌜hā ajja|utta, sumarīasi.⌟

7.45 PṚTHIVĪ: āḥ! kas tav' ārya|putraḥ?

SĪTĀ: *(sa|lajj"|âsram)* ⌜jadhā vā ambā bhaṇādi.⌟

---

[i] Fire corroborated Sītā's chastity after the death of Rāvaṇa.

RAMA: *(watching)* This is fortunate indeed—but a source of deep pity,* too.

BHAGI·RATHI: Even Earth who bears all can tremble—what force love for a child exerts. But then, this is something common to all, a knot of infatuation,* an internal source of turmoil for any sentient being, the very thread of worldly life.* Child Vaidéhi, goddess Earth, compose yourselves, I beg you.

EARTH: *(regaining her composure)* Goddess, how can I compose myself, I who gave birth to Sita?

Her long sojourn among *rákshasas* was one thing,* 7.40
another her being disowned, a terrible disrgrace.

BHAGI·RATHI:

Yet what creature has the power to seal the doors
of fate when it is on the verge of bearing fruit?

EARTH: Quite so.* But was that seemly of dear Rama?

To pay no heed to the hand he grasped
in childhood, when he was a child,*
or to me or Jánaka or Fire[i]
or her deference or his progeny.

SITA: Oh my husband, they have reminded me once again of you.*

EARTH: Ha! Do you have a husband? 7.45

SITA: *(with tears of shame)* It's as my mother says.

RĀMAḤ: amba Pṛthivi, īdṛśo 'smi.

BHĀGĪRATHĪ: bhagavati Vasundhare, śarīram asi saṃsārasya. tat kim a|saṃvidān" êva jāmātre kupyasi?

ghoraṃ loke vitatam a|yaśo.
yā ca vahnau viśuddhir
Laṅkā|dvīpe, katham iva janas
tām iha śraddadhātu?
Ikṣvākūṇāṃ kula|dhanam idaṃ,
yat samārādhanīyaḥ
kṛtsno lokas. tad ativiṣame
kiṃ sa vatsaḥ karotu? [6]

7.50 LAKṢMAṆAḤ: a|vyāhat'|ântaḥ|prakāśā hi devatā bhūteṣu.

BHĀGĪRATHĪ: tath" âpy eṣa te 'ñjaliḥ.

RĀMAḤ: amba, anuvṛttas tvayā Bhagīratha|gṛhe prasādaḥ.

PṚTHIVĪ: nityaṃ prasann" âsmi vaḥ. kin tv āpāta|duḥsahaḥ sneha|saṃvegaḥ. na punar na jānāmi Sītā|snehaṃ Rāma|bhadrasya.

dahyamānena manasā
daivād vatsāṃ vihāya saḥ
lok'|ôttareṇa sattvena
prajā|puṇyaiś ca jīvati. [7]

---

[i] To ask her forgiveness on Rāma's behalf. [ii] An ancestor of Rāma, whom Gaṅgā once favored by purifying the ashes of his ancestors.

RAMA: Mother Earth, I am the man you describe.

BHAGI·RATHI: O Earth, you are the body of all of mortal life. How can you be angry then with your son-in-law, as if you were wholly unaware?

The dreadful infamy had spread abroad
and the purifying trial by fire
took place on Lanka—how were people here
to be expected to give it credence?
The ancestral wealth of the Ikshvákus
lies in propitiating all the world.
So in these straits, truly dreadful straits,
what was my child supposed to do?

LÁKSHMANA: The deity's inner light shines unimpeded into 7.50
all creatures.

BHAGI·RATHI: Nevertheless, I fold my hands in homage to you.[i]

RAMA: Mother, you have extended your grace to the House of Bhagi·ratha[ii] as well.

EARTH: I have always been graciously disposed toward you all.* It was only distress due to my love, which was at first so hard to bear; it is not that I did not appreciate dear Rama's love for Sita.

With a heart in flames he was forced by fate
to abandon Sita, and only now
survives by some supernatural courage
and the good karma of his subjects.

7.55 RĀMAḤ: sa|karuṇā hi guravo garbha|rūpeṣu.

SĪTĀ: *(rudatī, kṛt'|âñjaliḥ)* ⌜ṇedu maṃ attaṇo aṅgesu vilaaṃ ambā.⌟

RĀMAḤ: kim anyad bravītu?

BHĀGĪRATHĪ: śāntam. a|vilīnā saṃvatsara|sahasrāṇi bhūyāḥ.

PṚTHIVĪ: vatse, avekṣaṇīyau te putrakau.

7.60 SĪTĀ: ⌜a|ṇādha mhi. kiṃ edehiṃ?⌟

BHĀGĪRATHĪ: kathaṃ tvaṃ sa|nāth" âpy a|nāthā?

SĪTĀ: ⌜kīdisaṃ mama a|bhaggāe saṇādhattaṇaṃ?⌟

RĀMAḤ: hṛdaya, vajram asi.

DEVYAU:

jagan|maṅgalam ātmānaṃ
  kathaṃ tvam avamanyase
āvayor api yat|saṅgāt
  pavitratvaṃ prakṛṣyate? [8]

RAMA: How deep the pity elders have for everyone they consider their offspring. 7.55

SITA: *(weeping; with hands folded)* Mother, take me to you and dissolve me in your body.

RAMA: What else could she ask for?

BHAGI·RATHI: Heaven forbid. May you live a thousand years before such a dissolution.

EARTH: My child, your two little boys must be looked after.

SITA: I have no protector; what am I to do with them? 7.60

BHAGI·RATHI: How can you say you are unprotected when indeed you are not?

SITA: What sort of protector have I, cursed as I am?

RAMA: Heart, you are cold steel.

THE TWO GODDESSES:

> How can you disdain yourself,*
> the source of good fortune to the world,
> since it is from our relationship with you
> that our own purity is increased?

7.65 LAKṢMAṆAḤ: ārya, śrutam?

RĀMAḤ: śṛṇotu lokaḥ.

nepathye kalakalaḥ.

RĀMAḤ: adbhutataraṃ kim api.

SĪTĀ: ⌜kiṃ ti saalaṃ antarikkhaṃ pajjaladi?⌟

7.70 DEVYAU: jñātam.

Kṛśāśvaḥ, Kauśiko, Rāma
  iti yeṣāṃ guru|kramaḥ
prādurbhavanti tāny eva
  śastrāṇi saha Jṛmbhakaiḥ. [9]

NEPATHYE:

devi Sīte, namas te 'stu.
  gatir naḥ putrakau hi te
ālekhya|darśane devo
  yath" āha Raghu|nandanaḥ. [10]

SĪTĀ: ⌜diṭṭhiā attha|devadāo edāo! hā ajja|utta, ajja vi de pasādā paripphuranti.⌟

LAKṢMAṆAḤ: uktam āsīd āryeṇa, «sarvath" êdānīṃ tvat|prasūtim upasthāsyant'» îti.

LÁKSHMANA: Brother, did you hear? 7.65

RAMA: Let the world hear.

Offstage a tumult.

RAMA: Something yet more wondrous is at hand.

SITA: How is it the whole sky is engulfed in flames?

THE TWO GODDESSES: We know: 7.70

> Those whose succession of gurus has been
> Krisháshva, Káushika, and Rama,
> those magical weapons and Jrímbhakas
> are now manifesting themselves.

OFFSTAGE:

> Queen Sita, homage to you,
> our destiny now lies with your sons
> as the joy of the Raghus proclaimed
> at the time of viewing the paintings.

SITA: What good fortune, the weapon deities! Oh my husband, your acts of kindness are even today still coming to light.

LÁKSHMANA: My brother did tell her, "From now on without fail they will serve your offspring."*

DEVYAU:

7.75 namo vaḥ param'|âstrebhyo.
dhanyāḥ smo vaḥ parigrahāt.
anudhyātair upetavyaṃ
vatsayor. bhadram astu vaḥ. [11]

RĀMAḤ:

kṣubhitāḥ kām api daśāṃ
kurvanti mama sāmpratam
vismay'|ānanda|sandarbha|
jarjarāḥ karuṇ'|ôrmayaḥ. [12]

DEVYAU: modasva vatse. Rāma|bhadra|tulyau te putrakāv idānīṃ saṃvṛttau.

SĪTĀ: ⌜bhaavadi, ko edāṇaṃ khatti'|ôcidaṃ kamma karissadi?⌟

RĀMAḤ:

eṣā Vasiṣṭha|guptānāṃ
Raghūṇāṃ vaṃśa|vardhinī
kaṣṭaṃ Sīt" âpi sutayoḥ
saṃskartāraṃ na vindati. [13]

7.80 BHĀGĪRATHĪ: putri, kiṃ tav' ânayā cintayā? etau hi vatsau stanya|tyāgāt pareṇa bhagavato Vālmīker arpayiṣyāmi. sa etayoḥ kṣatra|kṛtyaṃ kariṣyati.

yathā Vasiṣṭh'|Āṅgirasāv
ṛṣī, Prācetasas tathā
Janakānāṃ Raghūṇāṃ ca
vaṃśayor ubhayor guruḥ. [14]

[i] A patronymic of Śatānanda, family priest of the Janaka kings.

THE TWO GODDESSES:

Homage to you, supreme weapons, 7.75
how blessed we are that you have favored us.
Be pleased to attend upon these children
whenever you are summoned in thought.

RAMA:

Waves of pity have been sent surging
and break in pools of astonishment and bliss,
reducing me now to some condition
that is impossible to describe.

THE TWO GODDESSES: Rejoice, child, your two little boys have now become the equals of dear Rama.

SITA: Blessed one, who is there to perform for them the rites required of Kshatriyas?

RAMA:

How awful that Sita herself— the strength
of the Raghu clan, which Vasíshtha priests
have always guarded—can find no one
to perform the sacraments for her sons.

BHAGI·RATHI: My daughter, no need to fret over this. After 7.80
the two boys are weaned I will commit them to the care of Valmíki, and he will perform the Kshatriya rituals for them.

No less than the seers Vasíshtha and Ángirasa[i]
is Prachétas' son a guru to both Raghu and Jánaka clans.

RĀMAḤ: su|vicintitaṃ bhagavatyā.

LAKṢMAṆAḤ: ārya, satyaṃ vijñāpayāmi: tais tair upāyair vatsau Kuśa|Lavāv utprekṣe.

etau hi janma|siddh'|âstrāv
 ubhau Prācetasān muneḥ
vīrau samprāpta|saṃskārau
 vayasā dvādaś'|ābdikau. [15]

7.85 RĀMAḤ: vatsa, ity ev' âhaṃ pariplavamāna|hṛdayaḥ sampramugdho 'smi.

PṚTHIVĪ: ehi, vatse, pavitrī|kuru rasātalam.

SĪTĀ: ⌜ṇedu maṃ attaṇo aṅgesu vilaaṃ ambā. ṇa sahissaṃ īdisaṃ jīa|loa|parivattaṃ aṇubhaviduṃ.⌟

RĀMAḤ: kim uttaraṃ syāt?

PṚTHIVĪ: vatse, stanya|tyāgaṃ yāvan man|niyogataḥ putrayor avekṣasva. pareṇa tu yathā rocişyate.

7.90 BHĀGĪRATHĪ: evaṃ nāma.

niṣkrāntā GAṄGĀ/PṚTHVĪ/SĪTĀḤ.

RĀMAḤ: kathaṃ, vilaya eva Vaidehyāḥ sampannaḥ? hā devi, Daṇḍak"|âraṇya|vāsa|priya|sakhi, hā cāritra|devate, lok'|ântaraṃ paryavasit" âsi. *(mūrchati)*

RAMA: Bhagi·rathi has thought it all through most carefully.

LÁKSHMANA: My brother, I tell you truly, for a whole host of reasons I feel certain that those two children are Kusha and Lava:

> They too commanded the weapons from birth,
> both young heroes received the sacraments
> from the sage, the son of Prachétas,
> and both of them are twelve years old.

RAMA: Dear brother, the very thought is throwing my heart into turmoil and driving me to distraction. 7.85

EARTH: Come with me now, my child, and purify the netherworld.*

SITA: Mother, take me to you and dissolve me in your body. I can no longer bear the vicissitudes* of this world.

RAMA: How will she reply?

EARTH: My child, do as I bid and wait until your two sons are weaned. Thereafter, however, it will be as you wish.

BHAGI·RATHI: So be it. 7.90

Exeunt GANGA, EARTH, *and* SITA.

RAMA: What, has Vaidéhi's dissolution taken place? Oh my queen, dear companion in my sojourn in Dándaka wilderness, oh goddess of virtue, have you then resolved to go to the other world? *(falls faint)*

LAKṢMAṆAḤ: bhagavan Vālmīke, paritrāyasva, paritrāyasva! eṣa kiṃ te kāvy'|ârthaḥ?

NEPATHYE: apanīyatām ātodyakam. bho bhoḥ sa|jaṅgama|sthāvarāḥ prāṇabhṛto martyāḥ: paśyata Vālmīkin" âbhyanujñātaṃ pavitram āścaryam.

7.95 LAKṢMAṆAḤ: *(vilokya)*

manthād iva kṣubhyati Gāṅgam ambho.
  vyāptaṃ ca deva'|rṣibhir antarikṣam.
āścaryam! āryā saha devatābhyāṃ
  Gaṅgā|Mahībhyāṃ salilād udeti. [16]

NEPATHYE:

Arundhati jagad|vandye,
  Gaṅgā|Pṛthvyau juṣasva naḥ.
arpit" êyaṃ tav' âbhyāśe
  Sītā puṇya|vratā vadhūḥ. [17]

LAKṢMAṆAḤ: diṣṭyā, aho āścaryam! ārya, paśya, paśya. *(vilokya)*… kaṣṭam, ady' âpi n' ôcchvasity āryaḥ.

tataḥ praviśaty ARUNDHATĪ SĪTĀ *ca.*

ARUNDHATĪ:

7.100 tvarasva, vatse Vaidéhi,
  muñca śālīna|śīlatām.
ehi, jīvaya me vatsaṃ
  priya|sparśena pāṇinā. [18]

LÁKSHMANA: Help, Valmíki, help! Is this the moral of your poem?*

OFFSTAGE: Away with the orchestra. You there, mortal creatures one and all, moving and unmoving: Behold the purifying miracle that Valmíki has vouchsafed.

LÁKSHMANA: *(glancing)* 7.95

The Ganga's waters are surging as if churned,
the sky is pervaded by heavenly seers.
A miracle! Sita and the deities,
Ganga and Earth, are emerging from the deep.

OFFSTAGE:

Arúndhati, honored by the world,
look kindly upon us, Ganga and Earth:
We hereby entrust Sita to your care,
a good wife who keeps her holy vows.

LÁKSHMANA: What good fortune, what a miracle! Brother, look, look. *(glancing)*... Alas, brother has still not regained his composure.

Enter ARÚNDHATI *and* SITA.

ARÚNDHATI:

My child, this modesty of yours 7.100
is uncalled-for, have done with it.
Come quickly and revive my child Rama
with the beloved touch of your hand.

SĪTĀ: *(sa|sambhramam spṛśantī)* ⌜samassasadu, samassasadu ajja|utto.⌟

RĀMAḤ: *(samāśvasya s'|ānandam)* bhoḥ kim etat? *(dṛṣṭvā sa|harṣ'|âdbhutam)* aye, devī! *(sa|lajjam)* katham, amb" Ârundhatī, sarve ca prahṛṣyad|Ṛṣyaśṛṅga|Śāntā|sametā guravaḥ.

ARUNDHATĪ: vatsa, eṣā bhagavatī Bhagīratha|gṛha|devatā su|prasannā Gaṅgā.

NEPATHYE: jagat|pate Rāma|bhadra, smaryatām ālekhya|darśane māṃ praty ātmano vacanam. «sā tvam, amba, snuṣāyām Arundhat" îva Sītāyāṃ śiv'|ânudhyānā bhav'» êti. tatr' ân|ṛṇ" âsmi.

7.105 ARUNDHATĪ: iyaṃ te śvaśrūr bhagavatī Vasundharā.

NEPATHYE: uktaṃ ca pūrvam āyuṣmatā vatsā|parityāge: «bhagavati Vasundhare, ślāghyāṃ duhitaram avekṣasva Jānakīm» iti. tad adhunā kṛta|vacan" âsmi, prabho, vatsāyām.

RĀMAḤ: katham, kṛta|mah"|âparādho 'pi bhagavatībhyām anukampito Rāmaḥ. *(praṇamati)*

ARUNDHATĪ: bho bhoḥ paura|jānapadāḥ! iyam adhunā Jāhnavī|Vasundharābhyām evaṃ praśasya mam' Ârundhatyāḥ samarpitā. pūrvaṃ ca bhagavatā Vaiśvānareṇa nirṇīta|puṇya|cāritrā, sa|brahmakaiś ca devaiḥ saṃstutā Sāvitra|kula|vadhūr deva|yajana|sambhavā Sītā devī parigṛhyatām, iti kathaṃ bhavanto manyante?

---

[i] Act 1.101 [ii] Gaṅgā. [iii] A wife celebrated in the epics for giving up her life for the sake of her husband's.

SITA: *(touching him in alarm)* Compose yourself, my husband, I beg you.

RAMA: *(regaining his composure; with delight)* Oh, what can this be? *(looking; with joy and wonder)* Why, my queen! *(ashamed)* And mother Arúndhati, and all my elders, along with a joyous Rishya·shringa and Shanta.

ARÚNDHATI: My child, there is the gracious Ganga, deity of the House of Bhagi·ratha.

OFFSTAGE: Lord of the world, dear Rama, remember what you asked of me at the time of viewing the paintings: "Be as kindly disposed to your daughter-in-law Sita as Arúndhati is."[i] I am now free of that debt.

ARÚNDHATI: And there is Earth, your mother-in-law. 7.105

OFFSTAGE: Years ago, at the time of disowning Sita you asked (and long may you live), "O Earth, watch over Jánaki, your esteemed daughter." Today, Your Majesty, I have fulfilled that request with regard to my child.

RAMA: How can this be? Though Rama is guilty of terrible wrongdoing both these blessed ones have shown him mercy. *(bows)*

ARÚNDHATI: You there, people of the city and countryside! This woman has been entrusted to Arúndhati, and been showered with praises from Jáhnavi[ii] and Earth. Earlier her virtuous conduct was certified by Vaishvánara, the god of fire. She has been extolled by gods and Brahmans as a woman of the clan of Savítri.[iii] Accept Sita back, the queen who was born at a sacred rite. What say you sirs?

LAKṢMAṆAḤ: evam āryay" Ârundhatyā nirbhartsitāḥ prajāḥ kṛtsnaś ca bhūta|grāma āryāṃ namaskaroti, loka|pālāś ca sapta'|ṛṣayaś ca puṣpa|vṛṣṭibhir upatiṣṭhante.

7.110 ARUNDHATĪ: jagat|pate Rāma|bhadra,

niyojaya yathā|dharmaṃ
  priyāṃ tvaṃ dharma|cāriṇīm
hiraṇmayyāḥ pratikṛteḥ
  puṇya|prakṛtim adhvare. [19]

SĪTĀ: *(sva|gatam)* ⌜avi jāṇādi ajja|utto Sītā|dukkhaṃ pamajjiduṃ?⌟

RĀMAḤ: yathā bhagavaty ādiśati.

LAKṢMAṆAḤ: kṛt'|ârtho 'smi.

7.115 SĪTĀ: ⌜jīvida mhi.⌟

LAKṢMAṆAḤ: ārye, eṣa nirlajjo Lakṣmaṇaḥ praṇamati.

SĪTĀ: ⌜vaccha, īdiso ciraṃ jīva.⌟

ARUNDHATĪ: bhagavan Vālmīke, upanīyetām imau Sītā|garbha|sambhavau Rāma|bhadrasya Kuśa|Lavau. *(niṣkrāntā)*

RĀMA|LAKṢMAṆAU: diṣṭyā tath" âiva tat.

7.120 SĪTĀ: *(sa|bāṣp'|ākulam)* ⌜kahiṃ me puttakā?⌟

LÁKSHMANA: How Arúndhati has dressed down the subjects, while the whole world of living beings pays homage to sister-in-law, while the world-guardians and the seven seers attend her with a rain of flowers.

ARÚNDHATI: Lord of the world, dear Rama: 7.110

> In accordance with *dharma* assign your beloved
> companion in *dharma*—
> the holy original of the golden copy—her sacrificial
> tasks.

SITA: *(aside)* Does my husband know how to assuage Sita's sorrow?

RAMA: As the blessed one commands.

LÁKSHMANA: My ends have been achieved.

SITA: I have been brought back to life. 7.115

LÁKSHMANA: Sister-in-law, here he prostrates himself before you—that Lákshmana who knows no shame.

SITA: My child, may you live long, just as you are.

ARÚNDHATI: Valmíki, please bring forward Kusha and Lava, the two sons born to Rama of Sita's womb. *(exit)*

RAMA *(and)* LÁKSHMANA: What good fortune, it's all true.

SITA: *(overcome with tears)* Where are my two little boys? 7.120

tataḥ praviśati VĀLMĪKIḤ KUŚA|LAVAU *ca.*

VĀLMĪKIḤ: vatsau Kuśa|Lavau, eṣa Raghu|patiḥ pitā yuvayoḥ, Lakṣmaṇaḥ kaniṣṭha|tātaḥ, Sītā|devī jananī, eṣa rāja'|rṣir Janako mātāmahaḥ.

SĪTĀ: *(sa|harṣa|karuṇ'|âdbhutaṃ vilokya)* ⌜kadhaṃ, tādo?⌟

KUŚA|LAVAU: hā tāta, hā amba, hā mātāmaha!

7.125 RĀMAḤ: *(sa|harṣam āliṅgya)* nanu vatsau puṇyaiḥ prāptau sthaḥ.

SĪTĀ: ⌜ehi, jāda Kusa, ehi, jāda Lava. cirassa parissajadha puṇo jamm'|antara|gadaṃ jaṇaṇiṃ.⌟

KUŚA|LAVAU: *(tathā kṛtvā)* dhanyau svaḥ.

SĪTĀ: ⌜bhaavaṃ, paṇamāmi.⌟

VĀLMĪKIḤ: vatse, īdṛśy eva ciraṃ bhūyāḥ.*

7.130 *nepathye kalakalaḥ.*

VĀLMĪKIḤ: *(utthāy' âvalokya ca)* utkhāta|Lavaṇo Mathur"|ēśvaraḥ prāptaḥ.

LAKṢMAṆAḤ: s'|ânuṣaṅgāṇi kalyāṇāni.

---

[i] Śatrughna.

Enter VALMÍKI *along with* KUSHA *and* LAVA.

VALMÍKI: Kusha and Lava, dear children: This is the lord of the Raghus, your father, and Lákshmana, your uncle, and Queen Sita, your mother. And this is the royal seer Jánaka, your maternal grandfather.

SITA: *(glancing with joy, pity, and wonder)* What, is my father present too?

KUSHA *(and)* LAVA: Oh father, mother, grandfather!

RAMA: *(embracing them joyfully)* Surely it was only through 7.125
good karma that I have recovered you, my two children.

SITA: Come Kusha, my child, and you too, Lava. Hold your mother in a long embrace—it is as if she has been reborn.

KUSHA AND LAVA: *(doing so)* How fortunate we are.

SITA: I bow before you, blessed one.

VALMÍKI: My child, may you live long just as you are.

Offstage a tumult. 7.130

VALMÍKI: *(rising and looking about)* It's the lord of Máthura[i] arriving, after uprooting Lávana.

LÁKSHMANA: When good things come they come in spate.

RĀMAḤ: sarvam idam anubhavann api na pratyemi. yad vā prakṛtir iyam abhyudayānām.

VĀLMĪKIḤ: Rāma|bhadra, ucyatāṃy kiṃ te bhūyaḥ priyam upakaromi?

7.135 RĀMAḤ: ataḥ param api priyam asti? tath" âp' îdam astu:

pāpmabhyaś ca punāti vardhayati ca
śreyāṃsi y" êyaṃ kathā,
māṅgalyā ca manoharā ca, jagato
māt" êva, Gaṅg" êva ca,
tām etāṃ paribhāvayantv abhinayair
vinyasta|rūpāṃ budhāḥ
śabda|brahma|vidaḥ kaveḥ pariṇata|
prajñasya vāṇīm imām. [20]

niṣkrāntāḥ sarve.

iti mahā|kavi|śrī|Bhavabhūti|praṇīta
Uttara|Rāma|carita|nāṭake
sammelanaṃ nāma saptamo 'ṅkaḥ.
samāptaṃ c' êdaṃ nāṭakam.

[i] The *Rāmāyaṇa*.

RAMA: Though all this is really happening to me I still cannot believe it. Then again, such is the nature of good fortune.

VALMÍKI: Dear Rama, is there some further good turn I can do for you?

RAMA: What can be better than all this? Still, perhaps the 7.135
following:

This is a story[i] that purifies from evil
and lavishes all benefits as well—
it is at once auspicious and enchanting
like the Mother of the world and the Ganga.*
May the learned come to relish it
embodied in dramatic performance,
the verbal art of a seasoned poet, a master
of the sacred mystery of language.*

Exeunt all.

End of Act VII.
The end of Bhava·bhuti's play,
"Rama's Last Act"

CHĀYĀ

The following is a Sanskrit paraphrase (chāyā) *of the Prakrit passages (marked with* ⌜corner brackets⌟ *in the play). References are to chapter and paragraph.*

1.25 jānāmy, ārya|putra, jānāmi. kin tu santāpa|kāriṇo bandhu|jana|viprayogā bhavanti.

1.30 ārya, tataḥ kiṃ vilambyate?

1.35 namas te. api kuśalaṃ me samagrasya guru|janasya, āryāyāś ca Śāntāyāḥ?

1.37 asmān vā smarati?

1.51 ata eva Rāghava|dhurandhara ārya|putraḥ.

1.61 bhavatv, ārya|putra, bhavatu. ehi prekṣāmahe tāvat te caritam.

1.64 ka idānīm eta upari nirantara|sthitā upastuvant' îv' ārya|putram?

1.68 nama etebhyaḥ.

1.70 anugṛhīt" âsmi.

1.72 amhahe. dalan|nava|nīl'|ôtpala|śyāmala|snigdha|masṛṇa|māṃsalena deha|saubhāgyena vismaya|stimita|tāta|dṛśyamāna|saumya|sundara|śrīr an|ādara|khaṇḍita|Śaṅkara|śar'|âsanaḥ śikhaṇḍa|mugdha|maṇḍana ārya|putra ālikhitaḥ.

1.77 ete khalu tat|kāla|kṛta|go|dāna|maṅgalāś catvāro 'pi bhrātaro vivāha|dīkṣitā yūyam. ammo, jānāmi tasminn eva pradeśe tasminn eva kāle varte.

1.80 vatsa iyam apy aparā kā?

1.82 kampit" âsmi.

1.86 suṣṭhu śobhasa, ārya|putr', âitena vinaya|māhātmyena.

1.96 ammo, eṣa jaṭā|saṃyamana|vṛttāntaḥ.

1.98 eṣā prasanna|puṇya|salilā bhagavatī Bhāgīrathī.

1.103 smaraty etaṃ pradeśam ārya|putraḥ?

1.107 alaṃ idānīṃ tāvad etena. paśyāmi tāvad ārya|putra|sva|hasta|dhṛta|tāla|patr'|ātapa|vāraṇam ātmano 'kṣibhyāṃ dakṣiṇ'|âraṇya|praveśam.

1.114 hā ārya|putra. etāvat te darśanam.

1.116 yathā tathā bhavatu. dur|jano '|sukham utpādayati.

1.119 ayi deva Raghu|kul'|ānanda. evaṃ mama kāraṇāt klānta āsīḥ.

1.124 hā dhik, hā dhik! aham apy atibhūmiṃ gatena raṇaraṇaken' ārya|putra|śūnyam iv' ātmānaṃ prekṣe.

1.126 hā tāta nirvyūḍhas te 'patya|snehaḥ.

1.129 atra kil' ārya|putreṇa vicchardit'|âmarṣa|dhīratvaṃ pramukta|kaṇṭhaṃ ruditam āsīt.

1.133 eṣa sa cira|nirviṇṇa|jīva|loka|samuddharaṇa|guruk'|ôpakārī mahā|bhāgo mārutiḥ.

1.135 vatsa, eṣa kusumita|kadamba|tāṇḍavita|barhiṇaḥ kin|nāma|dheyo girir yatr' ânubhāva|saubhāgya|mātra|pariśeṣa|dhūsara|śrīr mūrchaṃs tvayā praruditen' âvalambitas taru|tala ārya|putra ālikhitaḥ?

1.139 ārya|putra, etena citra|darśanena pratyutpanna|dohadāyā asti me vijñāpyam.

1.141 jāne punar api prasanna|gambhīrāsu vana|rājiṣu vihariṣyāmi, pavitra|saumya|śiśir'|âvagāhāṃ ca bhagavatīṃ Bhāgīrathīm avagāhiṣye.

1.145 ārya|putra yuṣmābhir api tatra gantavyam.

1.147 tena hi priyaṃ me.

1.150 evaṃ bhavatu. apahriye khalu pariśrama|janitayā nidrayā.

1.155 sthira|prasādā yūyam. ita idānīṃ kim aparam?

1.157 priyaṃ|vada, ehi saṃviśāvaḥ.

1.160 asty etad, ārya|putra, asty etat...

1.163 deva, upasthitaḥ.

1.165 āsanna|paricārako Durmukho devasya.

1.168 hā katham idānīṃ Sītā|devīm antareṇ' ēdṛśam a|cintanīyaṃ jan'|âpavādaṃ devasya kathayiṣyāmi? atha vā niyogaḥ khalu ma īdṛśo manda|bhāgasya.

1.169 hā ārya|putra saumya, kv' âsi?

1.172 jayatu devaḥ.

1.174 upastuvanti devaṃ paura|jānapadā vismāritā vayaṃ mahā|rāja|Daśarathasya Rāma|deven' êti.

1.176 śṛṇotu devaḥ.

1.178 āśvasitu devaḥ.

1.188 katham idānīm agni|pariśuddhāyā garbha|sthita|pavitra|Raghu|kula|santānāyā devyā durjana|vacanād evaṃ vyavasitaṃ devena?

1.192 hā devi.

1.210 hā saumy' ārya|putra...

1.210 hā dhik, hā dhik! duḥ|svapnakena vipralabdh" âham ārya|putram ākrandāmi.

1.210 hā dhik, hā dhik! ekākinīṃ māṃ prasuptām ujjhitvā gata ārya|putraḥ. kim idānīm etat? bhavatu. tasmai kopiṣyāmi—yadi taṃ prekṣamāṇ" ātmanaḥ prabhaviṣyāmi. ko 'tra parijanaḥ?

1.211 devi, kumāra|Lakṣmaṇo vijñāpayati: «sajjo rathaḥ. ārohatu devī.»

1.212 iyam ārohāmi.

1.212 parisphurat' îva me garbha|bhāraḥ. śanair gacchāmaḥ.

1.213 ita ito devī.

1.214 namo Raghu|kula|devatābhyaḥ.

3.24 ammahe, jānāmi priya|sakhī me Vāsantī vyāharati?

3.26 kiṃ tasya?

3.28 ārya|putra, paritrāhi, paritrāhi mama taṃ putrakam!

3.28 hā dhik, hā dhik! tāny eva cira|paricitāny akṣarāṇi Pañcavaṭī| darśanena māṃ manda|bhāginīm anubadhnanti. hā ārya|putra!

3.31 ammahe, jala|bhṛta|megha|manthara|stanita|gambhīra|māṃsalaḥ kuto nv eṣa bhāratī|nirghoṣo bharan karṇa|vivaraṃ mām api manda|bhāginīṃ jhaṭity uddhūsarayati?

3.34 bhagavati, kiṃ bhaṇasi, «a | parisphuṭam» iti? mayā punaḥ svara|saṃyogena pratyabhijñātam ārya|putra eva vyāharati.

3.36 diṣṭyā a|parihīna|rāja|dharmaḥ khalu sa rājā.

3.38 hā kathaṃ, prabhāta | candra | maṇḍal' | āpāṇḍura | parikṣāma | durbalen' ākāreṇ' âyaṃ nija|saumya|gambhīr'|ânubhāva|mātra|pratyabhijñeya ārya|putra eva. tan māṃ dhāraya.

3.44 hā, katham etat?

3.46 hā dhik, hā dhik. māṃ manda|bhāginīṃ vyāhṛty' āmīlita|netra|nīl'|ôtpalo mūrchita eva. hā kathaṃ dharaṇī|pṛṣṭhe nirutsāha|niḥsahaṃ viparyastaḥ? bhagavati Tamase, paritrāhi, paritrāhi. jīvay' ārya|putram.

3.48 yad bhavatu tad bhavatu. yathā bhagavaty ājñāpayati.

3.50 jāne punar api pratyāgatam iva jīvitaṃ trailokyasya.

3.54 etāvad ev' êdānīṃ me bahutaram.

3.56 hā dhik, hā dhik! kimity ārya|putro māṃ bhaṇiṣyati?

3.58 bhagavati Tamase, apasarāvaḥ. yadi tāvan māṃ prekṣiṣyate tato 'n|abhyanujñāta|sannidhānen' âdhikaṃ mama rājā kopiṣyati.

3.60 ām. asty etat.

3.62 ārya|putra, a|sadṛśaṃ khalv etad asya vṛttāntasya.

3.62 atha vā kim iti vajramayī janm'|ântare 'pi punar a|sambhāvita|labdha|darśanasya mām eva manda|bhāginīm uddiśya vatsalasy' âivaṃ|vādina ārya|putrasy' ôpari niranukrośā bhaviṣyāmi? aham etasya hṛdayaṃ jānāmi, mam' âiṣa iti.

3.64 bhagavati Tamase, tathā niṣkāraṇa|parityāgino 'py etasy' âivaṃ|vidhena darśanena kīdṛśya iva me hṛday'|âvasthā iti na jānāmi.

3.69 ete khalu te '|gādha|darśita|sneha|sahāyā ānanda|niṣyandinaḥ Sītāmayā ārya|putrasy' ôllāpā yeṣāṃ pratyayena niṣkāraṇa|parityāga|śalyito 'pi bahu|mato me janma|lābhaḥ.

3.75 ka idānīm abhiyokṣyate?

3.78 kathaṃ, priya|sakhī me Vāsantī.

3.82 hā tāta Jaṭāyo. śūnyaṃ tvayā vinā Janasthānam.

3.85 bhagavati, satyam eva vana|devatā api māṃ na prekṣante.

3.87 tato 'nusarāvaḥ.

3.92 ammahe, īdṛśaḥ sa saṃvṛttaḥ.

3.95 a|viyukta idānīṃ dīrgh'|āyur asyāḥ saumya|darśanāyā bhavatu.

3.98 bhagavati Tamase, ayaṃ tāvad īdṛśo jātaḥ. tau punar na jānāmi Kuśa|Lavāv etāvatā kālena kīdṛśāv iva bhavataḥ.

3.100 īdṛśy ahaṃ manda|bhāginī yasyā na kevalaṃ nirantara ārya|putra|virahaḥ putra|viraho 'pi.

3.102 kiṃ vā mayā prasūtayā yena tādṛśor api mama putrakayor īṣad|kalita|virala|komala|dhvala|daśan'|ôjjvala|kapolam anubaddha|mugdha|kākalī|vihasitaṃ nibaddha|kāka|śikhaṇḍakam amala|mukha|puṇḍarīka|yugalakaṃ na paricumbitam ārya|putreṇa?

3.104 bhagavati Tamase, eten' âpatya|saṃsmaraṇen' ôcchvasita|prasnuta|stanī tayoś ca pituḥ sannidhānena kṣaṇa|mātraṃ saṃsāriṇy asmi saṃvṛttā.

3.109 eṣa saḥ!

3.111 evaṃ bhavatu.

3.115 suṣṭhu pratyabhijñātam ārya|putreṇa.

3.120 sakhi Vāsanti, kiṃ tvayā kṛtam ārya|putrasya mama c' âitad darśayantyā? hā dhik, hā dhik. sa ev' ārya|putraḥ. tad eva Pañcavaṭī|vanam. s" âiva priya|sakhī Vāsantī. ta eva vividha|visrambha|sākṣiṇo Godāvarī|kānan'|ôddeśāḥ. ta eva jāta|nirviśeṣā mṛga|pakṣi|pādapāḥ. mama punar manda|bhāginyā dṛśyamānam api sarvam etan n' âsti. īdṛśo jīva|lokasya parivartaḥ.

3.123 prekṣe, sakhi, prekṣe.

3.125 hā daiva, eṣa mayā vin", âham apy etena vin" êti kena sambhāvitam āsīt? tan muhūrtakam api janm'|ântarād iva labdha|darśanaṃ bāṣpa|salil'|ântareṣu prekṣe tāvad vatsalam ārya|putram.

3.136 sakhi Vāsanti, kiṃ tvam asy evaṃ|vādinī? priy'|ârhaḥ khalu sarvasy' ārya|putro, viśeṣato mama priya|sakhyāḥ.

3.142 sakhi Vāsanti, virama, virama.

3.148 tvam eva, sakhi Vāsanti, dāruṇā kaṭhorā ca yā evaṃ pradīptaṃ pradīpayasi.

3.152 ārya|putra, dharāmy eṣā dharāmi.

3.154 hā dhik, hā dhik. ārya|putro 'pi pramukta|kaṇṭhaṃ praruditaḥ.

3.161 evam etat.

3.168 mohit" âsmy etair ārya|putra|vacanaiḥ.

3.173 evam asmi manda|bhāginī punaḥ punar apy āyāsa|kāriṇy ārya|putrasya.

3.176 eten' ārya|putrasya dur|vāra|dāruṇ'|ārambheṇa duḥkha|saṅkṣobheṇa pramuṣita|nija|duḥkham iva vepate me hṛdayam.

3.180 sandīpanāny eva duḥkhasya priya|sakhī vinodan'|ôpāya iti manyate.

3.183 dāruṇ" âsi, Vāsanti, dāruṇ" âsi, yā etair hṛdaya|marma|gūḍha|śalya|ghaṭṭanaiḥ punaḥ punar māṃ manda|bhāginīm ārya|putraṃ smārayasi.

3.187 hā dhik, hā dhik! punar api pramūḍha ārya|putraḥ.

3.189 hā ārya|putra, māṃ manda|bhāginīm uddiśya sakala|jīva|loka|maṅgal'|ādhārasya te janma|lābhasya vāraṃ vāraṃ saṃśayita|jīva|dāruṇo daśā|pariṇāma, iti hā hat" âsmi.

3.201 apasartum icchāmi. eṣa punaś cira|sad|bhāva|saumya|śītalen' ārya|putra|sparśena dīrgha|dāruṇam api santāpaṃ jhaṭity ullāpayatā vajra|lep'|ôpanaddha iva svidyan|niḥsaha|viparyasto vepate '|vaśa iva me hastaḥ.

3.204 ārya|putra, sa eva. idānīm jānāsi.

3.207 hā dhik, hā dhik. ārya|putra|sparśa|mohitāyāḥ pramādaḥ khalu saṃvṛttaḥ.

3.213 hā dhik, hā dhik. ady' âpy an|avasthita|stimita|mūḍha|ghūrṇamāna|vedanaṃ na paryavasthāpayāmy ātmānam.

3.216 ammahe, a|vaśen' âiten' ātmanā lajjāpit" âsmi bhagavatyā Tamasayā. kim iti kil' âiṣā maṃsyate: «eṣa te parityāg,a eṣo 'bhiṣaṅga» iti?

3.218 satyam a|karuṇ" âsmi y" âivaṃ|vidhaṃ tvāṃ prekṣamāṇā dharāmy eva jīvitam.

3.220 ayi ārya|putra, viparītam eva.

3.223 may" âiva dāruṇayā vipralabdha ārya|putraḥ.

3.226 ārya|putra, tāto vyāpādyate. aham apy apahriye. paritrāhi!

3.229 ammo, unmattik" âsmi saṃvṛttā.

3.232 «niravadhir!» iti hā hat" âsmi.

3.235 bahu|mānayit" âsmi pūrva|viraham.

3.237 bhagavati Tamase, gacchaty ārya|putraḥ!

3.239 bhagavati, prasīda. kṣaṇam api tāvad dur|labhaṃ janaṃ prekṣe.

3.241 ārya|putra, kā?

3.243 ārya|putra idānīm asi tvam. ammahe, utkhātam idānīṃ me parityāga|lajjā|śalyam ārya|putreṇa.

3.245 dhanyā sā y" ārya|putreṇa bahu|manyate, y" ārya|putraṃ vinodayanty āśā|nibandhanaṃ jātā jīva|lokasya.

3.247 parihasit" âsmi bhagavatyā.

3.249 pratikūl" êdānīṃ me Vāsantī saṃvṛttā.

3.251 evaṃ kurvaḥ.

3.254 namo '|pūrva|puṇya|janita|darśanābhyām ārya|putra|caraṇa|kamalābhyām.

3.256 kiyac|ciraṃ vā megh'|ântareṇa pūrṇa|candrasya darśanam?

4.4 svāgatam an|adhyāya|kāraṇānāṃ viśeṣato jīrṇa|kūrcānām.

4.6 bho Bhāṇḍāyana, kiṃ|nāmadheya eṣa idānīṃ mahataḥ sthavirā|sârthasy' âgra|dhaurya|dharo 'tithir āgataḥ?

4.8 huṃ, Vasiṣṭhaḥ?

4.10 mayā punar jñātaṃ vyāghro vṛko v" âiṣa iti.

4.12 yena parāpatiten' âiva sā varākikā kalyāṇikā maḍamaḍāyitā.

4.14 bho! nigṛhīto 'si.

4.16 yen' āgateṣu Vasiṣṭha|miśreṣu vatsatarī viśasitā. ady' âiva paścād āgatasya rāja'|rṣer Janakasya bhagavatā Vālmīkin" âpi dadhi|madhubhyām eva nivartito madhu|parkaḥ. vatsatarī punar visarjitā.

4.18 kiṃ|nimittam?

4.20 tataḥ kim|ity āgataḥ?

4.22 apy adya sambandhinībhiḥ samaṃ saṃvṛttam asya darśanaṃ na v" êti?

4.24 yath" âite sarve sthavirāḥ parasparaṃ militās, tath" āvām api baṭukaiḥ samaṃ militv" ân|adhyāya|mah"|ôtsavaṃ khelantau sambhāvayāvaḥ.

4.44 īdṛśe kāle Mithil"|âdhipo draṣṭavya iti samam eva sarva|duḥkhāni samudbhavanti. na śaknomy udvartamāna|mūla|bandhanaṃ hṛdayaṃ vyavasthāpayitum.

4.47 kathaṃ ca vatsāyā vadhvā evaṃ gate tasya rāja'|rṣer mukhaṃ darśayāmaḥ?

4.49 eṣa sa mahā|rājasya hṛday'|ānando vatsāyā vadhvāḥ pitā rāja'|rṣiḥ. hā dhik, hā dhik. smārit" âsmy anuṣṭhita|mah'|ôtsavān divasān. hā deva, sarvam eva tan n' âsti.

4.58 ammo, unmīlanti vedanāḥ.

4.69 hā vatse Jānaki, kv' âsi? smarāmi te vivāha|lakṣmī|parigrah'|âika|maṅgalam utphulla|śuddha|hasitaṃ mugdha|mukha|puṇḍarīkam. āsphurac|candra|candrikā|sundarair aṅgaiḥ punar api me jāte uddyotay' ôtsaṅgam. sarvadā mahā|rājo bhaṇati, «eṣā Raghu|kula|mahattarāṇāṃ vadhūḥ. asmākaṃ tu Janaka|sambandhena duhitṛk" âiva.»

4.74 jāte Jānaki, kiṃ karomi? dṛḍha|vajra|lepa|pratibandha|niścalaṃ hata|jīvitaṃ māṃ manda|bhāginīṃ na parityajati.

4.76 kuto 'tikrānte mano|rathe?

4.81 su|labha|saukhyam idānīṃ bālatvaṃ bhavati.

4.81 ammahe, eteṣāṃ madhye ka eṣa Rāma|bhadra|lakṣmī|pariśobhitaiḥ s'|âvaṣṭambha|mugdha|lalitair aṅgair asmākam api locanaṃ śītalayati?

4.91 kiṃ manyadhve, evaṃ bhaṇita āgamiṣyat' îti?

4.93 kathaṃ sa|vinayaṃ niśāmita|Gṛṣṭi|vacano visṛjya' ṛṣi|dārakān ito|mukhaṃ prasṛta eva sa vatsaḥ?

4.98 jāta, ciraṃ jīva.

4.100 jāta, ito 'pi tāvad ehi.

4.100 ammahe, na kevalaṃ dara|vispaṣṭa|kuvalaya|śyāmal'|ôjjvalena deha|bandhena, kavalit'|âravinda|kesara|kaṣāya|kaṇṭha|kala|haṃsa|ghoṣa|gharghara|nināda|dīrgheṇa ca svareṇa Rāma|bhadrasy' ânuharati. nanu kaṭhora|kamala|garbha|pakṣmalaḥ śarīra|sparśo 'pi tādṛśa eva. jāta, prekṣe tāvat te mukham.

4.100 rāja'|ṛṣe, kiṃ na paśyasi? nipuṇaṃ nirūpyamāṇo vatsāyā vadhvā mukha|candreṇa saṃvadaty eva.

4.102 ammo, unmattī|bhūtam iva me hṛdayaṃ kim api cintayantyā bahu vipralapati.

4.104 jāta, asti te mātā? smarasi vā tātam?

4.106 tataḥ kasya tvam?

4.108 ayi jāta, kathitavyaṃ kathaya.

4.112 vatsa|Lakṣmaṇasya putraka «ājñāpayat'» îty amṛta|bindu|sundarāṇy akṣarāṇi śrūyante.

4.129 bhrātā 'pi te 'sti?

4.131 jyeṣṭha iti bhaṇitaṃ bhavati.

4.137 hā vatse mugdha|candra|mukhi, ka idānīṃ te śarīra|kusumasya jhaṭiti daiva|durvilāsa|pariṇāma ekākinyā nipatitaḥ?

4.145 bhagavati, paritrāhi, paritrāhi! prasādaya kupitaṃ rāja'|rṣim.

4.157 bhagavati, jānāmy, etam an|avekṣamāṇā vañcit" êva. tad ito 'nyato bhūtvā prekṣāmahe tāvad gacchantaṃ dīrgh'|āyuṣam.

6.6 tat kim|iti punar a|kāṇḍa|tāṇḍavit'|ôddaṇḍa|taralita|taḍic|chaṭā|kaḍāram iv' âmbaraṃ jhaṭiti saṃvṛttam?

6.12 diṣṭy" âitena vimala|muktā|phala|śītala|snigdha|masṛṇa|māṃsalena nātha|deha|sparśen' ānanda|manda|mukulita|ghūrṇamāna|locanāyā antarita eva me santāpaḥ.

6.15 katham a|virala|vilola|ghūrṇamāna|vidyul|latā|vilāsa|maṇḍitair matta|mayūra|kaṇṭha|śyāmalair avastīryate nabho|'ṅgaṇaṃ jala|dharaiḥ?

6.17 priyaṃ me, priyaṃ me!

6.20 nātha, ka idānīm eṣa sa|sambhram'|ôtkṣipta|kara|bhramita|paṭṭ'|âñcalo dūrata eva madhura|vacana|pratiṣiddha|yuddha|vyāpāra etayoḥ kumārayor antare vimāna|varam avatārayati?

7.13 hā ārya|putra, hā kumāra Lakṣmaṇa, ekākinīm a|śaraṇām araṇya āsanna|prasava|vedanāṃ hat'|āśāḥ śvāpadā mām abhilaṣanti. s" êdānīṃ manda|bhāginī Mandākinyām ātmānaṃ nikṣepsyāmi.

7.25 diṣṭyā dārakau prasūt" âsmi. hā ārya|putra!

7.28 bhagavati, kā tvam? tvaṃ ca?

7.30 bhagavati, namas te.

7.34 hā amba, īdṛśy ahaṃ tvayā dṛṣṭā.

7.44 hā ārya|putra, smāryase.

7.46 yathā v" âmbā bhaṇati.

7.56 nayatu mām ātmano 'ṅgeṣu vilayam ambā.

7.60 a|nāth" âsmi. kim etābhyām?

7.62 kīdṛśaṃ mam' â|bhāgyāyāḥ sa|nāthatvam?

7.69 kim iti sakalam antarikṣaṃ prajvalati?

7.73 diṣṭy" âstra|devatā etāḥ! hā ārya|putra, ady' âpi te prasādāḥ parisphuranti.

7.78 bhagavati, ka etayoḥ kṣatriy'|ôcitaṃ karma kariṣyati?

7.87 nayatu mām ātmano 'ṅgeṣu vilayam ambā. na sahiṣya īdṛśaṃ jīva|loka|parivartam anubhavitum.

7.101 samāśvasitu, samāśvasitv ārya|putraḥ.

7.112 api jānāty ārya|putraḥ Sītā|duḥkhaṃ pramārṣṭum?

7.115 jīvit" âsmi.

7.117 vatsa, īdṛśaś ciraṃ jīva.

7.120 kutra me putrakau?

7.123 kathaṃ, tātaḥ?

CHĀYĀ

7.126 ehi, jāta Kuśa, ehi, jāta Lava. cirasya pariṣvajethāṃ punar janm'|ântara|gatāṃ jananīm.

7.128 bhagavan, praṇamāmi.

NOTES

An asterisk (*) in the body of the text marks the word or passage being annotated.

RAMA'S LAST ACT

1.1 Being less familiar and slightly harder (as masc.) to construe with *idam*, *namovākam* is more probable (both words are *hapax* in Bh).

1.3 H: "He was known as Śrīkaṇṭha by the name carried by his father, and familiarly as Bhavabhūti" (p. 12). N takes the expression much more concretely, and perhaps more credibly given the usual meaning of *lāñchana*: "Out of deep devotion he wore on a part of his body a golden cloth upon which the foot of Śrīkaṇṭha was marked." It could even mean: "branded with the foot of Śrīkaṇṭha" (though it is unclear to me how common the practice was among Shaivas; it is even today obligatory among orthodox Mādhvas).

1.4 The husband of Language and creator god.

1.5 In the choice between *kāryavaśāt* and *kavivaśāt* the echo of the previous verse (besides the agreement of Ne and N) seems decisive.

1.5 *Āyodhyaka* need not imply "native of Ayodhyā," as shown conclusively by Śabara's comment on *Pūrvamīmāṃsāsūtra* 1.3.20 (in reference to the word *māthura*). B's failure to see this led him to accept what I find to be a corrupt (if old) version of the text at Act 1.8ff. (see Notes to the Edition p. 435).

1.6 Demonic creatures, against whom Rāma fought to recover his wife. A few went over to Rāma's side.

1.6 I follow Ne and N, whose reading is slightly more difficult than B's, insofar as *rājarṣi* would account for Janaka (as V points out).

1.6 B's reading is corroborated by N and V; G's *-āgatāḥ* appears to be a simplification (*pace* K).

1.6 Ne, B alone read *saṃprati hi*, linking the conclusion of the festivities in Ayodhyā with the departure of the elders to Ṛṣyaśṛṅga's ritual. All C, reading *anyac ca,* understand their departure as a second unrelated condition.

1.12 See N: *paddhatir mārgaḥ saṃdarbhaparipāṭīty arthaḥ.*

1.14 "It is our duty to act," *vyavahartavyam.* C understand more narrowly, "speak," i.e., perform the royal eulogy. But the word can also mean simply act in the world, which would provide another premonition of Rāma's dilemma. K rightly hears a rebuke by Bh to his critics, of the sort that occasioned the great verse in MM (1.16; see Introduction).

1.16 When Rāma recovered her Sīta was forced to undergo a fire ordeal in Laṅkā to prove her chastity.

1.24 N is right to note that the first half of the verse is a reference to the particular events at hand (the departure of the elders), and the second a more general corroboration. "Hazards," *pratyavāya*: Dangers that arise from the failure to perform obligatory religious acts.

1.26 "Feel such revulsion," *bībhatsamānāḥ*. A technical term of Sanskrit aesthetic theory, the first of many such allusions throughout the play (see Introduction). The verse no doubt offers a foreshadowing, if ironically, of the events to follow.

1.45 Mirashi and others are troubled by the timeline here: If Rāma returned to Ayodhyā right after the battle in Laṅkā and the recovery of Sītā, and the coronation ceremony took place immediately, then her advanced pregnancy would indeed be suspicious (1974: 266). But there is no reason whatever to assume Bh shared so crude a conception of realism.

1.48 "Life itself," *svasmāt* (literally, "oneself" or "one's self"). The northern reading *tasmāt*, which is contradicted by all C (including V and G, *pace* their editors' constituted texts), certainly seems like a simplification. N persuasively glosses, *svasmāt sarvebhyo 'pi preyastamād ātmanaḥ. vibhakte pañcamī.*

1.50 "To propitiate," *ārādhanāya*. The word is often used of placating a god. See also v. 1.182 [42].

1.53 Aṣṭāvakra's departure seems awkward enough to imply some kind of dramaturgical rule, that only three actors were permitted on stage simultaneously (cf. Sophocles' innovation in ancient Greek drama, according to Aristotle). But other scenes in the play belie this (for example, in Act 4 there are already four people on stage [Kausalyā, Arundhatī, Janaka, and Lava] when a group of boys enters).

1.54 It is curious that the theme of the painting exhibition, though absent from the *Uttarakāṇḍa*, is alluded to in *Raghuvaṃśa* (14.25).

1.59 There is a crucial textual problem here. I translate *te ... praṇāmaḥ*, the reading of Ne, N, and B, though it is weak. V and G read more powerfully *te ... pravādaḥ* ("slur on you"). But it is impossible to believe Rāma would say such a thing to Sītā. What the context demands—though attested by none of the mss. available to me—is *me ... pravādaḥ*, "This is a slur on me that I will have to bear for the rest of my life."

1.60 V interprets the verse as pertaining only to the present circumstances: It is wrong to trouble people who are already sad by reminding them of past troubles. This explanation is of course impossible to construe with *kuladhanaiḥ*. K reports the v.l. *kaṣṭam*, which despite his objection strikes me as an improvement.

1.62 B's dual seems improbable. It was Rāma who was seated at the opening of the scene and begins to walk about (Ne reads *parikrāmanti*).

1.65 A quasi etymology of the name Viśvāmitra, with the figure "apparent contradiction" (*virodhābhāsa*): though he appears to be *Viśva-amitra* ("foe to all") he is really *Viśva-mitra* ("friend to all"). (The name is presumably originally based on a *devatādvanda, viśvā-mitra*)

1.72 G (*pace* K's edition) reads *anāyāsa-*, "without effort."

1.74 The "others," including Daśaratha, are more strictly Janaka's new relatives. Presumably for hierarchy's sake Vasiṣṭha is mentioned first.

1.76 Viśvāmitra, who arranged the marriage between Rāma and Sītā, and can therefore metaphorically be termed the giver and receiver of the bride.

1.78 The southern reading (i.e., the bracelet is "tied on") is contextually superior to the northern ("outstretched").

1.79 Lakṣmaṇa uses this kinship term for the wife of his younger brother, in contrast to the term used for the wives of his older brothers Bharata and Rāma.

1.81 Bhavabhūti uses *apavārya*, *svagatam*, and *ātmagatam* without distinction in the sense of "aside."

1.85 Or: diverting [him], K.

1.91 Absent a fuller census of manuscripts one is inclined to regard the reading *ambānām* (the curiosity "of my mothers") for *aṅgānām* as the work of Victorians *avant la lettre*. Bh uses *kutūhala* only once elsewhere and it is in an erotic context (MM 9.44). See also 6.124 [35] below. For Bh as for much of the later tradition (though not for Vālmīki, see Pollock 1986: 358–59), Sītā was prepubescent when married, though the marriage would not have been consummated until her first menstruation. N understands the verse aright, noting that "the skill in handling a completely innocent young girl is the highest secret of connoisseurship; this is well understood among the multitude [*samavāya*; or read, *samaya*, from the characteristic practices] of sophisticated men."

1.95 Recall that in Vālmīki's text, Lakṣmaṇa had wanted to kill Kaikeyī and seize control of the kingdom (*Rāmāyaṇa* 2. 20).

1.100 One might be inclined to read *purā* in place of G, V, and B's *pituś ca* (which seems like an awkward attempt to get the kin relationship correct). The v.l. *purā* however is found only in

N's ed., not even in N himself (though Ne corroborates N's *[pituḥ] prapitāmahān*).

1.105 Though supported by Ne, B's *lulita-* for C's *lalita-* is dubious. N attractively explains the latter by saying that her limbs became especially alluring when exhausted.

1.105 Were B's simple-minded *saṃjāta-* original it is hard to see how it would have generated the variant *saṃpāta-* (all C), which I therefore accept (see also Act 1.144).

1.107 The original reading of Sītā's speech here may be irrecoverable. I follow N (corroborated to an important degree by Ne, and by G, *pace* K) over against B (to some degree supported by BN).

1.110 Bh typically uses *sarasa-* in the sense of "sap-full" or "fresh" (e.g., in reference to flowers, see Index s.v.), has no application to "fords."

1.112 I read *āsakti-* with N and V (so too ŚP p. 859) for B's *āsatti-*, but construe it with what follows rather than what precedes (so N, K). I have accepted *avicalita-* (attested also in MM) because of the agreement of Ne (*avicalati* I assume to be metathesis) and N, in preference to the (*hapax*) *aviralita-* though *avirala-* is a favorite Bh word and the reading is widely attested (including Bhoja ŚP p. 859). With regard to what is probably the most celebrated *anusvāra* in all of Sanskrit literature, mss. are split; C unanimously corroborate *eva*, as does Bhoja.

1.116 The exact nuance here escapes me (the memory of a bad person is disquieting? even though not present a bad person can cause troubles?), but the echo of verses 5–6 is clear enough.

1.118 An oft-quoted verse, the citations like the mss. and C being divided in their reading of *c*, *vikalakaraṇair* (which I accept, so all C, *pace* K) and the almost unintelligible *vikalakaruṇair* (B; Ne's *karuṇavikalair* may be a *lectio facilior* of this, though see textual note to 3.122 [23]). Bhoja, who cites the verse four times in ŚP, once reads *viśadakaruṇair* (p. 688) in the context of a discussion of *rasa*. The verse beautifully foreshadows the action of Act 3.

1.128 *Rāmāyaṇa* 3.65.15ff. indicates that *kabandha* is here to be taken as a proper name.

1.128 Comparing MVC 5.27 it appears that Bh understood *Śramaṇī* to be a proper name, in contrast to R 3.69.19ff., which gives her name as *Śabarī*.

1.128 Beginning with this speech Lakṣmaṇa is describing things Sītā never witnessed.

1.129 I cannot see how N's reading of the compound as a *dvandva* makes sense. The lection is disputed.

1.131 My reading is corroborated by ŚP p. 1021; in addtion, *bhuvoḥ* would require an asyndeton uncharacteristic of Bh.

1.135 Peacocks are said to dance at the start of the rainy season, and it is then that the *kadámba* trees blossom.

1.136 The meter of the verse, *mandākrāntā*, would have recalled to every reader the *Meghadūta*, Kālidāsa's classic poem of a demigod who is separated from his beloved and asks a cloud to carry her a message.

1.154 With V I want to hear a set of binaries throughout the verse and so follow him in my understanding of the contrastive verbs in *d*, which I reverse in the trans.; the v.l. *samunmīlayati* (for *ca sammīlayati*) would make things much easier but has no C support (V does not read this, *pace* K). I also agree that *a* refers to mental as opposed to physical states, the latter being described in *b*. Note that ŚP p. 855 reads *pramādo* in *b*.

1.160 There is something slightly confusing about stage directions in Sanskrit plays. This one of course refers to the actress's action. The character Sītā is actually falling asleep, not pretending to fall asleep. She is not privy to the awful events that now unfold, and in any case the next stage direction is "she sleeps"—though technically this too should refer to the actress and so should be "mimes sleeping."

1.164 Rāma understands the doorkeeper to be referring to the torture of separation just mentioned.

1.171 The language of the verse suggests an analogy between love and transcendence, since "unity," *advaita*, and "veils," *āvaraṇa*, are terms of Vedānta metaphysics. I accept B's *hi tat*, which is read by all C; ŚP reads *hitam* on p. 675, but—unless it is an oversight of the editor—*hi tat* on p. 859). K's principal explanation of the verse is not acceptable. For the general construction of the v. I follow BN, though not in his supplying, like N, the verb *bhūyāt* in *d*. (N's *anugatam* for *anuguṇam* is read by Bhoja, ŚP pp. 675 and 1250, but not on p. 859.)

1.176 I follow Ne in taking *evam eva* as part of the stage direction (here and in the two other occurrences in the play; see the explicit discussion in *Nāṭyadarpaṇa* (*Vivaraṇa*) 1.18; the same usage is found elsewhere, e.g. *Bālarāmāyaṇa* 3 (on which the commentator remarks *karṇe evam evaṃ rahasyakathanaprakāra eṣaḥ*). N, G, V read as Prakrit, *evvaṃ via*, making it clear that for them the words were to be spoken aloud, "It's like this . . ." (so *Mālavikāgnimitra* 1). The locution occurs only here (and in 1.193 and 2.42) in the works of Bh; MVC has several instances of *karṇe kathayati* or the like.

1.182 Daśaratha died of grief when in order to keep his word to his wife Kaikeyī he sent Rama into exile.

1.187 V and G are certainly right to hear a negative overtone ("unpracticed" and "heartless" respectively).

1.188 But for the agreement of Ne and N, I would be inclined to accept B's *adhyavasitam* ("come to [such] a conclusion") since the objection concerns the nature of the inference he is making, not just his decision.

1.189 Or: Heaven forbid (that anything I am about to do is wrong, so N).

1.194 I accept *-āśayāṃ-*, the reading of Ne, N, and B, though not N's explanation (*harṣaśokādyanuvidhāyinīm*); V's *-āśrayāṃ* strikes me as a latter emendation made in a mistaken interpretation of *āśaya* (illustrated by K).

1.198 It is not easy to see how life-breaths can wound one's vitals, *marmopaghātibhiḥ* (C), and one might at first glance be inclined to understand the second half of the verse altogether differently by taking the phrase more passively (though the word *upaghātin* is attested only in an active sense)—however "fatal the blows" his life receives—and understanding the impersonal passive *vajrakīlāyitam* as "seems bolted ... by iron bolts" (literally, "seem as if acting like iron bolts," i.e., is as hard to remove). But unlike most characters in Sanskrit literature Rāma may not be asking why he cannot die in the face of terrible suffering (N's understanding, which is grammatically impossible, though Rāma complains in this way later, see for example Act 3.160 [32], 3.167 [34]; 6.121 [33]); he seems rather to be saying that life itself has been a source of unbearable suffering for him (so essentially G).

1.207 "Destitute," *śūnyām*: So read by N in place of B's *ślāghyām*, "commendable," though of course Rāma could be emphasizing the injustice of what he is about to do (since his wife is "praiseworthy" and innocent) rather than its consequences. This is suggested by V, who proposes unpersuasively that the adjective be taken as proleptic ("so as to be free from harm").

2.12 *udgītha-*: The term technically refers to *Sāmaveda* chant, but often connotes the syllable *om*.

2.22 N: philosophy, economy, and polity; G: writing, soldiery, weapons-and-chariots; V: medicine, weaponry, music.

2.28 Bh seems to draw a parallel here—the idea of "fulfillment" for him means perpetuation of the family line through the birth of a son—with the fate of Rāma, see Act 5.74 [24], 5.76 [25].

2.29 We must read the nominative here. It is not the verse forms as such that are new but their non-Vedic embodiment.

2.49 A Vedic rite on behalf of political sovereignty: A king claimed control of all the territory in which the sacrificial horse was permitted to wander freely.

2.52 Vedic rites require the presence of the sacrificer's duly wedded wife.

2.64 BN suggests taking *apas-kiramāṇa-* as an *aluksamāsa* ("sprinkling water"), modifying *-drumāḥ*.

2.69 I take this as a pure (archaic) optative (comparable to optative + *epi* in Greek). Differently N: "The particle *api* loses its interrogative quality here and connotes supposition" (*jījñāsāyām*).

2.73 As in the case of *-upāya* in 2.74, I take *puṇyābhisaṃbhavāḥ* as a *bahuvrīhi*.

2.82 The geography here is somewhat unclear, though it was evidently critical for Bh. The key point is that (as *Rāmāyaṇa* 3.10–12 makes plain), Pañcavaṭī, the peaceful forest where Rāma and Sītā spent the greater part of the exile, is to the north of the regions (Janasthāna, etc.) inhabited by the *rākṣasa*s. Traveling beyond the "woods in the middle distance" in Act 2.88ff. that comprise Pañcavaṭī took one deeper and deeper into demon country. What remains uncertain is why Janasthāna is now said to be horrific (2.83 [16]) when in 2.80 it was just said to be a *siddhakṣetra*.

Also obscure is what is intended by the use of contrapuntal registers here: Śambūka's bombastic and turbid descriptions of nature, and Rāma's heart-rendingly simple confessions of guilt and pain. Is this perhaps a mixture of rasas? But the comic—if that is what Śambūka's represents, a sort of *vidūṣaka* (as would be expected on the analogy with the *Śākuntala*, see Introduction)—is not typically combined with the pitiful (and note this is indeed *karuṇa* and not *śṛṅgāra*).

2.83 N, "Weak creatures are always in fear of more powerful ones, and so never sleep tranquilly." B's *-ghora-* is corroborated by BN (v.l. *-bhoga-*).

2.85 The logic behind the choice of reading here is brought out clearly in N's comment, which is reflected in the translation. The reading derives further corroboration from Act 2.87 [19]*d*.

2.92 The one that leads to liberation from transmigration

2.99 Or, with N: "But why has this befallen Rāma now?"

2.100 B's reading violates the parallelism with the images of the first three *pāda*s.

2.104 "Killed," *vināśita-*: This could also mean, less harshly, just "drove away."

2.110 The reading is widely attested, but S may be right in preferring *krauñcābhido*, given the epic precedents, though it seems very likely to be a *lectio facilior*.

3.1 N notes that their entrance is foreshadowed in the last verse of the previous act.

3.4 "Hidden," *anirbhinno*. My reading is corroborated by Bhoja, ŚP pp. 1097, 1634.

3.9 It is clear from Act 7.13 that Sītā was attempting to commit suicide.

3.11 Observe the use of *vinipāto* in Act 3.5 (though see Act 4.38 [6]*d* below).

3.19 There seems to be one too many similes here, but no good v.l. presents itself. How, in light of the Gaṅgā's promise of invisibility, do the two rivers see Sītā? Compare below, Act 3.86: the "deities" must refer only to the forest spirits, not to the river spirits.

3.31 The reading of G and B (Skt. *utsukāpayati*, *utsukayati*), "to cause to yearn," does derive some support from *utkaṇṭhitam* in 3.33 [7]*d*; BN translates as *ucchvāsayati*, "revive."

3.36 The exact nuance here is unclear: does this imply that Sītā believes Rāma had renounced righteousness when he exiled her?

At all events, it is obvious that Sītā like everyone else (except Rāma himself) endorses the execution of Śambūka.

3.46 The short *-i* form is read by both G and B; the word is *hapax* in Bh.

3.47 N, G, V's *nirato janaḥ*, "[to which] this man [i.e., Rāma] is devoted," seems somewhat redundant.

3.56 I hesitantly accept Ne (which, erroneously in my view, drops the *maṃ*); almost equally good is N's *maṇṇisadi* (*maṃsyate*), "should be thinking." BN, B's reading (Skt. *mārgiṣyati*), "should search for," anticipates too much.

3.62 N, K [though not G himself, who has *saṃ-* rather than *asaṃ-*] read *puṇo asaṃbhāviatulaggaladdha-* (see also below endnote to 3.125), whose authenticity is suggested by its obscurity, which however has stumped me. BN gives the *chāyā*: *vajramayīm … asaṃbhāvitadurlabhadarśanām* (i.e, addressing me whom he had never expected to see again; *asaṃbhāvita* and *durlabha* seem redundant). N's reading here, *-tulāgralabdha*, is obscure to me, though its very obscurity suggests its authenticity (the phrase seems to be unattested elsewhere).

3.69 As the two emendations made here show, N's readings can be at once less expected (*sīdāmaaā* for *sudā mae*) and simpler (note that BN also omits *-māṇasa-*) than B's.

3.94 "Good fortune," *kalyāṇa*. N (citing the *Mātaṅgalīlā*) calls attention to the technical sense of the word when used of elephants, alluding to their physical grandeur and strength in battle. But more likely the poet is hereby referring to the luck of having benefited from Sītā's maternal care.

3.97 The allusion is no doubt to the incident recounted in Act 1.107.

3.99 It is unclear whether this means: like Rāma (i.e., in appearance), or (with N) like the young elephant (i.e., in strength and daring), or whether the boys have simply grown up the way the elephant has.

3.102 N's *īsikalida* (*īṣatkalita-*) is preferable since *īṣat* typically requires a verb and only with considerable awkwardness can be made to modify *virala* directly.

3.104 N (first interpretation) is correct here, I believe ("feel for a moment as if I have received the gift of a happy life"), not K ("a woman with a family").

3.106 As N explains, "after the birth of a child a transformation of consciousness is inevitably produced, which unites the hearts of a man and woman even when they were previously not much in love." (V is adrift on the compound, which he takes as a *samāhāradvandva*, "love-and-closeness," and the ablative as *nimitta* of the "knot of bliss").

3.108 Though I follow N here, the phrase *padatāṇḍava* strikes me as dubious.

3.112 C disagree sharply about *a–b*, and the lines are indeed complex. B and N agree in their reading, which I accept. BN correctly notes *bhramiṣu arthāt tava bhramiṣu*. According to N the *pādas* are meant to prove that Sītā has the skills for teaching the peacock how to dance. The brutally literal sense is: "beautifying her eye, of which a circular movement was made within the sockets, by means of the *tándava* dances...."

3.121 It is not entirely clear what Vāsantī intends. N believes the implication to be that, imagining Sītā present before her, Vāsantī is rebuking her for her indifference, though this strikes me as improbable.

3.122 Three time-periods are referred to in this verse: before Rāma and Sītā were married, during their married life together, and the present (which makes *te* essential, *pace* K). B's *navaṃ navam* is not only contradicted by all C but is very awkward, given the need for a predicate. N's *-śyāmaḥ* (for B's *so 'yam*; G, V's *-cchāyaḥ*) is less certain. He explains that Rāma's paleness is a result of brooding, and his darkness a result of sleeplessness.

3.124 I translate B (Ne, G) but one wonders whether the reading isn't a learned emendation for that of N (V), *paśya priyaṃ bhūyaḥ*, "Look further on your beloved," i.e., take your time gazing. I see no point in Tamasā's offering a blessing at this juncture in the narrative.

3.125 Again note the reading of N, *tulāgralabdha-* (above endnote to 3.62).

3.127 N hears *śleṣa* in this verse, unnecessarily in my view.

3.132 *Pace* K I see no problem with the compound *prasavodbheda* (read by B, N, and G) except for the word order.

3.137 I accept N's reading in place of B's, given that Bh typically uses *anurudhya* in the sense of "comply with, acknowledge."

3.145 The precise sense of this phrase is unclear, but it is altogether unlikely that Rāma should be taken as speaking ironically (S) let alone as leveling a criticism against the people, something he refrains from doing throughout the play (note that he is still obsequious to them in verse 3.163 [33]). It may be instead that he cannot bring himself to utter the reason. The phrase echoes part of the poet's celebrated self-defense in MM 1.6 (*jānanti te kim api*) cited in the Introduction (Somadeva Vasudeva, personal communication), where the sense is close to "they may have some point." G believes it expresses shame.

3.146 B's placement of the line, immediately after verse 3.147 [28] (where it would mean "The reproach comes at last"), is impossible in view of the agreement of Ne and N, who however disagree about the reading itself. N has *upalambhaḥ* and rather simplemindedly understands this as further explanation of Rāma's statement: "Because he recovered [Sītā] so late" (that is, because she had lived with another man). Ne (with G, V) reads *upālambhaḥ* but this cannot be taken sarcastically ("A rather too late criticism"), given that, as just noted, Rāma consistently refuses to blame the people. The translation aims to capture some sense of this refusal.

3.154 G, V alone add before this *aṇṇo via* (*anya iva*), "like any other [i.e., undisciplined] person" (see S ad loc.), but this is certainly an interpolation—as the agreement of Ne, BN, and N virtually assures—to explain the slightly unanticipated *avi* (*api*).

3.158 I agree with N—and compare the following verse—that this is another one of Rāma's troubles, not part of the blessing (so K).

3.163 BN tries to square the use of the singular *mām* (also read by Ne) in *c* over against the plural in *d*. The reading of N, *adyāsmābhiḥ*, has merit.

3.170 "Honey," *madhu*: Possibly instead "liquor," thus explaining *mohita* in Sītā's preceding statement.

3.172 "Heated arrowhead" follows BN; or perhaps "flaming." "Athwart," *tiraścīnam*, in accordance with N and as vague as the Sanskrit. In truth I fail to see how a dart embedded obliquely would be any more painful than one embedded straight (so K).

3.175 B's reading is hard to construe with *ujjṛmbhaṇa*.

3.185 *viśvaṃ* (N) would seem to be an emendation or corruption of *viśvaṅ* (G B), which I therefore accept, though the resulting intransitive use of *sthagayati* remains awkward (Ne reads the hypometric *viśva-*). There is a similar v.l. in MM 9.20, where the verse is repeated.

3.194 "Parts," *-dhātūn*. Or perhaps "senses," with N, who compares Act 6.96 [22] (*cetanādhātur*).

3.201 I retain B's (Ne) *ollavanteṇa* (*ullāpayatā*), dubious though it is (G V's *ullāhaanteṇa*, [*ullāghavatā*], is presumably a *lectio facilior*). N reads *avaṇudanteṇa* (*apanudatā*).

3.204 "Now you know," i.e., but did not seem to know when you disowned me (so essentially N). In addition to sense, the echo with v. 3.205 [41cd] (*sa eva*) indicates that the reading of B, despite its wide support, should be rejected.

3.213 The following verse and the succeeding prose show that Sītā must here be referring to herself, and thus N's reading alone can be correct.

3.231 The reading *pravilayaḥ* is certified by the agreement of N and Ne (I am assuming that Ne's *pravilayayaḥ* is dittography) and by ŚP pp. 1544, 1632. In *c*, by contrast (here *pace* ŚP), *-rasa-* must construe with *vimardair*, not with *viyogo*.

3.234 The references recapitulate the chronology of the recovery of Sītā from Laṅkā.

3.236 N reverses the subjective and objective genitives here (erroneously, given the next sentence).

3.248 I follow N here.

3.257 I agree with V (who glosses *apūrvarūpakanirimāṇam*; N misses the critical metaliterary reference, glossing "acts done in a previous birth, in short, the fickleness of fate"). The word's rare technical sense is found in the *prastāvanā* of the lost *Rāmābhyudaya* of Yaśovarman (*śuddhiḥ prastutasaṃvidhānakavidhau*, "purity in the construction of the relevant plot," cited ŚP p. 712).

3.258 Mirashi correctly explains that this verse refers only to the present play, and that the different forms of *karuṇa* are a result of the different characters feeling the pity—Rāma, Sītā, Janaka, Kausalyā, Vāsantī, and so on (1974: 281).

3.262 N spells out the implications here: Earth is the mother of Sītā; Gaṅgā is the family deity of the Raghu clan; "others like us" means other forest and river deities.

4.3 N notes that the wild rice is meant for ascetics, buttered rice for Brahman guests.

4.4 A much disputed reading. N offers (I give only the *chāyā*s here) *sāvaśeṣabhūtajīrṇakūrcānām* (the graybeards and as yet unreceived guests [?]); BN *āgatam anadhyāyanakāraṇam saviśeṣabhūtam adya jīrṇakūrcānām.* I see no propriety for B's *viśeṣato* but also see no simple way to revise it.

4.10 B's *vakka* in the sense of *vṛka* seems to be unattested; K reads *vio*, which is also *hapax* in Bh

4.31 N glosses *durita* as *pāpa*, BN as *duḥkha*.

4.31 BN glosses *manyu* as *krodha*, N as *duḥkha* (Amara supports both). See the use of the word in Act 4.54, which vindicates BN.

4.32 An allusion to *Īśa Upaniṣad* 3 (so V). K takes *andhatāmisrāḥ* as the proper name of a hell, which would be improbably pedantic of Bh and more troubling than the slight redundancy with "sunless."

4.32 I follow N (*cintayā*) and V (*vicāreṇa*) though this is not the typical meaning of the word in Bh (see, e.g., Act 1.198 [48]; 4.55; 4.139 [23]; 4.146 [25])

4.32 The syntax may be a bit awkward but earlier usage (Act 2.57) shows that this is meant as the common general exclamation (very frequent in Prakrit, e.g., *Sattasaī*), and is not specifically addressed to Sītā (*pace* N ["'mother' in the sense of someone who 'brings distinction on our family'"], S).

4.35 I agree with N, who understands this optatively.

4.52 An allusion to *Bṛhadāraṇyaka Upaniṣad* (5.14), appropriately given that Janaka is a central figure in that text.

4.54 Going first to the sacrifice of Ṛṣyaśṛṅga and then to Vālmīki's ashram, Kausalyā avoided seeing Rāma from the moment he abandoned Sītā—that is, for twelve years.

4.56 That is, her name itself is guarantee of her purity; she has no need of purification by fire.

4.66 Only B reads *-niṣṭhuram*. N's *-visphuraṇam* is an attractive variant.

4.69 To regard Sītā as daughter rather than daughter-in-law has a special significance in the Indian context, where the relationship of mother-in-law and daughter-in-law is traditionally a fraught one.

4.80 The compound is obscure. C interpret as "vacation due to the arrival of learned persons," which Janaka would hardly use of himself (though Vasiṣṭha and Arundhatī could be meant). The conjecture *śiṣya-* suggests itself, unless that be thought redundant.

4.81 Glossed *saviśeṣaiḥ* by N, citing the *Śabdaratnākara*.

4.83 See Sītā's words above in reference to the young Rāma, Act 3.122 [23].

4.83 The correct *anvaya* is given by N: *kaḥ ayaṃ dṛṣṭaḥ ... -añjanaṃ kurute*. S's construction, of *kurute dṛṣṭaḥ* as some sort of passive verbal phrase, is improbable.

4.86 The reading *aparaḥ* seems a patent and awkward emendation for *apare* designed to save the poet from a supposed solecism (expect *aparasmin*, and note the "erroneous" use of both *-e* and *-mmi* in Prakrit, Mall, 1928: xxxviii; Bh's many small ungrammaticalities are noted *passim* in the commentary of S).

4.93 The reading *isi-* (*ṛṣi-*) strikes me as dubious (N, V read *-asesa-* [*-aśeṣa-*]) though obviously not impossible. BN glosses *ṛṣīṇāṃ dārakāḥ pālakāḥ*.

4.95 BN calls attention to the difficulty of construing this adjective in the simile, for if (as N and V also assume) the verse forms a single sentence, then *parilaghu* must formally parallel "extraordinary [degree]." I accordingly understand the second half of the verse as a separate sentence, *parilaghu* then paralleling the implied "boy," who is at once small but powerful.

4.96 I do not see how *-paryāya* can mean "according to your rank and order" (K) when Lava has just said he does not know their rank and order. I follow N.

4.99 See endnote to 1.81. Arundhatī's words are spoken in soliloquy, and are not meant to be heard by Kausalyā (as the stage direction *apavārya* strictly used would require).

4.121 Logically necessary though read by no ms.

4.146 N preserves the correct attribution; see K's sensible remarks, and contrast S's convolutions. For the sentiment (now in the mouth of Rāma), see act 6.50 [14]. (MALL 1928: xxxvii comments on Bh's predilection for dividing single verses between or among speakers.)

4.149 *Kumāra* cannot mean prince since the boys are unaware of Lava's paternity.

4.152 The verse is not supposed to be sarcastic: the schoolboys had lived their whole lives in the forest and had never before seen a horse.

4.157 BN reads (in the *chāyā*) *na jivāmīva*, "I feel no longer alive."

4.174 Ne, N, G, V all read *jālmān*, and see Act 5.26. But the vocative is used in the next speech (*capala*).

4.177 B's translation indicates he meant to print *saumyāpūrv-* (so Ne), which remains, however, a rather odd epithet.

5.1 I take this as a singular (Candraketu's heroism is not at issue), despite the title of the next act, which is presumably intended as a dual. N (alone among the C) remarks on this act—which contemporary readers are likely to find intrusive—with the observation that "[The author] is here concerned to produce an act marked by the composition of a narrative characterized by *rasa*, because a narrative devoid of *rasa* and *bhāva* cannot be considered fully developed." He means, I believe, that this is the act in which are displayed all the *rasa*s beyond those that dominate the rest of the play, *(vipralambha-)śṛṅgāra* and *karuṇa* (as well as *hāsya*, it would seem, which is closely allied to *śṛṅgāra*, see above on Act 2). N remarks on the production of these other *rasa*s frequently in his commentary on the act. See for example his note on v. 5.14 [6], "In this verse we find a mixture (*saṃkara*) of all six *rasa*s, that is, excluding *śṛṅgāra* and *hāsya*"; on v. 5.36 [11] he comments on the "transition" between feelings (*śabalatā*) that make up the heroic "energy" (*utsāha*) in the verse, and on v. 5.47 [14] he notes the mixture of the *rasas* of fury and amazement that function subordinately to the *rasa* of the heroic in the verse

5.2 A type of tree, meant here as an insignia.

5.5 A form of tonsure traditional for particular Vedic lineages; see, e.g., *Pūrvamīmāṃsāsūtra* 1.3.16, 17.

5.7 It is hard to believe that Bh would have written the verse as printed in B, requiring an impossible syntax (impossible at least to my eyes) of the locative in *a* with *-śara-* (along with *sāpekṣatva*, since it is embedded in a compound.) in *d*. N's *saṃvṛtaḥ sainyasaṅghaiḥ* looks like an emendation but it is at least intelligible. Equally hard is taking *c* as an adverb; this I emend in accordance with all C.

5.9 "Same," i.e., as Rāma's. The awkawardness originates in the Sanskrit, which defers the referent of *tulya-* until the next line.

5.11 The agreement of Ne and N on the rare *samabhareṇa* (G, V, *madabhareṇa*; BN, *samarareṇu-*), already persuasive, is corroborated by the reading of the C in the companion verse, Act 5.39 [12]*d* (where B's *parikaras* seems a patent simplification).

5.15 And therefore, presumably, have learned of their commitment to preserving their honor in combat at all costs.

5.26 My reading and understanding are corroborated by v. 5.36 [11] *b*, *paścād balair anusṛtaḥ*. B's *yuddhābhisāriṇaḥ*, though confirmed by Ne, seems patently inferior.

5.27 A fire-breathing mare believed to live in the ocean and to keep it from overflowing by burning the water. The god Indra cut off the wings of mountains, some of which fell into the ocean.

5.40 At Candraketu's suggestion that Lava is an unworthy opponent (N).

5.45 Literally, "seizing and releasing" (note the N reads *srastamuktam*). I follow BN's explanation: *tamaḥsaṃbandhena grastam vidyutsaṃbandhena muktam.*

5.53 For *prativīra* (supported by Ne but otherwise not found in Bh's works) N's *pravīra*, "proven hero" (used in Act 6.5 and twice in MVC) may be preferable.

5.56 So BN: *grahamaitryādi jyotiḥ śāstraprasiddham*. Or "eye-love," according to V.

5.57 Bhoja cites the verse in ŚP p. 662, corroborating the reading of C.

5.59 N, "softened in the process of ritual purification." Is there a slight inconsistency in investing Lava, raised in the forest, with this accoutrement?

5.60 Literally, "by which even the most tremendous force is overcome" (preferring N to V or K).

5.60 In such a phrase this would normally be translated as "character" or "nature" were it not for the reflexive, metaliterary quality of Bh's writing throughout the play (see Introduction).

5.67 Translated in accordance with the argument in the previous note. Otherwise *sāhasaikarasa-* would mean simply "of pure recklessness."

5.83 An allusion to the most famous of all Rigvedic mantras, the *Gāyatrī*.

5.89 B's *yathocitam* strikes me as barely possible though it has no support among C or mss. consulted (N *yadācaritam*; Ne *yathācaritam*) and is grammatically dubious.

5.91 B's *api matsarāḥ* is supported by BN; N reads *avimatsarāḥ*, which amounts to the same thing. The implication in either case however is not entirely clear to me.

5.98 N: Am I to fulfill my obligations in only some instances—i.e., and not in a case relating to Rāma? Less strictly and hence less likely V: rights for which only some— Rāma—are authorized. The sense of "qualities" (B) or "virtues" (K) is not pertinent here.

5.100 G, B's *nātinirvaktum* may appear to be strange enough to be authentic, but it is completely unattested in Sanskrit. Ne's *na tu nirkvaktum* looks like a *lectio facilior*. The southern reading adopted in the text may have been disfavored because of the relatively rare use of *arhati* with a direct object.

5.104 N's second explanation; less likely is his first "some new breed of man, or hero."

5.106 N's *huṃ vartate* (glossed "Bah! Keep them hidden" on the basis of a text unknown to me called the *Avyayasūtra*) may well be the original for which B's reading is a simplification. It is also given by Kṣemendra in *Aucityavicāracarcā* p. 10.

5.106 Literally, "face-front," with the implication "but moving backward," following V's explanation ("he uses the phrase 'face-front' since he is too disgusted to actually say 'turning his back'"), which also preserves the sarcasm that we are to hear in "finesse." BN v.l., G, B's *kutomukhāni* is unattested. BN's *akutobhayāni*, "fearless," is the easiest reading of all but can hardly be original, since it leaves unexplained how the more difficult ones could have displaced it.

5.106 Three of Rāma's most questionable deeds were slaying a woman (Sunda's wife Tāṭakā), retreating in battle (with the demon Khara, brother of Rāvaṇa), and killing an enemy (Indra's son Vālin, king of the monkeys) from within a place of concealment.

5.110 N, "groundless," since they don't know that they are cousins, but this is inappropriate for later uses of the word (e.g., Act 6.6).

6.2 Not all repetition is significant, and *-udbhrānta* seems to be a case in point (*pace* S), see Act 5.110 [36]*d*.

6.4 B's *āmandram* (G's *amandam* is a *lectio simplicior*) is supported by BN and found in MM (9.33a). N reads *ānanda-*.

6.5 N takes this literally: the buds were jewels, as the lotuses were made of gold.

6.12 Women do not say such things in Sanskrit poetry, but B's *āṇandamandamuulidaghummantaloaṇāe* is supported by BN, and

N's alternative (at least on his explanation of it) is not much of an improvement.

6.20 *-potañcalo* seems odd enough to retain (and is supported by BN, G, V); N reads *-kodaṃḍo*, with greater narrative relevance (given the reference to Śambūka in the next line).

6.28 N observes, "The idea here is that Rāma's heart is burning at having failed to pay his debt to his ancestors by renouncing his wife [and so failing to father a son], but by embracing Candraketu, who is carrying on the family line, his pain is assuaged."

6.32 The world (so N, V). Possible also: the treasure that is the Brahmans (BN); the treasure of the Brahmans; the treasure that is the Veda.

6.33 See 4.103 [22]. The parallel makes improbable N's gloss, "to be beheld only through the power of good karma," and V's, "whose countenance and majesty are pure."

6.37 It is improbable that Rāma is addressing Candraketu, and so it might seem that the addition of the stage direction "*aside*" is necessary, though it is not reported by any ms. but then the same might be thought of Lava's preceding speech.

6.38 N: "It is impossible to say for sure whether the blossoming of the lotus and the running of the moonstone are dependent or not on the touch of the rays as their cause. As in the case of fire's burning upward and wind's blowing crosswise, the cause cannot be fully grasped by the mind. The same is true in the case of the affections." See also Jagaddhara on MM 1.27, where the verse is repeated: "From the blossoming of the soft lotus petals at the rise of the sun with its harsh beams, and from the splitting of the hard stone at the rise of the soft-rayed moon we conclude that the cause of attraction must be something innate. What external cause can be found in either of these two cases?"

6.45 The double comparison in B is awkward, and not alleviated by alliteration. N reads: *ānandayati hi candana-*. (V finds a hypermetric *mātra* in the reading he shares with B, but I do not see where.)

6.46 *Pace* K, B's *duryogaḥ* is corroborated by N, who glosses "*duṣṭayogaḥ sannahanam.*"

6.64 This follows the construction of N, who refers back to Act 5.39 [12].

6.95 B's reading (translated "Is this boy my son?") offers an inference that seems premature in view of Rāma's reasoning in what follows.

6.102 The northern readings here, which B follows, show the general weakness of that recension. The variant *kāntimat* (sc., *vapuḥ*) seems designed to eliminate a putative error in the trope, whereby a feminine entity (*kānti*) is compared with a masculine (*candra*, emended to a neuter in BN, *ratna*) and a neuter (*utpala*), a difficulty noted and dismissed by N (*liṅgabhedo na virasatām āvahati*). It is impossible to believe that an emendation was made in the opposite direction. *Aviyutasiddhāḥ* (in place of *avihita-*), moreover, harmonizes with the other philosophical jargon used throughout the play. "In every part": N glosses instead *pratikṣaṇa-*, "continuously" (so V); I agree with G's implicit interpretation, which certainly construes better with the *upamānas*.

6.104 N, BN, G gloss *taruṇa* as young, that is, no longer a child (note Bh's repeated use of *kaṭhoragarbha*, full-grown fetus).

6.104 Despite Ne, the reading *-āśayaḥ* is attested in no C and seems hardly be translatable by "posture" (so B). Even BN agrees in reading *-aṃsayoḥ* here.

6.107 As N notes, *-mudrā* is basically otiose.

6.107 Literally "snare-like," see the use of *-pāśa* in v. 6.128 [37] below. This is an *upamitasamāsa; pāśa-* cannot be a commendatory suffix to *karṇa*, as N notes.

6.108 Act 1.69

6.115 N notes *śliṣṭaparaṃparitam caitad rūpakam*, but this is obscure to me (read *śiṣṭa*-?).

6.116 Comparable though not identical verses are found in the last *sarga* of *Rāmāyaṇa* 1.76.15–16 (which incidentally rules out N's reading *anyatame sarge*).

6.120 "That lack all *rasa*," -*virasa*-, more readily to be translated something like "that leave a bad taste in the mouth" were it not, again, for Bh's metaliterary concerns here (see endnote to 6.28 [8]). This line is given quite differently in N, and it is impossible to decide on the original. N's v.l., in literal translation: "your [Sītā's] affairs of life that brought frustrated love with its incoherent reversals, and that ended only in a song of praise" (i.e., that in the end are simply gone and only provided matter for poetry).

6.127 N remarks, "The shame comes from his grasping that Vālmīki knew of those very private affairs; he smiles at Lava's lack of full understanding; the deep affection Rāma feels comes from seeing the child's complete innocence; his teary-eyed piteousness from remembering his abandonment of the woman who trusted him."

6.127 Note the clear antiphony with Act 2.99. For *atiprasaṅga*- see Act 2.99 and *Index* s.v. B's reading seems to be unattested elsewhere in Bh.

6.130 I take this as more of Bh's display of *mīmāṃsā* learning; possibly, instead, "vision" (B, K). But Rāma just had the vision in the previous verse; why would he say it is now impossible?

7.2 Ne's reading here, where it is not corrupt, corroborates N: *martyāmartyasadevamanusyatiryaṅnarakanikāyasāntarābhavasthāvaro bhūtamayaḥ*.

7.2 N perhaps correctly offers a v.l. that frames the sentence as a question: "Why is it that Vālmīki today..." The point is that no one is supposed to know Vālmīki's plan for a performance intended to resolve the doubts about Sītā.

7.9 So far as I am aware, Lakṣmaṇa is never shown to sit in Rāma's presence. B's reading, though old and hard to explain, seems to me therefore suspect.

7.12 The allusion is perhaps again (see endnote to 4.52) to *Bṛhadāraṇyaka Upaniṣad* 5.14. 4ff.

7.13 Bh typically uses *hatāśa* only of threatening creatures or things. Hence the reading of B (and Ne, BN, G) is to be preferred to *hadāsaṃ* (*hatāśām*) of N, V (so also K).

7.17 I.e., Lakṣmaṇa is back (literally, "look at Lakṣmaṇa"). I adopt the reading of N, V, but without accepting their explanation ("have regard for Lakṣmaṇa"). Ne shows a lacuna here.

7.19 The agreement with Ne and N is conclusive (N [V] interprets *vipākaḥ* [cf. Act 4.38 [6]] to mean the same thing as the reading of G, B). The addition of *daivadur-* does however serve to enhance the paradox (of a "fated" turn of events being owing to some person's agency). And this paradox seems indeed to be part of Bh's assessment of Rāma's predicament. Observe that in Act 7.54 [7], Rāma is said to have been forced by fate to abandon Sītā; and note further the echo with Act 1.180 [41].

7.23 I follow N here, who points to a rare use of *pada* (citing Amara). Possible too, though more banal, "where I cannot stand," or, "where I cannot take a step" (V).

7.32 N: "This blessing is a 'favor' since there is no good fortune greater than once again accepting her who had earlier been rejected."

7.37 N's *kalyāṇāntaram* is certainly possible (Sītā's being rescued is "another benefit," in addition to the birth of the sons), but is rendered improbable by the adversative *tu*. (Ne reads *karuṇottaram*).

7.38 B's reading *mohagranthiḥ* may be an emendation for an original (and slightly awkward) *mūḍhagranthiḥ* (preserved in N, V), of which Ne's *mūlagranthiḥ* may in turn be a mislection.

7.38 Or with N: of rebirth (though Bh does use the word as translated here elsewhere in the play; see for example Act 7.48).

7.40 B's *ekaś* is quite uncertain, but neither Ne's *trasto 'ciram* nor N's *soḍhaś* seems a compelling alternative.

7.42 I repunctuate B's text, which is impossible as it stands. There are numerous variants, but without important change in meaning. Possibly correct is N's *vo* (for *vā*): "*your* dear Rāma," sarcastically flagging Gaṅgā's close ties to the Raghu clan, as their family deity (Act 7.29).

7.43 N tries to mitigate the tautology (*bālenānena*) by what seems a clear emendation.

7.44 Again there are multiple variants: N, "you are remembered"; BN, G, "I have been caused to remember you"; V, "do you remember?" None is especially compelling.

7.53 Neither the plural (*pace* K) nor the singular *tava* (N, V) seems quite right here. What is wanted is the dual.

7.64 N curiously glosses "your own body."

7.74 Act 1.69

7.86 For Earth here to ask Sītā to depart, only to refuse in response to Sītā's entreaty, seems completely inconsistent. It could only make sense if a distinction were being drawn between "purifying the netherworld" and dissolving into Earth's body (thus B, in a note to his translation ad loc.; so also essentially K), and presumably it was there that Bh imagines Sītā to have dwelled during the twelve years of her repudiation (in the *Uttarakāṇḍa* she lived in Vālmīki's hermitage). Still, this is improbable in itself, and Rāma's following exclamation ("What, has Vaidéhi's dissolution taken place?") does not quite fit. It would improve things substantially if the line were deleted; yet all C support the reading of the passage, and I see no alternative to letting it stand.

7.87 N, G, V read instead, "bear such humiliation."

7.93 N reads differently, and understands, "He (Rāma) is the whole point of your poem." G and V share his reading but interpret less metanarratively.

7.129 BN G (with variants) B [Ne lacuna] add: *Sītā: ammahe, tādo, kulagurū, ajjāaṇo sabhattuā a ajjā santādevī, salakkhaṇā suppasaṇṇā ajjaüttacalaṇā samaṃ kuśalavā 'vi dīsanti. tā ṇibbhara mhi āṇandeṇa.* ("Sita: Why, there I see my father, guru of the clan, and my mothers-in-law, with their husbands, and my sister-in-law Shanta·devi with her husband, and my most honored and gracious husband along with Lakṣmaṇa, and Kusha and Lava too. I am filled to overflowing with bliss.") The reference to Kuśa and Lava is clearly inconsistent with what has just occurred.

7.136 I.e., respectively (*pace* K). N (implicitly) understands: like the Mother of the world the *Rāmāyaṇa* is auspicious and removes all evils; like the Gaṅgā it is enchanting and affords the highest delight. One might have expected the two to be reversed. *mātā*: N, Mahāmāyā; G, Lakṣmī; B, Earth (thinking back to the scene just concluded); V, "a mother" (construing *jagato* as objective genitive with *śreyāṃsi*).

7.136 Bh ends as he begins, invoking the poets of old—here Vālmīki —and the powers of speech (that is, especially, his own, which replicate those of Vālmīki, see Act 2.30). For this reason, inter alia, I disagree with N and other C that *śabdabrahmavidaḥ* in *c* modifies both *budhāḥ* as well as *kaveḥ*.

Notes to the Edition

1.1 *namovākam* N BN G V : *namovākyam* Ne B

1.4 *anvavartata* Ne N V : *anuvartate* G B

1.4 *prayoksyate* Ne N G V : *prayujyate* B

1.5 *kavi-* Ne N V : *kārya-* G B

1.6 *deva-* Ne N V : *rāja-* G V B

1.7 *sūtra(dhāra)ḥ: evam etat* add Ne B

1.8 *sūtradhāraḥ* N G V *naṭaḥ* Ne B

1.9 *naṭaḥ* N G V *sūtradhāraḥ* Ne B

1.11 om. B.

1.26 *-bhāgā* Ne N V : *-bhāvā* G B

1.48 *svasmāt* N G V : *tasmāt* Ne B

1.62 *parikrāmati* N G V : *parikrāmataḥ* B

1.78 *āgṛhīta-* N G, V : *udgṛhīta-* Ne BN B

1.80 *vi* G V (om. N) : *pi* [passim] B

1.91 *patana-* Ne N G V : *pratanu-* BN B

1.91 *kuḍmalair* Ne N V : *kuntalair* BN G B

1.91 *kusumair* Ne N V : *mukulair* BN G B

1.91 *aṅgānām* N V : *ambānāṃ* Ne BN G B

1.100 *udatītarat* Ne N G V : *udadīdharat* BN B

1.105 *-saṃpāta-* Ne N G V : *-sañjāta-* B

1.107 *ajjaüttasahattadharidatālavattādavavāraṇaṃ attaṇo akkhīhiṃ dakkhiṇāraṇṇappavesaṃ* N G : *ajjaüttahatthadharidatālaveṇṭādavattaṃ attaṇo dakkhiṇāraṇṇapahiattaṇaṃ* B

1.109 *-parirabdha-* N G V : *-pariṇaddha-* Ne B

1.110 *-nīrāṃ* N : *-tīrāṃ* Ne G V B

1.112 *āsakti-* N G V : *āsatti-* Ne B

1.112 *avicalita-* Ne N : *aviralita-* G V B

1.112 *eva* N BN G V : *evam* Ne B

1.118 *-karaṇair* N G V : *-karuṇair* B

1.121 *lagati* N : *luṭhati* Ne G V B

1.131 *mayā* N V : *bhuvo* Ne G B

1.176 *evam eva* Ne : *evam evam* B

1.177 *-saṃveśo* N V : *-saṃvego* Ne G B

1.187 *evam eva* Ne : *evam evam* B

1.188 *vavasidaṃ* Ne N BN V : *ajjhavasidaṃ* G B

1.197 *kāṣṭha-* Ne N V : *kaṣṭa-* G B

1.207 *śūnyāṃ* N : *(su)ślāghyāṃ* Ne G V B

2.27 *avyatikīrṇavarṇām* N : *avyatikīrṇām* Ne G B

2.29 *nūtanaś* N G : *nūtana-* Ne V B

2.39 *-vastu-* N : *-bandhu-* B

2.39 *prāsaṅginīnāṃ* Ne N : *prāsaṅgikīnāṃ* G V B

2.39 *-dṛśyām* Ne N : *-dṛṣṭām* G V B

2.41 *evam eva* Ne : *evam evam* B

2.47 *matir* N : *vāco* Ne G B

2.64 *-ākampena* Ne N G V : *-otkampena* B

2.64 *-klānta-* N G V : *-kānta-* Ne BN, B

2.77 *-garta-* N G V : *-garbha-* B

2.77 *-vindhya-* Ne N : *-araṇya-* G V B

2.85 *priyarāmā* Ne N BN : *priyārāmā* G V B.

2.98 *vitatānokahaśyāmalaśrīr* N : *vitataśyāmalānokahaśrīr* Ne G B

2.100 *purābhūtaḥ* N V; *ghanībhūtaḥ* G B (*ghanābhūtaḥ* Ne)

3.4 *anirbhinno* N G V : *anirbhinna-* Ne BN B

3.5 *prakarṣaṃ* Ne N : *prakarṣa-* B

3.11 *idṛśāṃ vinipāto* N : *īdṛśānāṃ vipāko* Ne G V B

3.12 *grahāpacāra-* N : *gṛhācāra-* Ne G V B

3.31 *uddhūsarei* N : *ussuāvedi* G B

3.56 *bhaṇissadi* Ne: *maggissadi* BN B

3.62 *vi puṇo* N BN G V : *via puṇo* Ne : B *via*

3.64 *kīlisīo via* (*kīdisī vi* Ne) *me hiaāvatthā* N Ne (G V) : *kīdiso via me hiaāṇubandho* BN B

3.66 *ghaṭanāt stambhitam* N G V : *ghaṭanottambhitam* Ne B

3.68 *ānandayati* N G V : *evārdrayati* B (*cārdrayati* Ne)

3.69 *agādhadaṃsidasiṇehasahāā* (*-sabbhāvā* Ne) Ne N : *agādhamāṇasadaṃsidasiṇehasambhārā* G V B

3.69 *sītāmaā* Ne N : *sudā mae* BN B

3.94 *-mūlāt* Ne N G V : *-pūrāt* B

3.102 *-kalida-* N : om. Ne BN G V B

3.108 *atulitapadatāṇḍavotsavānte svayam* N : *ataruṇamadatāṇḍa-votsavānteṣv ayam* Ne (*-antād*) B

3.122 *navo nava* N G V : *navaṃ navam* Ne B

3.122 Ne reads *-karuṇaḥ*, see 1.118 [28] and endnote to 1.118.

3.122 *pāṇḍuśyāmaḥ* N G V : *pāṇḍuḥ so 'yam* Ne B

3.125 *viṇetti* N : *viṇatti* B

3.128 *-ścyutaḥ* Ne N G V : *-ścyutaiḥ* B

3.137 *anubadhya* Ne N : *anurudhya* G V B

3.138 *iti muhyati* Ne N G V: *mūrchati* B

3.173 *puṇo* Ne N BN : om. G V B

3.174 *atinirutsukasya* N (*atinirutkampa-* Ne) : *atiniṣkampa-* G B

3.174 *-priyavastu-* N : *-tattatpriyavastu-* G B

3.175 *helo-* Ne N : *lolo-* BN B

3.175 *-karuṇ-* Ne N BN G V : *-karaṇ-* B

3.175 *iva* Ne N G V: *eva* B

3.176 *pamusia-* Ne N G V : *pupphurida-* BN B

3.189 *-jīa-* Ne (*-jīva-* N) : *-jīvida-* BM G V B

3.191 *kaṣṭam* Ne N : *katham* G V B

3.204 *so evva. dāṇiṃ jāṇāsi* N : *so jjevva dāṇiṃ si tuṃ* Ne BN G V B

3.213 *pajjavatthāvemi* N : *pajjavatthāvedi* Ne G B

3.230 *anya evāyam adhunā pralayo* N (G V *viparyayo*, *pace* K) : *an-vartha evāyam adhunā pralāpo* Ne (with v. l.) B

3.231 *-rasaiḥ* N : *-rasaḥ* Ne G V B

3.231 *kaṭus* Ne N V : *katham* G B

3.231 *tu pravilayaḥ* Ne N V : *tv apratividhaḥ* BN G B

3.234 *-viṣaye* N V : *-viṣayaḥ* Ne B

4.4 *-kucchāṇaṃ* N BN G V : *-kuccālāṇaṃ* B

4.17 *kalpam* add BN G V B

4.49 *sumārida* N G V : *sambharāvida* BN B

4.49 *aṇuṭhṭhida-* N BN : *aṇecchia-* B

4.83 *iva* N : *api* G V B

4.86 *'pare* v.l. V : *'paraḥ* N G V B

4.95 *-śiśiro* N V :*-śiśutā-* BN G B

4.95 *nirgrāhyo* N BN V : *nirgāhyo* B

4.96 *sataḥ* N V : *svataḥ* G B

4.104 *sumarasi* N G V : *sambharasi* B

4.146 *lavaḥ* N : *arundhatī* G V B

4.151 *are* N (V *aye*) : om. G B

4.157 *vañcidā* N G V : *vañcaāmi* Ne B

4.162 *praviśya* N G V : om. Ne B

4.175 *adya* Ne N G V : *anyā* B

4.177 *so py apūrv-* N G V : *saumyapūrv-* B

5.2 *udkhāta-* N G V : *udghāta-* B

5.7 *saṃvṛttaḥ sainyasaṅgaiḥ* N : *sarvataḥ sainyakāye* G B

5.7 *-ghora-* N G V : *-aṃ* Ne B

5.11 *samabhareṇa* Ne N : *samarabhāra-* B

5.14 *āgarjad-* N G V : *āguñjad-* Ne B

5.26 *pṛṣṭhānu-* N V : *yuddhābhi-* Ne G B

5.27 *-helā-* Ne N BN G V : *-senā-* B

5.39 *samabharas* Ne N G V : *parikaras* B

5.54 *uddiśya* N : *prati* G V B

5.57 *-bhūtāni* Ne N G V : *-marmāṇi* B

5.58 *uddiśya* N G V : omit B

5.71 *apratirūpaṃ* N G V : *pratirūpaṃ* Ne B

5.100 *na hi nirbandham* N V (K) : *nātinirvaktum* G B

5.106 *trīṇy akuto-* N V : *trīṇi kuto-* Ne G B

6.11 *-paṭuraṭaccaṭula-* N : *-paṭutara-* Ne B

6.71 *sakrodhākūta-* N : *sādbhuta-* B

6.95 *kim iti ayam* Ne : *kim iti ayaṃ ca* N V : *kim apatyam* G B

6.96 *nijaḥ snehajo dehasāraḥ* N G V (*nija-*) : *nijasnehasārasya sāraḥ* Ne B

6.96 *iva bahiś* N G V : *ita itaś* Ne B

6.96 *ekaḥ* N G V : *iva* Ne B

6.96 *(iva) sikto* N (*ava-*) V: *(iva) mṛṣṭo* Ne B

6.102 *aviyuta-* N G V : *avihita-* Ne BN B

6.102 *kāntim udbhedayanti* N G V : *kāntimat ketayanti* Ne BN B

6.102 *candraṃ* N G V : *ratnaṃ* Ne BN B

6.102 *sve yathā vā* N G V : *te manojñā* B

6.104 *subandhurāṃsayoḥ* N V : *abandhur āśayaḥ* Ne B

6.105 *-vaṃśa-* Ne N V : om. B

6.107 *śukla-* N G V : *muktā-* Ne BN B

6.107 *rakta-* N BN G V : *naiva* Ne B

6.116 *antye* Ne K : *ante* B

6.125 *citrakūṭamandākinī-* N : *mandākinīcitrakūṭa-* Ne G B

6.127 *-atiprasaṅgasya* N G V : *-atiśayaprasaṅgasya* Ne BN B

6.135 *-samavasthita-* N G V : *-samupasthita-* Ne BN B

7.2 *bhoḥ kiṃ nu* Ne N V : *bho bhoḥ adya* G B

7.2 *martyāmartyadevāsuranaranārītiryaṅnikāyaḥ sāntarābhavacarasthāvaro* N : *sadevāsuratiryaguraganāyakanikāyo jaṅgamaḥ sthāvaraś ca* B

7.7 *kumāra-* Ne N G V : om. B

7.9 *upaviśati* N G : *upaviśataḥ* Ne B

7.17 *avekṣasva* N G V : *kṣaṇam apekṣasva* B

7.19 *vipākaḥ* Ne N V : *daivadurvipākaḥ* G B

7.31 *cāritrocitāṃ* Ne N G V: *cāritropacitāṃ* B

7.38 *upaplavaḥ* Ne N G V : *anupaplavaḥ* B

7.40 *ca* Ne N : *tu* V B

7.87 *sahissaṃ* N G V : *sahamhi* B

7.112 *avi* N V : om. Ne BN B

INDEX

Sanskrit words are given in the English alphabetical order, according to the accented CSL pronunciation aid. They are followed by the conventional diacritics in brackets.

affection, 71, 81, 89, 99, 107, 109, 117, 139, 151, 157, 159, 167, 183, 187, 195, 199, 217, 219, 227, 251, 297, 299, 303, 307, 327, 329, 331, 341, 343, 347, 349, 351, 353, 363, 429, 431

Agástya *(Agastya)*, 129, 135, 153, 159, 165

Aikshváka *(Aikṣvāka)*, 291, 307, 309

anger, 42, 91, 101, 121, 183, 223, 243, 251, 255, 272, 273, 279, 285, 291, 293, 313, 337, 371

Ángirasa *(Āṅgirasa)*, 377

animal, 151, 177, 195, 197, 271, 361
  wild, 149, 205, 363

Ánjana *(Añjanā)*, 101

ápsaras *(apsaras)*, 39, 269, 361

army, 139, 277, 285, 287, 289, 293

arrogance, 279, 307, 309

Arúndhati *(Arundhatī)*, 48, 67, 79, 91, 113, 119, 137, 231, 235, 239, 245, 247, 249, 261, 273, 277, 355, 381, 383, 385, 424

ascetic, 49, 86, 91, 93, 121, 127, 141, 145, 155, 235, 237, 293, 335, 361, 422

asceticism, 85, 91, 93, 127, 135, 139, 141, 145, 147, 177, 237, 243

ashram, 67, 75, 99, 135, 137, 147, 235, 239, 257, 267, 271, 279, 281, 337, 355, 423

Ashta·vakra *(Aṣṭavakra)*, 75, 81

Atréyi *(Ātreyī)*, 129, 137, 141

audience, 37, 40, 48, 51, 65, 361

avatar, 311

Ayódhya *(Ayodhyā)*, 47, 65, 89, 137, 147

battle, 67, 149, 223, 285, 287, 293, 299, 301, 303, 305, 313, 317, 339, 409, 418, 428

Bhagi·ratha *(Bhagīratha)*, 90, 91, 371, 383

Bhandáyana *(Bhāṇḍāyana)*, 235, 335

Bharad·vaja *(Bharadvāja)*, 93

Bharata *(Bharata)*, 302, 411

Bhárgava *(Bhārgava)*, 87

Bhrigu *(Bhṛgu)*, 311

bow, 85, 261, 271–273, 281, 285, 287, 293, 303, 317, 337, 339, 340, 387

brahma *(brahma)*, 321

Brahma *(Brahmā)*, 65, 85, 132,

327, 335, 341
Brahman, 29, 49, 65, 67, 86, 139, 145, 259, 273, 308, 311, 361, 383, 422, 429
challenge, 289, 307
Chandra·ketu *(Candraketu)*, 37, 139, 267, 269, 279, 285, 289, 291, 293, 303, 305, 307, 309, 319, 321–323, 327, 331, 333, 341, 361, 426, 429
chariot, 103, 121, 141, 159, 177, 221, 229, 285, 287, 289, 293, 301, 305, 307, 319, 321, 415
flying, 140, 317
child, 32, 35, 36, 79, 85, 89, 99, 119, 121, 135, 139, 145, 169, 193, 195, 227, 243, 251, 253, 257, 259, 261, 263, 265, 269, 271, 273, 275, 279, 285, 287, 297, 349, 353, 355, 357, 361, 367, 369, 373, 375, 377, 379, 387, 419, 431
unborn, 119, 205, 347
childbirth, 167, 271, 363, 365
cloud, 95, 103, 155, 161, 177, 221, 229, 281, 289, 293, 295, 317, 320, 321, 337, 343, 413
compassion, 81, 118, 139, 145, 157, 213, 295, 349, 357, 369, 373, 422
crime, 243
custom, 29, 35, 46, 47, 49, 52, 53, 58, 139, 303, 333, 335, 347, 411
kshatriya, 131, 301
Dándaka *(Daṇḍaka)*, 36, 99, 129, 147, 149, 179, 365, 379
Dasha·ratha *(Daśaratha)*, 67, 111, 235, 245, 248, 253, 257, 267, 269, 303, 355, 414
debt, 57, 383, 429
deer, 97, 155, 197, 201, 279
golden, 97
deity, 48, 64, 65, 67, 69, 85, 91, 101, 108, 117, 119, 121, 123, 129, 133, 135, 167, 169, 183, 189, 193, 224, 225, 231, 245, 249, 251, 287, 304, 305, 317–320, 333, 335, 343, 349, 361, 365, 369, 371, 375, 379, 381, 383, 408, 410, 417, 426
family, 367, 422, 433
forest, 49, 127, 189, 422
tutelary, 40
dharma *(dharma)*, 39, 71, 139, 155, 177, 225, 237, 245, 301, 303, 309, 327, 329, 341, 363, 385
disgrace, 119, 271, 273, 277
disowning, 49, 165, 167, 185, 187, 207, 219, 227, 369, 383, 421
dream, 109, 121, 221, 259, 265
Dúrmukha *(Durmukha)*, 109, 115

Dúshana *(Dūṣaṇa)*, 149
Dushyánta *(Duṣyanta)*, 34
duty, 67, 69
  caste, 67
dynasty, 77, 81, 115, 176, 249, 304, 345, 367, 429
  Solar, 291, 305, 317, 327, 339, 349
emotion, 33, 41, 42, 44, 56
enemy, 34, 221, 223, 227, 257, 279, 287, 410, 428
fate, 37, 47–49, 113, 115, 137, 207, 237, 245, 251, 255, 257, 265, 297, 301, 369, 371, 375, 415, 422, 432
fear, 42, 97, 99, 149, 271, 273, 317, 416
festival, 65, 67, 249, 345
  of the Lord of Kala·priya, 65
flower, 83, 103, 107, 127, 139, 141, 153, 169, 171, 175, 195, 201, 207, 253, 271, 317, 353, 385, 412
forest, 46, 95, 103, 107, 127, 141, 147, 151, 155, 157, 165, 171, 197, 201, 205, 209, 271, 353, 365, 416, 417, 422, 425, 427
gallery, 36, 38, 81
Ganga *(Gaṅgā)*, 36, 40, 48, 51, 57, 90, 166–169, 188, 245, 361, 365, 367, 370, 379, 381–383, 389, 417, 422, 433, 434
Gáutama *(Gautama)*, 85, 87
Godávari *(Godāvarī)*, 95, 135, 141, 155, 161, 165, 167, 169, 177, 189, 197, 213
Grishti *(Gṛṣṭi)*, 245, 249, 261, 263, 277
grove, 93, 135, 137, 161, 167, 197, 237
guest, 67, 93, 127, 235, 237, 422
guru, 77, 85, 131, 179, 249, 305, 335, 375, 377, 434
  family, 48, 245, 257
Hánuman *(Hanumān)*, 101, 119, 224
happiness, 51, 65, 79, 105, 111, 113, 127, 147, 151, 181, 183, 187, 193, 199, 215, 219, 253, 259, 285, 319, 329, 343, 347, 351, 375, 377, 383, 387, 434
hero, 77, 223, 267, 279, 285, 287, 289, 293, 299, 301, 303, 317, 327, 333, 341, 379, 427, 428
honor, 67, 235, 237, 257, 361, 426
  family, 83
horse, 91, 275, 277, 279, 281, 285, 293, 307, 333, 425, 426
  sacrificial, 139, 267, 277, 416
hunter, 133
Ikshváku *(Ikṣvāku)*, 91, 115, 177, 289, 371
Indra *(Indra)*, 305, 313, 339, 426, 428
Índrajit *(Indrajit)*, 303

íngudi *(iṅguḍī)*, 91
Jáhnavi *(Jāhnavī)*, 383
Jamadágnya *(Jāmadagnya)*, 309, 311
Jámbavan *(Jāmbavān)*, 225
Jánaka *(Janaka)*, 71, 77, 85, 113, 119, 121, 237–239, 243, 255, 272, 273, 345, 355, 357, 369, 376, 377, 387, 408, 423, 424
Jánaki *(Jānakī)*, 67, 81, 89, 103, 121, 135, 169, 171, 179, 183, 205, 213, 217, 255, 257, 383
Jana·sthana *(Janasthāna)*, 40, 95, 97, 99, 135, 141, 149, 151, 167, 177, 189, 211, 416
Jatáyus *(Jaṭāyus)*, 99, 189, 221, 222
Jrímbhaka *(Jṛmbhaka)*, 83, 295, 297, 333, 375
Kabándha *(Kabandha)*, 99
Kakútstha *(Kakutstha)*, 305
Kápila *(Kapila)*, 91
karma
  bad, 309
  good, 229, 327, 335, 371, 387, 429
Káshyapa *(Kaśyapa)*, 65, 99
Kausálya *(Kausalyā)*, 48, 239, 245, 247, 253, 273, 277, 423, 424
Khara *(Khara)*, 149, 151, 313, 428
knowledge, 29, 131, 133, 245, 321, 431
  three forms of, 131
  Vedánta, 129
Kraunchávata *(Krauñcāvata)*, 161
Kshatriya, 259, 261, 277, 279, 307, 309, 311, 317, 327, 333, 337, 339, 340, 361, 377
Kumbhi·nasi *(Kumbhīnasī)*, 121

Kusha *(Kuśa)*, 40, 129, 169, 193, 225, 259, 271, 335–337, 343, 345, 361, 379, 385, 387, 434
Kúshika *(Kuśika)*, 87
Lákshmana *(Lakṣmaṇa)*, 36, 39–41, 81, 95, 103, 115, 121, 137, 139, 167, 200, 201, 224, 267, 269, 271, 302, 305, 361, 363, 365, 385, 387, 411, 432
Lakshmi *(Lakṣmī)*, 109, 259, 434

Lanka *(Laṅkā)*, 67, 119, 371, 409, 422
Lava *(Lava)*, 37, 40, 44, 50, 129, 169, 193, 225, 259, 263, 265, 273, 275, 289, 299, 321, 323, 327, 331, 333, 337, 345, 361, 379, 385, 387, 424–427, 431, 434
Lávana *(Lavaṇa)*, 36, 121, 387
Loma·pada *(Lomapāda)*, 67
longing, 75, 199, 217, 229, 299, 309
Lopa·mudra *(Lopāmudrā)*, 159,

165, 167, 169
lotus, 85, 93, 99, 101, 133, 165, 179, 191, 193, 199, 201, 205, 213, 261, 265, 303, 313, 317, 329, 331, 345, 428, 429
love, 30, 31, 34, 36, 49, 57, 75, 99, 105, 109, 111, 117, 119, 127, 133, 151, 157, 159, 171, 177, 179, 185, 187, 191, 193, 195, 197, 199, 205, 207, 209, 211, 219, 225, 229, 297, 299, 303, 317, 319, 321, 329, 345, 349, 351, 353, 355, 369, 371, 385, 413, 414, 419, 420, 427, 431
Máithili *(Maithilī)*, 201
malice, 69, 115, 251, 271, 337
Mályavan *(Mālyavān)*, 103
Mánava *(Mānava)*, 169
Mandákini *(Mandākinī)*, 189, 353, 363
Mándavi *(Māṇḍavī)*, 87
Mánthara *(Mantharā)*, 89
mantra, 297, 305, 335, 427
Manu *(Manu)*, 339
marriage, 67, 87, 107, 217, 248, 255, 350, 352, 357, 411, 416, 419
Matánga *(Mataṅga)*, 99
Máthura *(Mathurā)*, 387
miracle, 51, 103, 277, 285, 295, 319, 329, 381
Míthila *(Mithilā)*, 85, 247, 269
Mitra *(Mitra)*, 304
modesty, 89, 381
monkey, 67, 103, 118, 225, 428
monster, 99
music, 65, 415
musician, 65
Nala *(Nala)*, 225
Naráyana *(Nārāyaṇa)*, 321
Nimi *(Nimi)*, 113
Nisháda *(Niṣāda)*, 91, 133
obligation, 51, 99, 227, 377, 427
ordeal
  fire, 46, 69, 371, 409
outcaste, 49, 117, 139, 147
pain, 99, 117, 151, 165, 167, 171, 183, 217, 219, 271, 351, 416, 429
Pampa *(Pampā)*, 99
Pánini *(Pāṇini)*, 30
passion, 95, 353
Paulástya *(Paulastya)*, 65, 221
picture, 36, 38–41, 81, 97, 99, 103, 109, 295, 347, 375, 383, 410
Prachétas *(Pracetas)*, 129, 133, 167, 239, 277, 297, 331, 343, 347, 363, 377, 379
Prásravana *(Prasravaṇa)*, 95, 135, 155
pregnancy, 34, 67, 79, 347, 409
  cravings, 79, 103
pride, 253, 291, 307, 339
priest, 66, 85, 138, 247, 376, 377
  family, 66, 85, 138, 247, 376
propitiation, 81, 113, 257, 371,

410
punishment, 49, 145, 177
pupil, 29, 251, 263, 271, 309, 331, 335, 343
purification, 51, 67, 81, 115, 249, 251, 343, 363, 370, 371, 379, 381, 389, 423, 427, 433
Púshpaka *(Puṣpaka)*, 141, 145, 159, 327
Rághava *(Rāghava)*, 81, 307
Raghu *(Raghu)*, 91, 97, 115, 121, 123, 137, 168, 245, 255, 265, 285, 301, 303, 304, 345, 357, 365, 367, 377, 422, 433
Raghu·nándana *(Raghunandana)*, 187, 261, 273
Raghu·pati *(Raghupati)*, 341
rákshasa *(rākṣasa)*, 67, 69, 97, 103, 118, 120, 121, 149, 223, 307, 309, 369, 416
Rama *(Rāma)*, 29, 34, 36, 37, 39–41, 44–51, 65, 67, 75, 76, 79, 97, 107, 111, 113, 115, 117, 119, 133, 137, 139, 141, 145, 151, 157, 159, 165–167, 169, 181, 187, 197, 201, 207, 209, 215, 217, 221, 225, 229, 248, 251, 256, 259, 265, 267, 273, 287, 297, 305, 307, 308, 311, 313, 322, 327, 349, 351, 357, 361, 365, 369–371, 375, 377, 381, 383, 385, 389, 408, 409, 411, 414–421, 423, 424, 426–434
rasa
heroic, 42, 44, 58, 339
of pity, 42, 44, 165, 229, 363, 416
of wonder, 42, 223, 351
rasa *(rasa)*, 38, 39, 41, 42, 44, 57, 58, 111, 127, 165, 223, 229, 269, 299, 301, 303, 329, 339, 343, 351, 363, 412, 416, 431, 439
Rávana *(Rāvaṇa)*, 64, 220, 278, 368
reproach, 69, 115, 205, 263, 420
Rishya·shringa *(Ṛśyaśṛṅga)*, 67, 75, 77, 79, 137, 235, 257, 383
ritual, 49, 67, 76, 82, 87, 91, 139, 166, 225, 244, 287, 307, 377, 409, 416, 427
birthday, 131, 166, 225
coronation, 65, 409
river, 95, 133, 135, 147, 155, 161, 165–167, 175, 187, 231, 365, 417, 422
rumor, 69, 109, 115, 251, 271
sacrifice, 66, 67, 79, 121, 137, 423
horse, 137, 159, 225, 277
Ságara *(Sāgara)*, 91
sage, 82, 99, 129, 231, 245, 269, 285, 379
Sarásvati *(Sarasvatī)*, 349
Sárayu *(Sarayū)*, 167

Saudhátaki *(Saudhātaki)*, 235
Saumítri *(Saumitri)*, 201, 225
scandal, 51, 113
seer, 39, 69, 77, 83, 89, 121, 129, 133, 159, 167, 237, 243, 263, 309, 363, 377, 381, 385
Brahman, 133, 153
royal, 237, 239, 247, 249, 251, 253, 265, 307, 341, 387
separation, 36, 37, 57, 75, 97, 103, 109, 121, 171, 185, 191, 193, 223, 225, 349, 413, 414
Shakúntala *(Śakuntalā)*, 34
Shambúka *(Śambūka)*, 42, 49, 139, 141, 145, 167, 323, 416, 418, 429
shame, 227, 243, 289, 293, 307, 369, 383, 385, 420, 431
Shánkara *(Śaṅkara)*, 85
Shanta *(Śāntā)*, 67, 77, 79, 257, 383
Shanta·devi *(Śāntādevī)*, 434
shastra, 301
Shatánanda *(Śatānanda)*, 85, 376
Shiva *(Śiva)*, 318
Shruta·kirti *(Śrutakīrti)*, 87
Shudra, 49, 141, 145, 177
Shurpa·nakha *(Śūrpanakhā)*, 39, 95
Shyama *(Śyāma)*, 93
Sita *(Sītā)*, 34, 36, 37, 39–41, 44–51, 75, 79, 91, 109, 117–119, 135, 137, 139, 145, 167, 169, 175, 181, 187, 189, 197, 201, 215, 219, 221, 223, 227, 229, 237, 239, 243, 248, 251, 257, 271, 349–351, 353, 365, 367–369, 371, 375, 377, 379, 381, 383, 385, 387, 409, 411, 413, 416–420, 422, 423, 431–434
soldier, 267, 285, 289, 309, 333, 337
sorrow, 57, 75, 99, 105, 111, 151, 157, 165, 169, 171, 179, 199, 205, 207, 209, 211, 213, 217, 225, 239, 243, 245, 247, 251, 303, 319, 329, 347, 349, 351, 385, 414
Subáhu *(Subāhu)*, 256, 257
Sugríva *(Sugrīva)*, 119, 224
Sumántra *(Sumantra)*, 285, 301
Sunda *(Sunda)*, 313, 428
Supárna *(Suparṇa)*, 305
Támasa *(Tamasā)*, 133, 165, 169, 179, 183, 185, 193, 219, 225, 420
Tátaka *(Tāṭakā)*, 83, 428
travel, 93, 416
hardships of, 93
Tvashtri *(Tvaṣṭṛ)*, 319
underworld, 167, 379, 433
Úrmila *(Ūrmilā)*, 87, 269, 341
Vádava *(Vaḍavā)*, 291
Vaidéha *(Vaideha)*, 247
Vaidéhi *(Vaidehī)*, 69, 75, 89, 113, 151, 221, 365, 369,

379, 433
Vaishvánara *(Vaiśvānara)*, 383
Valin *(Vālin)*, 428
Valmíki *(Vālmīki)*, 128, 129, 131, 137, 167, 230, 235, 237, 261, 267, 271, 277, 309, 336, 349, 355, 361, 377, 381, 385, 387, 411, 423, 431–434
valor, 291, 317
Vama·deva *(Vāmadeva)*, 139
Vasánti *(Vāsantī)*, 49, 135, 157, 175, 187, 189, 191, 197, 201, 203, 205, 211, 213, 215, 219, 221, 225, 227, 419
Vasíshtha *(Vasiṣṭha)*, 67, 77, 79, 85, 113, 119, 137, 138, 231, 235, 237, 239, 245, 247, 256, 304, 355, 357, 377, 424
Vedánta *(Vedānta)*, 29, 414
Vibhándaka *(Vibhāṇḍaka)*, 67
Vibhíshana *(Vibhīṣaṇa)*, 119
Vindhya *(Vindhya)*, 93, 147, 295
Virádha *(Virādha)*, 93
Vishnu *(Viṣṇu)*, 304, 305, 320
Vishva·mitra *(Viśvāmitra)*, 83, 86, 119, 287, 296, 335, 410, 411
vow, 75, 91, 113, 361, 381
vulture, 99, 155
Vyasa *(Vyāsa)*, 34, 38
water, 36, 91, 95, 103, 127, 149, 153, 161, 165, 191, 201, 207, 211, 229, 321, 343, 381, 426
  holy, 81, 91
weapon, 85, 281, 287, 295, 297, 320, 321, 327, 331, 333, 335, 337, 347, 375, 377, 379, 415
  divine, 40, 83, 139, 327
  Fire, 319, 321
  Jrímbhaka, 83
  magical, 35, 36, 131, 295, 339, 347, 375
wisdom, 225, 249
Yama *(Yama)*, 145

k	ṭ	t	p	ṅ	n	m	*(Except āḥ/aḥ)* ḥ/r	āḥ	aḥ	*Initial letters:*
k	ṭ	t	p	ṅ	n	ṃ	ḥ	āḥ	aḥ	k/kh
g	ḍ	d	b	ṅ	n	ṃ	r	ā	o	g/gh
k	ṭ	c	p	ṅ	ṃś	ṃ	ś	āś	aś	c/ch
g	ḍ	j	b	ṅ	ñ	ṃ	r	ā	o	j/jh
k	ṭ	ṭ	p	ṅ	ṃṣ	ṃ	ṣ	āṣ	aṣ	ṭ/ṭh
g	ḍ	ḍ	b	ṅ	ṇ	ṃ	r	ā	o	ḍ/ḍh
k	ṭ	t	p	ṅ	ṃs	ṃ	s	ās	as	t/th
g	ḍ	d	b	ṅ	n	ṃ	r	ā	o	d/dh
k	ṭ	t	p	ṅ	n	ṃ	ḥ	ā	aḥ	p/ph
g	ḍ	d	b	ṅ	n	ṃ	r	ā	o	b/bh
ṅ	ṇ	n	m	ṅ	n	ṃ	r	ā	o	*nasals* (n/m)
g	ḍ	d	b	ṅ	n	ṃ	r	ā	o	y/v
g	ḍ	d	b	ṅ	n	ṃ	*zero*[1]	ā	o	r
g	ḍ	l	b	ṅ	l̃[2]	ṃ	r	ā	o	l
k	ṭ	c ch	p	ṅ	ñ ś/ch	ṃ	ḥ	āḥ	aḥ	ś
k	ṭ	t	p	ṅ	n	ṃ	ḥ	āḥ	aḥ	ṣ/s
gg h	ḍḍ h	dd h	bb h	ṅ	n	ṃ	r	ā	o	h
g	ḍ	d	b	ṅ/ṅṅ[3]	n/nn[3]	m	r	ā	a[4]	*vowels*
k	ṭ	t	p	ṅ	n	m	ḥ	āḥ	aḥ	*zero*

Permitted finals:

[1]ḥ or r disappears, and if a/i/u precedes, this lengthens to ā/ī/ū. [2]e.g. tān+lokān=tāl̃ lokān.
[3]The doubling occurs if the preceding vowel is short. [4]Except: aḥ+a=o '.

Final vowels: a	ā	i	ī	u	ū	ṛ	e	ai	o	au	Initial vowels:
' â	" â	y a	y a	v a	v a	r a	e '	ā a	o '	āv a	a
' ā	" ā	y ā	y ā	v ā	v ā	r ā	a ā	ā ā	a ā	āv ā	ā
' ê	" ê	' î	" î	v i	v i	r i	a i	ā i	a i	āv i	i
' ē	" ē	' ī	" ī	v ī	v ī	r ī	a ī	ā ī	a ī	āv ī	ī
' ô	" ô	y u	y u	' û	" û	r u	a u	ā u	a u	āv u	u
' ō	" ō	y ū	y ū	' ū	" ū	r ū	a ū	ā ū	a ū	āv ū	ū
a' r	a" r	y ṛ	y ṛ	v ṛ	v ṛ	' ṛ̂	a ṛ	ā ṛ	a ṛ	āv ṛ	ṛ
' âi	" âi	y e	y e	v e	v e	r e	a e	ā e	a e	āv e	e
' āi	" āi	y ai	y ai	v ai	v ai	r ai	a ai	ā ai	a ai	āv ai	ai
' âu	" âu	y o	y o	v o	v o	r o	a o	ā o	a o	āv o	o
' āu	" āu	y au	y au	v au	v au	r au	a au	ā au	a au	āv au	au

THE CLAY SANSKRIT LIBRARY

Current Volumes

For more details please consult the CSL website.

1. The Emperor of the Sorcerers (*Bṛhatkathāślokasaṃgraha*) (vol. 1 of 2)
   by *Budhasvāmin*. Sir James Mallinson
2. Heavenly Exploits (*Divyāvadāna*)
   Joel Tatelman
3. Maha·bhárata III: The Forest (*Vanaparvan*) (vol. 4 of 4)
   William J. Johnson
4. Much Ado about Religion (*Āgamaḍambara*)
   by *Bhaṭṭa Jayanta*. Csaba Dezső
5. The Birth of Kumára (*Kumārasaṃbhava*)
   by *Kālidāsa*. David Smith
6. Ramáyana I: Boyhood (*Bālakāṇḍa*)
   by *Vālmīki*. Robert P. Goldman
7. The Epitome of Queen Lilávati (*Līlāvatīsāra*) (vol. 1 of 2)
   by *Jinaratna*. R.C.C. Feynes
8. Ramáyana II: Ayódhya (*Ayodhyākāṇḍa*)
   by *Vālmīki*. Sheldon I. Pollock
9. Love Lyrics (*Amaruśataka, Śatakatraya & Caurapañcāśikā*)
   by *Amaru, Bhartṛhari & Bilhaṇa*.
   Greg Bailey & Richard Gombrich
10. What Ten Young Men Did (*Daśakumāracarita*)
    by *Daṇḍin*. Isabelle Onians
11. Three Satires (*Kaliviḍambana, Kalāvilāsa & Bhallaṭaśataka*)
    by *Nīlakaṇṭha, Kṣemendra & Bhallaṭa*
    Somadeva Vasudeva

12. Ramáyana IV: Kishkíndha (*Kiṣkindhākāṇḍa*)
by *Vālmīki*. Rosalind Lefeber
13. The Emperor of the Sorcerers (*Bṛhatkathāślokasaṃgraha*) (vol. 2 of 2)
by *Budhasvāmin*. Sir James Mallinson
14. Maha·bhárata IX: Shalya (*Śalyaparvan*) (vol. 1 of 2)
Justin Meiland
15. Rákshasa's Ring (*Mudrārākṣasa*)
by *Viśākhadatta*. Michael Coulson
16. Messenger Poems (*Meghadūta, Pavanadūta & Haṃsadūta*)
by *Kālidāsa, Dhoyī & Rūpa Gosvāmin*. Sir James Mallinson
17. Ramáyana III: The Forest (*Araṇyakāṇḍa*)
by *Vālmīki*. Sheldon I. Pollock
18. The Epitome of Queen Lilávati (*Līlāvatīsāra*) (vol. 2 of 2)
by *Jinaratna*. R.C.C. Feynes
19. Five Discourses on Worldly Wisdom (*Pañcatantra*)
by *Viṣṇuśarman*. Patrick Olivelle
20. Ramáyana V: Súndara (*Sundarakāṇḍa*) by *Vālmīki*.
Robert P. Goldman & Sally J. Sutherland Goldman
21. Maha·bhárata II: The Great Hall (*Sabhāparvan*)
Paul Wilmot
22. The Recognition of Shakúntala (*Abhijñānaśākuntala*) (Kashmir Recension) by *Kālidāsa*. Somadeva Vasudeva
23. Maha·bhárata VII: Drona (*Droṇaparvan*) (vol. 1 of 4)
Vaughan Pilikian
24. Rama Beyond Price (*Anargharāghava*)
by *Murāri*. Judit Törzsök
25. Maha·bhárata IV: Viráta (*Virāṭaparvan*)
Kathleen Garbutt
26. Maha·bhárata VIII: Karna (*Karṇaparvan*) (vol. 1 of 2)
Adam Bowles

27. "The Lady of the Jewel Necklace" and "The Lady who Shows her Love" (*Ratnāvalī & Priyadarśikā*) by *Harṣa*. WENDY DONIGER
28. The Ocean of the Rivers of Story (*Kathāsaritsāgara*) (vol. 1 of 9) by *Somadeva*. SIR JAMES MALLINSON
29. Handsome Nanda (*Saundarananda*) by *Aśvaghoṣa*. LINDA COVILL
30. Maha·bhárata IX: Shalya (*Śalyaparvan*) (vol. 2 of 2) JUSTIN MEILAND

To Appear in 2007

"Friendly Advice" (*Hitopadeśa*) by *Nārāyaṇa* & "King Víkrama's Adventures" (*Vikramacarita*). JUDIT TÖRZSÖK

"How the Nagas were Pleased" (*Nāgānanda*) by *Harṣa* & "The Shattered Thighs" (*Ūrubhaṅga*) by *Bhāsa* ANDREW SKILTON

Life of the Buddha (*Buddhacarita*) by *Aśvaghoṣa* PATRICK OLIVELLE

Maha·bhárata V: Preparations for War (*Udyogaparvan*) (vol. 1 of 2) KATHLEEN GARBUTT

Maha·bhárata VIII: Karna (*Karṇaparvan*) (vol. 2 of 2) ADAM BOWLES

The Ocean of the Rivers of Story (*Kathāsaritsāgara*) (vol. 2 of 9) by *Somadeva*. SIR JAMES MALLINSON